THE STRATEGY OF GLOBAL BRANDING AND BRAND EQUITY

Why does a customer choose one brand over another? What are the factors which would make an individual more inclined to choose your brand?

This book offers a way to predict which brand a buyer will purchase. It looks at brand performance within a product category and tests it in different countries with very different cultures. Following the Predictive Brand Choice (PBC) model, this book seeks to predict a consumer's loyalty and choice. Results have shown that PBC can achieve a high level of predictive accuracy, in excess of 70% in mature markets. This accuracy holds even in the face of price competition from a less preferred brand.

PBC uses a prospective predicting method which does not have to rely on a brand's past performance or a customer's purchase history for prediction. Choice data is gathered in the retail setting – at the point of sale. *The Strategy of Global Branding and Brand Equity* presents survey data and quantitative analyses that prove the method described to be practical, useful and implementable for both researchers and practitioners of commercial brand strategies.

Alvin Lee is Lecturer of Marketing at Deakin University, Australia. He has researched the marketing of consumer goods across markets in Asia and the United States. He received his PhD in marketing from the University of Western Australia.

Jinchao Yang is Associate Professor at the College of Economics and Management, China Agricultural University. Dr Yang has PhD degrees in agriculture and marketing and has international marketing experience in consumer foods and beverages. He received his PhD in marketing from the University of Western Australia and his PhD in agriculture from China Agricultural University.

Richard Mizerski is Emeritus Research Professor of Marketing at the University of Western Australia. He has worked as a consultant for several international package goods marketers including Nestlé and Kraft on the marketing of consumer goods in the United States, Europe and Asia.

Claire Lambert is Lecturer at the School of Business of Edith Cowan University, Australia. She has extensive industry experience in quick service food marketing and sales promotion. She received her PhD in marketing from the University of Western Australia.

THE STRATEGY OF GLOBAL BRANDING AND BRAND EQUITY

Alvin Lee, Jinchao Yang, Richard Mizerski and Claire Lambert

Routledge
Taylor & Francis Group

LONDON AND NEW YORK

First published 2015
by Routledge
2 Park Square, Milton Park, Abingdon, Oxon OX14 4RN

and by Routledge
711 Third Avenue, New York, NY 10017

Routledge is an imprint of the Taylor & Francis Group, an informa business

British Library Cataloguing in Publication Data

A catalogue record for this book is available from the British Library

Library of Congress Cataloging-in-Publication Data
Lee, Alvin (Lecturer in Strategic Marketing)
   The strategy of global branding and brand equity / Alvin Lee, Jinchao Yang,
Richard Mizerski and Claire Lambert.
      pages cm
   Includes bibliographical references and index.
   1. Branding (Marketing)   2. Product management.   3. Brand name
products.   I. Title.
   HF5415.1255.L44 2015
   658.8'27—dc 3
   2014038777

ISBN: 978-0-415-74910-7 (hbk)
ISBN: 978-0-415-74911-4 (pbk)
ISBN: 978-1-315-72252-8 (ebk)

Typeset in Bembo
by Apex CoVantage, LLC

Printed and bound in Great Britain by
TJ International Ltd, Padstow, Cornwall

CONTENTS

Appendices

FIGURES

TABLES

WORKSHEETS

PREFACE

Thank you for choosing this book. Thank you for your interest in brands and branding. In these pages, we explain and test a way to measure and predict how customers choose between brands in a product category. The method is called the Predictive Brand Choice Model (PBC).

Marketers have long tried to accurately measure and predict how customers choose between brands. This measurement helps marketers improve the chances of their brand being chosen by customers.

One of the reasons for developing and testing the PBC model are the limitations in the models traditionally used to understand and predict how buyers choose brands, especially at "the moment of truth". This is when they are faced with a limited set of brands, and are deciding between their regularly bought brand and their less-preferred brand that is on sale. There appears to be no model that can reliably provide a test that predicts how the buyer will discriminate between these two choices at the point of sale. As such, we set out to develop a model that is:

- Easy to implement at the local level – i.e., in the store at the point of sale,
- Cheap to implement,
- Quick to implement,
- Highly predictive,
- A test that gives discrimination between brands based on Brand Knowledge,
- Reliable and has external validity in markets under different conditions (e.g., mature vs. growing markets, and in markets where Brand Knowledge for a category is different), and
- Predicts actual brand choice based buying behavior, not buying intentions for a brand.

A good way to introduce these improvements over previous methods to measure and predict buyer brand choice is to first discuss the constraints of traditional methods. One of the main limitations is that most models that use Brand Knowledge for prediction limit the prediction to intended purchase, not actual purchase. This severely limits the practical use of these models.

Limitations of previous methods

The traditional way to estimate and predict which brand a customer will chose uses measurements from consumer panels. This is where groups of consumers' purchases are tracked over time. These longitudinal data are used for prediction through regression based models. This method has many limitations. It is expensive. It takes a lot of time to build a good data set.

More importantly, this method is not typically accessible to smaller retailers – the cost and knowledge required to use these data are prohibitive. Traditional methods also cannot account for the limited choice of brands in typical purchase situations; not all brands are likely to be available. There is also the issue of price, where product prices may differ in different locations and some brands may be on sale. Traditional methods of predicting using panel data are also unable to easily predict and rank brand preference for groups of customers at the local (outlet) level – this is where there may be marked differences in Brand Knowledge and preferences – for example, for the same product category in different regions or countries.

A major limitation is that the methods used to measure Brand Knowledge are very poorly linked to actual purchase. As such, very few models are able to offer ways to predict purchase using a customer's brand knowledge. We are unaware of any method that offers a test that predicts a customer's discrimination between brands using their Brand Knowledge. What is more, there appears to be no model that can account for a customer's choice of brand when one of the brands they use in the category, but is their less preferred brand, is offering a discount. Based on their brand knowledge, how would we predict whether that customer will select the discounted brand?

The Predictive Brand Choice model (PBC)

This book presents the PBC. The model is presented as a brand measurement and prediction system. This system seeks to overcome many of the problems researchers face when using traditional methods to predict which brands a buyer will choose.

PBC offers a way to predict the performance of the top (or other ranked) brands. We tested the model in two countries, Australia and China, which have very different cultures. The market for the product used in the test is also in a different stage of maturity in each country (growing market vs. mature-declining market). In the mature-declining market, PBC can predict a buyer's choice in excess of 90% accuracy. This test is done in a field experiment that incorporates a price discount from the buyer's less preferred brand. This tests for the effect of brand equity, will the buyer continue to choose their preferred brand if the value of their less preferred brand increases with the price discount.

The field test to collect data for use by PBC is practical and easy to implement at the point of sale. It constitutes two interviews while the buyer is purchasing and consuming the product. The interview collects data about the buyer's brand knowledge and a list of their most often bought brands in the category. This is then used to predict the way a buyer chooses (discriminates) between the brands that are available.

This ability to collect data from a local venue and to use it to predict choices between the brands that are available is a step forward in the ability to predict buyer brand choice. This can help researchers and managers chart local brand knowledge. This understanding can help brand managers in their plans to enter new markets, or to improve their standing in current markets.

With PBC, researchers and practitioners now have a reliable method to predict a brand's sales performance, especially when the brand's buyers encounter competitive price discounting from competing brands.

PBC uses individual buyers' brand knowledge at the local level (outlet level) to predict brand choice. Most other methods have not successfully integrated buyer knowledge to predict actual purchase.

These other models, especially those using econometric analysis methods, are unable to predict at the local disaggregated level (e.g., at the outlet level). Rather, they predict at the aggregated level of "markets". These grouped industry comparisons are of limited use for brands that operate in localized markets – for example, in a pub/tavern/bar where only selected brands are available. As such, PBC gives brand managers and researchers a tool to help them manage brands better at the grassroots "outlet" level to measure localized "baskets" of brands.

The aggregation methods favored by many other brand measurement and prediction models cannot predict an individual buyer's "brand choice" – this is their choice of a brand at the point of purchase. Because of this, many practitioners have difficulty predicting in locales where some of the large international brands are unavailable, or where there is a local preference for a different "flavor" or a different set of brands. For example, in ethnic neighborhoods (Chinese, Latino, East European, South East Asian, South Asian, North Asian), or where customers cannot afford or avoid certain brands (e.g., because of boycott action). PBC does not face this constraint. In fact, it is designed to capture preferences and buyer choice behavior at the local level. This means that PBC can also work in markets where there are likely to be different cultures; where these cultural norms affect brand knowledge.

PBC can be used in markets at different stages of market maturity. PBC is tested on the same product category (beer) in countries where the beer category is in different stages of market maturity. PBC gives adequate to superior predictions in each market.

Aims of this book

The PBC model presents another method to predict brands' performance in different country markets. PBC is positioned as a systems and process innovation to enhance the practitioner's brand management processes. PBC also offers a springboard to conduct more brand-based research in markets where culture and life-cycle elements are different. At this point, it is unclear how these affect consumers' brand choice.

PBC helps clarify:

- How do buyers in each market view the top brands in the category?
- How does this view affect their choices when buying in the product category?
- How will buyers react if a brand discounts to gain market share or product trial?

Audience

This research monograph is written for:

- Academics, researchers and practitioners seeking easy access to a new way to predict brand performance across different countries, cultures, markets and geographic locales.
- Established researchers seeking a new system to predict brand performance across countries.
- Researchers and practitioners that require a system to compare the performance of different brands in different markets for the same product category.
- Practitioners seeking to predict the performance of their brands at the point of sale.
- Postgraduate and research students studying marketing, international marketing, cross cultural studies, branding, brewing, hospitality, retailing and predictive methods.
- Researchers and research students interested in international branding, international marketing and international business studies.
- Institutions and libraries that catalogue research monographs.

The way this book is organized

This book is organized as a linear series of chapters. These chapters review and use the extant knowledge surrounding international branding, brand performance, stochastic predictive methods and cultural studies. We aim for this monograph to serve as a practical guide to our system for measuring brand performance – the PBC model. As such, we have included worksheets in the final chapter to help readers work on some of the crucial stages for PBC. As far as possible, we have kept to the familiar structure of a research dissertation to aid readers familiar with the way research monographs are structured. Keep in mind as you are reading that each chapter builds on the last chapter, and that each chapter has a specific purpose. We will sometimes revisit material, tying different arguments together into the common themes of the book.

Finally

Previous publications tend to compare a single brand's performance (e.g., Budweiser beer in China and Australia). In reality, most markets do not operate in this way. The top brands for most countries differ. PBC gives researchers the ability to compare the mind-maps of buyers for the top brands in a category. This comparison can also be done between countries/markets without the brands having to be the same. This affords managers and retailers the opportunity to undertake thought exercises on what it will take to have their brand counted as a top brand in the market.

Most importantly, this book offers a prospective and predictive system to measure and predict brand performance. This is a departure from other work in this area that use retrospective systems to predict. These systems tend to have onerous requirements for historical data on brand performance. Further, no previous system (to our knowledge) can so accurately predict buyer choice in different markets. There is also no other model that predicts brand performance at the point of purchase when there is a discount.

We hope that these following chapters will help you research, practice, and teach better.

Happy reading,
Al Lee, Jinchao Yang,
Dick Mizerski and Claire Lambert

1

BRANDS – ORIGINS, HERITAGE AND IMPORTANCE

When asked how they form their decision on which brand to buy, many consumers are likely to explain the logic behind their decision. Consumers like to believe they use reason to inform their choice of purchases, not impulse. However, research has revealed the opposite; consumers discriminate very poorly between the many brand choices available in most markets, even for categories they frequently use and buy. While consumers often report reasoned decision-making, they happily select brands that represent less than optimal choices, often mistakenly perceiving their favorite brand as being the best brand. Many companies and governments have investigated the basis of consumers' decisions. Their studies seek to understand consumers' decision-making, trying to predict their future choices. Until now, none of the methods for prediction reported in the literature have been particularly accurate or reliable. This book documents the rationale and development of the PBC – Predictive Buyer Choice model – that can predict the brand choice of individual consumers exceptionally well, exceeding 95% accuracy under some circumstances.

Investigations into how people view successful brands indicate that consumers who have favorable knowledge about the brand (Brand Knowledge) tend to be more loyal to the brand (Brand Loyalty). They are also willing to pay a premium price (Brand Equity) and are more willing to buy other items from the same brand (Brand Extensions). But how is this possible if their Brand Knowledge is rarely based on an objective evaluation of the brand? While it is easy to credit good brand advertising for the consumers' Brand Knowledge, in truth, most buyers have developed knowledge of their brand from a wide variety of sources. These are sources that lie beyond the brand marketers' control. This book discusses how several product categories have nurtured successful brands. Some of these brands have even become international brands. These brands are seen by consumers to possess elements of what is often called favorable Brand Knowledge. These Brand Knowledge elements have enabled the brands to bridge cultures and age groups to become international leaders in their categories.

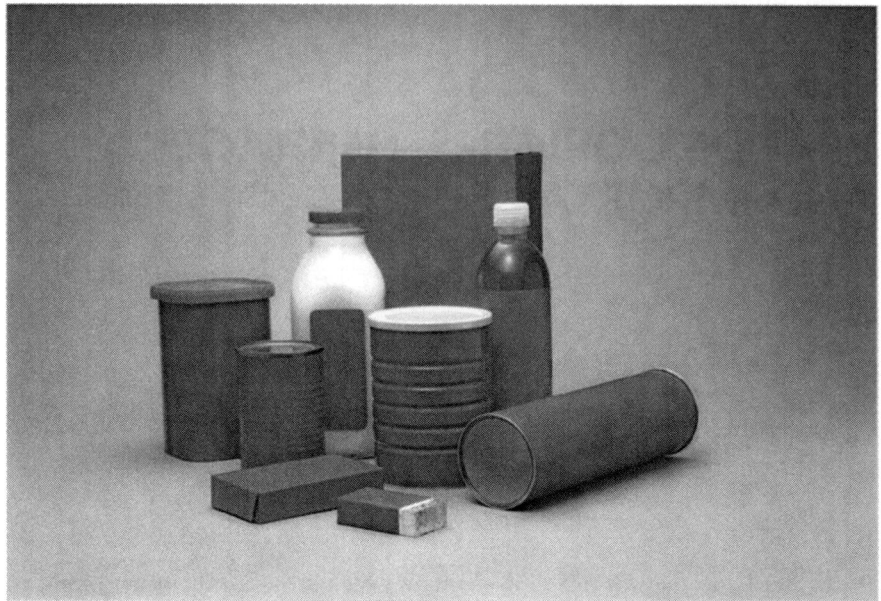

The first chapter provides an introduction to the topic of branding. Here we address the core characteristics of a brand and the differences between products and brands. We trace the origin of brands and what brands mean to business and consumers. Further, we introduce the importance of building a strong brand to maintain growth in increasingly competitive markets. This theme will be developed with much greater detail in subsequent chapters.

What is a product?

A product is anything that can be offered to a market that might satisfy a want or need (Armstrong, Adam, Denize and Kotler 2010). A product can be an idea (e.g., intellectual property such as an industrial process), a good (e.g., a computer) or a service (e.g., a haircut). A customer seeks a product to fulfil a need or want. In this case, the product serves to solve a problem for the customer. For example, if customers want to get from home to their workplace, they may choose an automobile to solve their transport problem. The automobile may compete with other products that provide a similar benefit, the customer may instead choose a bus, train, ride a bicycle or walk to work. To surmise, a product is a good or service, or a combination of goods and services that serve as a means to an end – that is, the product is a way to produce a desired outcome. This outcome solves a problem – i.e., a car solves the problem of transportation.

Most consumers will not buy products that do not provide any benefits. When they do, they are unlikely to buy again. Businesses that lose sight of the fact that they are selling benefits and not products tend to encounter economic trouble. Examples of companies that have failed to acknowledge this distinction and have consequently gone bankrupt include Kodak, Borders and Three Deer. Kodak forgot they were selling the benefit of recording memories. As such, they became too tied into the product format of film and film processing and were not focused on the emerging consumer benefit of digital photography – ironically, Kodak invented digital photography. When consumers migrated to the cheaper and more convenient method of storing their memories digitally, Kodak became a company with an outdated product, a product that was no longer desired by the brand's former customers.

Borders was very good at selling paper-based books. However, Borders became so tied to this format of distribution that the brand failed to transition to selling digital and online books. Borders is now a distant memory.

In China, Three Deer brand infant formula lost sight of its consumer benefit, the provision of safe and nutritious baby formula. When it did not control its supply chain tightly enough, contamination in the form of melamine (an industrial solvent), made its way into its product. This resulted in death and physical harm to many babies in China. The company selling Three Brand infant formula is now closed, and many directors have been tried and executed.

To enhance the chances of success, a company must define its products in terms of satisfying consumer needs. This will improve the prospect of successful branding the company's products and minimize the chances of encountering the same situation experienced by Kodak, Borders and Three Deer.

Tangible versus intangible

A product can be classified as tangible or intangible. A tangible product is a physical object that can be touched; for example, a computer, car, beer or smartphone. An intangible product is a product that cannot be touched. Usually, intangible products can only be perceived indirectly; examples include, digital files, a movie, or an insurance policy. Something that is tangible can also have an intangible aspect. For example, a DVD is tangible, but the movie stored on the DVD is intangible. The easiest way to verify if a product is tangible is to consider whether it can be touched or picked up. If it can be, it is a tangible product (e.g., DVD). However, if it cannot be touched or picked up, it is intangible.

What is a brand?

There may be many brands within a product category. For example, the automobile category has brands like Toyota, Mercedes Benz and Great Wall. While people buy products for the benefits the products offer, people buy brands because they perceive different brands to offer different kinds of value. As such, brands are designed to help consumers perceive the branded product as different from other products within the same product category.

The word "brand" is very commonly used (Stern 2006). When used by non-marketers, the word seems to have an imprecise meaning. Brand can refer to an idea, as in "The brand name is well-known". It can represent an item – "I am carrying a branded handbag", or even "That is a good brand" – referring to the product maker's reputation. Unsurprisingly, this varied use increases the confusion surrounding "brand". This murkiness surrounding the concept we call brand appears to have been around for more than a century (Stern 2006), and persists as the use of the word continues to evolve in the English language. It is due to the concept of brand still evolving. The ongoing relevance of the concept of brand, and the redefinition of the meaning ascribed to brand attests to the concept's importance and longevity.

To marketers, the word brand carries a very specific set of meanings. The American Marketing Association (2014) dictionary defines a brand as "a name, term, design, symbol, or any other feature that identifies one seller's good or service as distinct from those of other sellers". Kotler (1991) provides a near identical definition of a brand as, "a name, term, sign, symbol, or design, or combination of them which is intended to identify the goods and services of one seller or group of sellers and to differentiate them from those of competitors" (p. 442). In this definition, a brand appears to mean a name, term, symbol, design or other specially defining or differentiating feature to distinguish one seller's products from those of other sellers (Brown et al. 2006). Keller (1993) refers to these individual components as a brand's identity and in totality "the brand". This definition emphasizes the marketer-controlled differentiation and communication of a product in the market. However, Duncan defines a brand as "a perception resulting from experiences with, and information about, a company or a line of products" (Duncan 2005). Duncan's definition highlights the element of a customer's experience that is related to a brand.

A brand acts as a promise to its prospects and consumers. It represents the actual product or service the consumer expects to receive, its quality but also the emotions evoked when consumers use the product or service. If you think of the Heineken brand, the brand might represent quality, tradition, premium and indulgence. The Heineken brand promises something to its consumers.

For many a company, a brand is the most precious asset they own. It is something that cannot be touched, but is something the consumer feels about the product or service. From an accounting perspective, a brand is identified as an intangible asset. This asset is commonly the most valuable asset on a firm's balance sheet. Brands are carefully managed to generate shareholder value. They are a valuable intangible asset which will grow exponentially with investment and careful management. In fact, according to Brigham and Linssen (2010), Thomason Reuters and Interbrand reported that in the 1970s as much as much as 95% of the average corporation's value comprised of tangible assets. However, this has reduced to 75% today. This shows that its brands and reputation are normally regarded as a company's most valuable asset.

Product versus a brand

You may ask about the difference between a product and a brand. A product is manufactured by a company and is sold to a consumer in exchange for money. On the other hand, a brand is established based on what the customer perceives, experiences and expects of a product or service. A brand is not what a marketer of a product says it is, but what a consumer thinks it is. For this reason, a brand is more than a product. It is the emotional and behavioral relationship the consumer forms with the product. It is what sets the product apart from its competitors.

Products can be superseded, while brands can live on and on. Products such as cameras and photographic film have become obsolete as a result of technology advances that introduce more innovative products like the digital camera and smartphones into markets. The same has occurred for music cassettes and vinyl records – these have been superseded with the introduction of digital music devices such as iPods. The Beatles brand will forever live on, whilst the music cassette will be a distant memory that is relegated to history.

A brand cannot be copied; a product is easily copied. It did not take long for competitors to copy and launch their own branded product mimicking the Apple's iPad. But it is with the brand related to the product that consumers develop different perceptions, experiences and emotional connections.

A product can also be replaced if a competitor offers a better product or a similar product with the same features and benefits. For most of us, we see sugar as just sugar. You really only care that sugar is sweet, over what brand it is.

Products can very quickly become meaningful to consumers if the product offers unique and beneficial functions. However, it takes longer for a brand to create a meaningful relationship with a consumer. Time is required for a consumer to become aware of, to build an experience with, and to trust a brand. A positive relationship between the customer and brand only exists with awareness, experience and trust. To give an example, USB "thumb" drives were an instant hit with consumers. However, until today, there does not seem to be an especially strong brand in the market. Ones that come to mind are San Disk, Kingston and Transcend. The fact that brands do not feature strongly in this category is reflected in the number of brands and lack of differentiation among competing brands. For thumb-drives, it appears that consumers consider the products of different brands interchangeable and substitutable; USB thumb-drives are treated as a commodity.

As the specialty area of branding has grown in marketing, so has the number of specialist terms associated with brand and branding (Keller 2008). These combine "brand" with other words to literarily or metaphorically represent ideas to describe the different components that make the branding process work. For example, brand implementation, brand relationship spectrum, brand architecture, brand knowledge, brand structure and matrices, branded house and house of brands. Combinations of these terms also describe the outcomes of the branding process – brand equity, brand personality and brand identity. This explosion of specialist sub-terms within the study and practice of branding tends to increase the confusion novice readers are likely to have in identifying the differences between brand, branding and branded. To help better answer the question, "What is a brand?" let's explore the way the word brand has evolved.

Early references to brand

The word brand has a long history in the English language. Literature that has survived (Stern 2006) traces the word "brand" to the epic poem *Beowulf*. In *Beowulf*, brand is a synonym for sword (Oxford English Dictionary Online 2014), which is still a fitting association today, because brands now refer to a commercial tool that facilitates competition in marketplaces. *Beowulf* was first written around the year AD 1000 (Heaney 2002). However, the word brand is likely to have been used from around the fifth century, when the events that inspired *Beowulf* occurred (Klaber 1950). In the 1400s, brand was used as a verb in Wycliffe's *An Apology for Lollard Doctrines* (Todd 1842).

The word brand seems to have roots in the Old Germanic word, *brinn-an* (Stern 2006), meaning "to burn" (Diamond 1975, p. 267). The original meaning of *brinn-an* refers to the act, methods and results of burning. In the 1500s, *brinn-an* (or branding) began to be used in Europe to mark ownership of livestock like cattle and horses by way of a distinguishing symbol burnt into the cattle's skin with a hot iron stamp. This gave rise to adopting *brinn-an* as a way to describe items belonging to a specific person/group. By branding, the mark of ownership is burnt indelibly onto the animal (Schwartzkopf-Genswein et al. 1997). In fact, it was common to refer to a long and lasting impression as branding – for example, by "branding" a woman's heart, a knight is said to have left a lasting impression on a female suitor in Albion's England, a poem from the year 1586 (Warner 1971). This process was later adopted by marketers to distinguish their product or service from competitors, the distinguishing mark is referred to as a trademark.

In more modern times, the Oxford Dictionary documents the word brand as early as 1922. Used in relation to marketing, *brand name* appears in "Brand Names on Menus?" (Oxford English Dictionary Online 2014).

While brand in its use to describe permanently marking livestock traces back to Old Germanic languages, the tradition of branding livestock appears much, much older, a practice that predates the written word. Cave paintings from the late Stone Age and early Bronze Age have pictures of cattle with their flanks showing brands (Diamond 1983) that appear to be burnt on (Bonner 1908). This dates this way of marking property to be at least 50,000 years old.

The practice of branding livestock continues to this day. Today, in addition to a brand marking ownership, many livestock may receive other brands that serve to indicate the livestock's origin and pedigree. For example in Australia, livestock brands are registered and can be traced to individual farms. These marks can be used to identify the farm's trading name, owner of the business and the name of the property where the animal is bred and raised (Department of Agriculture and Food Western Australia 2013). Some brand marks even attest to the genealogy of the livestock. When used in this way, the brands combine to form identification of ownership and indicate the lineage of an animal. This becomes a useful mechanism to trace quality of livestock. A similar premise is also applied to products when they are branded to reflect company ownership and membership.

The uses of brand

Brands to mark ownership

People have probably been putting marks on objects since humans could make comprehensible marks. The earliest marks applied to goods were probably more marks of ownership than marks of trade (Simon 2002). Early marks of ownership that survive tend to be found on durable stone or pottery goods. This does not mean that marks and brands were confined to only these goods. They were just as likely to be prevalent on non-durable goods that did not survive through time.

Given that cavemen/women branded their cattle (Bonner 1908; Diamond 1975), they were just as likely to put a mark on other belongings like tools. A brand to mark ownership identifies the owner. This also serves to warn others to keep their hands off the marked object. To this day, people tend to mark their more treasured belongings, often using their name or monogram or other identifying mark. Even children write their names on their favorite toys and books. Having an ownership mark on an item also has the advantage of helping lost property find its way back to the owner.

Marks of ownership that survive time include crests signifying the occupant of ancient tombs (Bartsiokas 2000). Often these crests become brands themselves – e.g., when attached to royalty. Occupants of these tombs are buried with goods bearing their insignias, monograms, coats of arms, seals or names to signal ownership of the items (Greenberg 1951). This practice was most often seen in powerful or rich persons – kings and queens. However, common people are also likely to be buried with grave goods bearing their names. The practice of marking burial sites with a person's brand or crest continues to this day (e.g., crypt or tombstone). So does the practice of burial with grave goods.

Brands to warn others

Ancient peoples also used myths (e.g., stories and knowledge) to help others understand the meaning of certain marks and brands (Leonard 1997) – for example, the story about the curse of the Egyptian King Tutankhamen's tomb (Feder 1984). This story is used to spread knowledge that linked the name and brand to a negative outcome, perhaps serving as a deterrent to grave robbers to keep them away from the king's tomb. Similarly, marks like the Plague Cross were placed on the dwellings plague sufferers during the great plague that killed many in Europe (Society 1876). This served to warn others to stay away and to enable people who had contracted the plague to trade with each other, ensuring that they at least had the basic goods needed for survival.

Brands as marks of membership

Marks, signs and brands also signify a person's belonging or membership to a human collective. Rock petroglyphs along the Egyptian Nile from the sixth to fourteenth centuries depict crosses and star shapes that are linked to the Christian and Jewish religions. In this ancient "graffiti", some types of crosses are often drawn with camels (Kleinitz 2005), perhaps to show that the traveler "belongs" or identifies with a group of people or with a religion and that this religion is associated with travel (camels). This practice of using brands to signify belongingness continues to this day. People show their cultural membership through jewelry, clothing, and hairstyles. This iconography also appears on buildings and objects associated with particular groups. For example, the cross and circles for Christian societies, the star and crescent moon for Islamic societies, the mark of a lion to symbolize England or the rising sun for Japan and symbol of the dragon for China. Even the Chinese brand themselves as decedents of the dragon – 龙的传人. Many who belong to less conspicuous societies like the Freemasons wear the society's brand to signify membership. Some tribes like the Maori from New Zealand use tattoos as marks of belonging and racial pride. Similarly, Olympic athletes tend to get an "Olympic" tattoo to signify belonging to a special group.

Branding and marks can also have negative associations. For example, the marking of slaves (Pike 1967) and of different castes in society (e.g., in India) through skin markings like tattoos, painting, ornaments or through the use of different garments (Munshi and Rosenzweig 2006). Brands and marks of identification have also been used for purposes of identifying certain peoples, for example the branding of Jews during the holocaust using numbers tattooed on their bodies (Wyman 1984). This way of using brands to recognize membership is not new, for the Bible recounts the story of having slaves put a mark on their door during Passover to save their first born from harm (Exodus 12:7, 12:13, The Holy Bible).

More recently, a number of brands have become negatively associated with deleterious events. For example, Exxon is associated with the Valdez accident, BP with the oil spill in the Gulf of Mexico, NASA with space shuttle explosions, Philip Morris with health problems and Firestone with malfunctioning automobile tyres.

Brands as a mark of trade

Perhaps the most important role that brands have taken on, are as marks of trade. Brands started to become really important when trade started to spread across countries and to distant lands (Garnsey et al. 1983). When product is made and sold locally, many customers will know the product through the craftsperson's "reputation". If the reputation is good, then there will be goodwill for the product. In this case, there is no need for a brand. The producer's reputation is often enough. However, when the craftsperson is separated from their customer, then their brand becomes important – this is because the distant customer may not know the craftsperson personally. In this case, the distant customer needs a mark or brand affixed to the product in order to identify the craftsperson's reputation.

When used in trade, the brand mark is affixed by the object's producer. For example, by a craftsperson, or by the trader on their wares. These marks are abundant on surviving ancient pottery, bricks and tiles from Egypt, Mesopotamia, China,

Greece, Rome and other ancient civilizations. Brands continue their role today to promote trade and consumption. In today's marketplace there are brands of varying ages. However the most valuable brands are still relatively young (e.g., Apple, Google and Samsung). There are also brands with a lot of history which are still successful in today's marketplace. For example, HSBC was founded in 1865, Heinz in 1869 and Coca-Cola in 1886. All three brands are on Interbrand's 2014 Most Valuable 100 Brands list. The success of these brands is attributed to the benefits they offer, remaining relevant in the current marketplace and thus well regarded by consumers.

Early use of marks of trade

In ancient early trade, marks that facilitated trade were likely to have started the idea of "trade" marks. Some primitive artisans were likely to have been so proud of their creations that they affixed their mark as a signal of their craftsmanship (Diamond 1975). If customers and consumers in the marketplace liked the quality of the goods, and the goods were of consistent quality, these customers would begin to use the mark to identify and seek the artisan's products when buying or re-ordering (Shaw 1912). In this way, buyers and users begin to associate specific qualities with specific producers via the identifying mark used.

When an artisan's mark becomes a sought after indicator of quality or is associated with other desirable product attributes, the identification mark begins to take on the attributes of a brand. This is when the artisan's mark stands for some attributes. The mark is seen as a symbol of the quality; it helps to identify the product and consistency of the quality/features in the product. Because of these attributes and associations, the brand stands to distinguish products bearing the brand from other products bearing other brands. When there is a choice in the marketplace, customers begin comparing the attributes of different brands. This is when brands begin to take on a competitive characteristic. Brand managers often try to manipulate this competition by increasing the amount of knowledge in a market, by promoting the brand to be associated with desirable attributes.

With more widespread trade, the mark becomes increasingly removed (more remote) from the artisan. This may also happen with the passage of time, when the original artist stops making the product and others take over. This is when the brand's reputation contributes to the continuity of the brand. The brand's reputation, tied with associated product attributes and promises, begins to form a brand image. A brand's image has to stand independently of the brand's owner, maker and trader to represent the product. The fundamental reason for this is because customers in distant lands and time are unlikely to personally know the person who first made the product.

The spread of brands can be observed by studying ancient trading markets. Archaeologists have identified potter's marks on pottery; these pottery wares are at least four thousand years old (Schechter 1925). As early civilizations grew and trade flourished (3000–1500 BC), products carrying these brands were traded in places that were geographically far away from the producer. For example, jugs from Malta, particularly good at storing wine, are found as far away as Greece. Greek customers were interested in buying one particular brand of jugs, judging from the number of jugs bearing this brand found in Greece. It is likely that Greek traders used the brand to repeat orders with the producers (Diamond 1983). Thus, a brand functions as a means to identify products in a supply chain.

Traders played an important role in developing brands and trademarks. Greater volume of trade saw traders and merchants begin to play a more important role in the supply chain. Some merchants could source items from different artisans. Others provided a variety of wares. This provided customers with choice. Instead of having only locally produced jugs from one artisan, trade meant that customers could choose from a variety of different "brands" of jugs.

Often, the merchants who were particularly skilful at procuring products began to trade under their own "marks" and brands. This lent to greater importance being placed on the merchant's trading mark, especially when applied to unbranded commodities like tea or spices. In fact, merchants' brands often became more important than the individual artisan's mark. This is when the notion of a "house" mark or brand first emerged. It is where a merchant sourced from many artisans and then sold the commodity as a branded item using the merchant's own brand. In early history, merchant's or trader's marks were simply burned onto the container carrying the product, as documented in Chinese trading journals from as early as the fifth century BC. (Shao 2005), where spices and medicinal herbs from particular merchants were more prized than others because of their quality and freshness.

Even in ancient times, there is often more than one mark on the merchant's shipping container. Similar to the modern practice of branding livestock, these marks can include the merchant's mark and other marks to indicate the type and quality of the product in the containers. These containers may also have marks to signal the products' origin and the different ports/hands the merchandise has passed through. For example, early Roman traders sent cheese and wine to all corners of their empire using a marking and branding system that tracked the origin of the cheese, its quality, route and the different merchants and couriers that the cheese passed through on its way to the final consumer (Paster 1969). A more recent and well-known example of a merchant brand is the British East India Company, a mercantile organization that sold products under the East India brand, including the tea that was dumped into the sea during the famous Boston Tea Party raid (Harlow 2011). This tea did not bear the mark of the tea plantations in China that grew the tea, but the brand of the British East India Company.

Another use of tradesman's marks can be found in ancient Jerusalem. Stonecutter's marks have been found on stones in the ruins of the Temple of Solomon in Jerusalem, and in the cities of the early civilizations like Troy, Olympia and Damascus. These stonecutters chiseled or painted their mark onto the cut stones as the evidence needed to claim wages (Diamond 1975). Some of these marks also indicate the source of the stone (the name of the quarry) and type of stone – these are perhaps the earliest documented product ingredient and information labels.

Brands as marks of security

Since early history, people have branded and marked important containers and letters using "seals" (Bonner 1908). These seals are normally burnt on to ensure the security of the contents, acting as a mechanism to show that the container had not been tampered with. Many products today continue to use mechanisms and security "seals" that prevent tampering, for example, pharmaceutical products like Panadol branded headache tablets. These seal offers consumers an added sense of security.

A seal may also serve as a mark of authenticity (Bonner 1908). For example, wills, contracts, degrees and other important documents often bear the seals of issuing parties and authorities. This provides a way to verify the legitimacy and the authenticity of the document. In a sense, these seals convey a sense of safety that the document can be trusted because it bears the brand of a trusted agent or authority.

Popular products with sought after and trusted trademarks can become prone to counterfeiting, with these counterfeits faking the authentic brand, marks and seals. From very early times, counterfeiting resulted in the formation of laws to protect artisans and traders who legitimately owned the marks. More commonly, artisan guilds would enforce rules for artisans to sign and stamp their products – this was to ensure customers could identify artisans who made faulty products. A good example is the 1266 English law requiring bakers to mark loafs of bread. This meant customers were able to identify the bakers who made underweight loafs (Diamond 1983). This branding system for weight, and for purity, is enforced in many industries today; for example, for gold and silversmiths. These smiths have to stamp the quality, type and weight of items they manufacture, as well as stamp their own trademark on jewelry they have manufactured.

Marketing and brands

The Marketing Discipline in academy was formally established in the 1970s. Since then, the study and practice of branding has grown increasingly popular and important. A big part of marketing and branding resides on the notion of relationship-building; that is the building of relationships between the branded product and customers.

Life is all about relationships. From the moment of birth, children form a bonding relationship with their parents, their extended family, and as they grow up, they develop relationships with friends and peers. Having a solid relationship with someone usually entails knowing something about them: their personal history, their interests and the commonalities shared. Relationships are not only formed with special people in a person's life but also with brands. Without a doubt there will be brands that a person loves, hates, feels impartial towards or knows nothing about. A brand allows a customer to form a relationship with the product or service. A key to a consumer forming a relationship with a brand is information, for a brand represents what consumers understand about a particular seller's product.

In the 2010s, brand implementation increasingly focuses on technology that can diffuse brand information in the marketplace. This has increased the emphasis of the informational dimension of the branding process (Strauss and Frost 2001). Arguably, this results in more emphasis being placed on brands and less emphasis on some other product attributes. In other words, for products in branded categories, consumers are more likely to perceive information about the brand, and the brand itself, as being more important than information about the product. As a result, this increases the importance of the brand in the overall product package.

There are many methods for studying brands. These methods have resulted in the formation of many paradigms to describe the way brands work. One way to classify these studies is to draw the line between psychological studies that investigate consumers' perceptions of the brand (Fournier 1998), and studies that look at the financial equity a branded product can command (e.g., a higher price) (Ailawadi et al. 2003; Calder and Reagan 2001).

Herein lies the problem. There are very few studies that find a complementary middle between these competing paradigms. So far, we have not come across a study that uses consumer perceptions of brands in a category to predict their actual choice (not intended choice) of purchase. This highlights a large gap of knowledge blank area in the study of how consumers use brands to make purchase decisions.

Existing theory holds that a customer with positive and strong brand knowledge will have a higher consumer preference for the target brand. This increased brand preference will be positively correlated with the probability to purchase the brand. This is the extent of the research in the psychological paradigm.

The econometric paradigm tracks consumer's actual buying behavior. Buying behavior results in sales. In turn, increased sales mean the company makes more money, resulting in increased brand equity for the brand; higher brand equity makes the brand more valuable. Arguably, the more a brand is bought in a market, the larger its market share. The larger a brand's market share, the more knowledge there is about the brand in a market. This is a purchase cycle.

The continuum that stretches from brand knowledge to preference, to purchase to equity appears to be one continuous purchase cycle. Yet, researchers treat this continuum as two separate components. Very few studies make the link between brand knowledge, preference and actual purchase behavior. This book reports on the PBC model that makes this crucial link between brand knowledge, preference and behavior. Additionally, we test the effect of price discounts and premiums on more and less preferred brands.

Increasing importance of brands

Allison and Uhl (1964) conducted a blind taste study on male beer drinkers. They sought to establish whether they could discern the taste differences among major brands of beer when the bottles were unlabeled. The researchers report their participants were unable to distinguish the taste differences between the various beer brands that were tested. However, beer labels were found to influence the participant's evaluations of the beers – resulting in the respondents clearly discerning that differently branded beers tasted different. As such, Allison and Uhl surmised that it was not the physical product differences of the beers (e.g., taste) that developed the brand's success but rather the marketing efforts of the various firms to create a brand image for their product. This study highlights the importance and value of creating a good brand.

Brands are something people purchase, something people avoid, something people desire and something people outgrow. Consider the Coca-Cola brand; it is a product that people of different ages purchase, and it has enjoyed a long and famous reign as Interbrand's number one "Best Global Brand", for good reason. Coca-Cola is a brand classified as an enduring classic with over 125 years of experience, it continues to be highly recognized and is one of the world's most valuable brands. A key to its success is the millions of dollars the company has invested in marketing the brand around the world, with a lot of this effort recognized through numerous marketing and advertising awards. Coca-Cola's marketing investment has allowed the brand to remain strong and relevant in today's changing marketplace. The Coca-Cola brand is valued at $79.2 billion (Interbrand 2013).

Luxury brands such as Louis Vuitton, Prada and Rolex are brands people aspire to purchase as they mature. These brands seem to reflect wealth, success and superiority. Comparatively, brands such as Lego, Nickelodeon and Barbie are brands people love as children but outgrow as they mature into adulthood.

Brands are powerful. Brands are about belonging, providing a sense of connection to a tribe, acting as a badge or a symbol which signals to others a demonstration of differentiation. A brand is an attempt to differentiate one fast moving good or service from another. When products are very similar with little functional differences, there is a necessity to create an emotional difference. For example, Coca-Cola and Pepsi essentially offer the market the same product, a cola soft drink, and blind taste test experiments have indicated people perceive little difference in the two products when drunk "blind". In the 1970s and 1980s, Pepsi launched advertising campaigns in several markets (e.g., 1975 America, 1983 Australia) highlighting "The Pepsi Challenge" in which Pepsi portrayed more people prefer Pepsi over Coca-Cola. In the Australian advertisement, the challenge claimed research found, "In taste tests across Australia over 50% of people preferred the taste of Pepsi-Cola over the leading cola (Coca-Cola)". However, in the marketplace, Pepsi was and remains a perennial bridesmaid to Coca-Cola; holding the second position despite a (claimed) better tasting product.

This example highlights the necessity of creating an emotional difference between your product and a competitor's product in the market. For years, Coca-Cola's advertising has emphasized the brand first and foremost. It focuses on developing and creating happiness via communicating the shared experience of consuming its product, reminding consumers of their friends and family. When the word Coke is mentioned, most people will instantly think of the red colored can, the unique shape of the bottle, the refreshing taste of the drink and emotionally respond with feelings of happiness, fun, positivity and affirmation. Coca-Cola's advertising has had a strong impact on generating these responses with years of consistent messages reflecting what they stand for. Whilst Pepsi is considered a challenger brand – the company has a product that, may be argued, most people prefer over Coca-Cola. However, Pepsi lags behind the brand leader Coca-Cola in many markets. This may be the effect of superior branding.

When a company acquires another company, such as when Facebook bought Instagram in 2012 for 1 billion dollars, it is acutely clear the objective of the purchase is for the brand name owned by the acquired company. Most times, the price paid does not reflect the tangible assets that appear on the acquired brand's balance sheet (such as technology, offices and so forth). In simple terms, if all the theoretical company's assets are worth $10 million, and it is purchased for $100 million, then it could be said the value of the brand is worth $90 million. Procter and Gamble have made some significant brand acquisitions to stimulate its growth. The most significant of these in recent years is the 2005 purchase of the Gillette brand for $57 billion (Silverstein 2010). Such an acquisition adds renowned brands such as Oral B, Braun and Duracell to Procter and Gamble's stable of brands.

It is also well known that whenever brand names are neglected, they begin the slide. If this slide is not halted, the brand is relegated to commodity status. This results in the event of the brand's product passing naturally through the four stages of the product life cycle. Becoming regarded as a commodity makes the product easy to copy but hard to differentiate. Consider the Yahoo! brand, it is an aging internet company which struggles to compete in search, email, and data sharing. Yahoo was a brand that helped define the internet, it grew rapidly throughout the 1990s and at the time was the most accepted starting point for web users. However in the last 10 years, it has been in decline. Today Yahoo looks to acquisitions such as Tumblr (purchased for $1.1 billion in 2013) to essentially reinvigorate the Yahoo brand from an "aging" to a "cool" brand.

What this book adds to the science of brand measurement

This book documents and describes the PBC model, an innovative method to help managers and researchers predict brand performance at the point of purchase. This can be done for individual customers using the customer's brand knowledge and brand preference in a product category as predictors.

In this book, we report a test of the PBC model in two countries (Australia and China). These countries have different cultures. The product category (beer) is at different stages of maturity in each market. The test tries to predict a customer's choice between their "favorite" beer – their most top preferred brand of beer that was available for purchase in the test venue – and their "second favorite" brand. We test the robustness of our prediction using a price premium for the customer's favorite brand.

The results show that our PBC model predicts purchase choice extremely well, almost perfectly in the mature market where there is a high and stable level of brand knowledge about the product. PBC offers a less powerful prediction in the developing market, where there is still uncertainty surrounding the knowledge in the beer product category. This outcome supports our decision to use brand knowledge as a main predictor in the PBC model.

Researchers and managers can use this innovative method to quantify a customer's brand knowledge. This can then accurately predict a customer's choice of which brand to purchase under some circumstances. What makes PBC valuable is the model's ability to predict and compare the top brands in a category. The PBC process in this book also shows how researchers can do comparisons between countries, even when the top brands in each country are different. PBC can also be used with brands that are ranked in any position. Because brands that compete in different markets, tend to occupy different market positions as a result of their market share being different in each country/market, the PBC model offers a more useful tool over traditional ways for measuring and comparing brand performance – traditionally, those other models require a comparison of the same brands. PBC lets researchers compare the performance of each player in a specific market position (e.g., largest brand share, second largest brand share). Because of this, PBC can be used to compare the same brand's performance in different markets. These markets can be at different stages of development (e.g., growing versus mature markets). This means we have a model enabling researchers and practitioners to map and identify the types of brand knowledge and associations that resonate with a customer at different stages of the product life cycle.

Summary

This chapter has outlined the origins of brands and branding as well as the fundamental characteristics and functions of a brand. Brands are a very important part of marketing, and they provide important services to the expansion of the market and the increase of choices in the marketplace.

From the discussion, we can see that brands are more than marks, or symbols of trade. Brands serve many purposes. They are used as a means of identifying products, producers and sellers. Brands identify the product's origin and can be used to indicate ownership. Consumers may use brands to complement their ideal identity, as indications of their desired lifestyle. Most importantly, a brand serves to indicate, to promise the buyer, a level of quality for the product. When this promise is consistently delivered, the brand gains a good reputation. This promise serves to narrow the gap between the buyer and the seller, providing a symbol upon which to base and build common knowledge of the product. This is especially important when the customer and buyer are separated by space and time.

Brands give some producers reason to strive for consistency and quality. This drives them to improve quality and value. This is because a brand identifies the producer. Producers who operate behind a curtain of anonymity (e.g., no-brand products) do not feel a similar impetus to maintain consistent quality – for they cannot be identified when they make a bad product. As such, brands help to improve and advance product development. Having said this, having a brand is not a guarantee of quality – some brands are consistently bad quality. However, they may gain acceptance because they are sold at lower prices, providing value for the "bargain" market segment. With this, consumers use a brand to identify and position a product in terms of the brand's value proposition.

With consistency of quality and value, a brand's managers can advertise and associate the brand with particular attributes. When this communication is successful, the brand takes on the properties of these attributes – very successful brands come to symbolize these attributes. For example, Volvo cars symbolize safety, Mercedes denote success, BMW stands for performance and Toyota is associated with reliable and affordable automobiles.

These symbolic associations may sound very simple, but are the result of complex associations and building of brand maps and hierarchies within the brand's architecture. By unravelling the way consumers perceive and understand a company's brand architecture, researchers and managers obtain an understanding of the way consumers' see their brand. This can only come from brand measurement. That is why we continue to strive for better ways to measure brands.

Students and some managers often ask, "Why is branding important?" The short answer is, branding activities in marketing create brands. Brands are the way that the market can identify a product. Brands give a product an identity and act as an efficient way for buyers to identify which product best fits their needs, which they can afford, which they can aspire to and which they will buy. A brand can also signify value for a company and in most cases it represents their most valuable asset.

Imagine a world without brands, where items came in a white box or were measured to the quantity ordered. Imagine going into a shop in China and asking for a Kati of Mung Beans. Where did these beans come from? What is their quality? Which farm did they grow on? Are the beans organic? Do they contain pesticides? All of these questions can be answered simply by associating the beans with a brand name.

Brand and market managers have long searched for a stable and practical way to predict buyer brand choice at the moment of truth. Until now, researchers and managers mostly "guessed" how the market would react when a brand discounted its price. Would the customer continue with their most purchased brand? Or would the buyer move their purchase preference to the discounted brand? This book provides a system called the PBC – Predictive Brand Choice model – that is able to provide an answer to this question. PBC can reliably predict how a brand will perform under the threat of a discount, or when the brand has a premium price, at the point of purchase. This is important as the point of purchase is arguably the moment of truth, when branding efforts translate into sales. These sales will cumulate into brand equity – the worth of the brand. The next chapter will discuss in detail the different functions brands perform for the market, sellers and buyers. It will also provide the theoretical rationale that guided our thinking when developing PBC. We then describe the test and results of PBC using an experiment in two countries. This information will help you to better understand how we constructed this predictive brand measurement model.

Bibliography

Ailawadi, Kusum L., Donald R. Lehmann and Scott A. Neslin (2003), "Revenue Premium as an Outcome Measure of Brand Equity", *Journal of Marketing*, 67 (October), 1–17.

Allison, Ralph I. and Kenneth P. Uhl (1964), "Influences of Beer Brand Identification on Taste Perception", *Journal of Marketing Research*, 1 (3), 36–9.

American Marketing Association Dictionary (2014), (accessed November 21, 2014), [available at https://www.ama.org/resources/Pages/Dictionary.aspx].

Armstrong, Gary, Stewart Adam, Sara Denize and Philip Kotler (2010), Principles of Marketing (5th ed). Frenchs Forest, Australia: Pearson.

Bartsiokas, Antonis (2000), "The Eye Injury of King Philip II and the Skeletal Evidence from the Royal Tomb II at Vergina", *Science*, 288 (5465), 511–4.

Bonner, Robert J. (1908), "The Use and Effect of Attic Seals", *Classical Philology*, 3 (4), 399–407.

Brigham, Alexander F. and Stefan Linssen (2010), "Your Brand Reputational Value is Irreplaceable. Protect It!" in *Forbes* Vol. online. New York: Forbes.

Brown, Tom J., Peter A. Dacin, Michael G. Pratt and David A. Whetten (2006), "Identity, Intended Image, Constructed Image and Reputation: An Interdisciplinary Framework and Suggested Terminology", *Journal of the Academy of Marketing Science*, 34 (2), 99–106.

Calder, Bobby J. and Steven J. Reagan (2001), "Brand Design", in *Kellogg on Marketing*, Dawn Iacobucci, ed. New York: John Wiley.

Department of Agriculture and Food Western Australia (2013), "Stock Brands Enquiry Screen", (accessed Feb 7, 2014), [available at http://spatial.agric.wa.gov.au/brands/].

Diamond, Sidney A. (1983), "Historical Development of Trademarks, The", *Trademark Rep.*, 73, 222.

——— (1975), "Historical Development of Trademarks, The", *Trademark Rep.*, 65, 265.

Duncan, Tom (2005), *Principles of Advertising and Imc.* Boston: Tata McGraw-Hill.

Feder, Kenneth L. (1984), "Irrationality and Popular Archaeology", *American Antiquity*, 525–41.

Fournier, Susan (1998), "Consumers and Their Brands: Developing Relationship Theory in Consumer Research", *Journal of Consumer Research*, 24 (March), 343–73.

Garnsey, Peter, Keith Hopkins and Charles Richard Whittaker (1983), *Trade in the Ancient Economy*. Berkeley, CA: University of California Press.

Greenberg, Abraham S. (1951), "Ancient Lineage of Trade-Marks, The", *J. Pat. Off. Soc'y*, 33, 876.

Harlow, Unger G. (2011), *American Tempest: How the Boston Tea Party Sparked a Revolution*. Cambridge, MA: Da Capo.

Heaney, Seamus (Translation) (2002), *Beowulf: A Verse Translation*. New York: Norton.

Interbrand (2013), "Interbrand: Rankings", (accessed April 1, 2014), [available at: http://www.bestglobalbrands.com/2014/ranking/].

Keller, K. L. (2008), *Strategic Brand Management. Building, Measuring, and Managing Brand Equity* (3rd ed.). Upper Saddle River, NJ: Pearson Prentice-Hall.

Keller, Kevin Lane (1993), "Conceptualizing, Measuring, and Managing Customer-Based Brand Equity", *Journal of Marketing*, 57 (1), 1–22.

Klaber, F. (1950), *Beowulf and the Fight at Finnsburg* (3rd ed.). Boston: DC Heath.

Kleinitz, Cornelia (2005), "Rock Art Landscapes of the Fourth Nile Cataract: Characterisations and First Comparisons", in *Proceedings of the Second International Conference on the Archaeology of the Fourth Nile Cataract*. Berlin.

Kotler, P. (1991), *Marketing Management: Analysis, Planning, Implementation, and Control*. Englewood Cliffs, NJ: Prentice-Hall.

Leonard, Mark (1997), *Britain TM: Renewing Our National Identity*. London: Demos.

Munshi, Kaivan and Mark Rosenzweig (2006), "Traditional Institutions Meet the Modern World: Caste, Gender, and Schooling Choice in a Globalizing Economy", *The American Economic Review*, 1225–52.

Oxford English Dictionary Online (2014) in Oxford English Dictionary online [available at: http://www.oed.com/].

Paster, Benjamin G. (1969), "Trademarks-Their Early History", *Trademark Rep.*, 59, 551.

Pike, Ruth (1967), "Sevillian Society in the Sixteenth Century: Slaves and Freedmen", *Hispanic American Historical Review*, 344–59.

Schechter, F.I. (1925), "The Historical Foundations of the Law Relating to Trade-Marks", *HeinOnline*, 20.

Schwartzkopf-Genswein, K.S., J.M. Stookey and R. Welford (1997), "Behavior of Cattle During Hot-Iron and Freeze Branding and the Effects on Subsequent Handling Ease", *Journal of Animal Science*, 75 (8), 2064–72.

Shao, Ke (2005), "Look at My Sign – Trademarks in China from Antiquity to the Early Modern Times", *Journal of the Patent and Trademark Office Society*, 87 (8), 654–86.

Shaw, Arch Wilkinson (1912), "Some Problems in Market Distribution", *The Quarterly Journal of Economics*, 26 (4), 703–65.

Silverstein, Barry (2010), "Gillette's "Razor Guys": Fans Turned Brand Ambassadors," (accessed October 20, 2014), [available at: http://www.brandchannel.com/home/category/brand-ambassadors.aspx?page=6].

Simon, Harrison (2002), "The Politics of Resemblance: Ethnicity, Trademarks, Head-Hunting", *The Journal of the Royal Anthropological Institute*, 8 (2), 211–32.

Society, Chetham (1876), *Remains, Historical and Literary, Connected with the Palatine Counties of Lancaster and Chester*. Charleston, SC: Chetham Society.

Stern, Barbara B. (2006), "What Does Brand Mean? Historical-Analysis Method and Construct Definition", *Journal of the Academy of Marketing Science*, 34 (2), 216–23.

Strauss, Judy and Raymond Frost (2001), *E-Marketing*. New Jersey: Prentice Hall.

Todd, J.H. (1842), *An Apology for Lollard Doctrines*. London: Camden Society.

Warner, William (1971), *Albions England (1612)*. Great Britain: G. Olms.

Wyman, David S. (1984), *The Abandonment of the Jews*. Pantheon Books: New York.

2

THE ART OF BRANDING

The first chapter of this book explored what brands are and what they can help a company accomplish in a marketplace. This chapter discusses the process of branding. A lot of science exists to measure, categorize and identify the process to create a successful brand. This science helps managers in making better decisions when implementing the branding process. However, lying above the science of brand measurement is the art of making branding decisions. Why do we discuss the art of branding first? Because knowledge of how the different components of what constitutes a brand "hang" together, how they combine to form a successful brand, appears to be a prerequisite to understanding the science behind brand measurement. In essence, while the science increases understanding of brands and how they perform, the results of these measurements inform the decisions that must be made when building brands.

There are many products and services. The great majority of these have brand names. However, not all of these brands are successful. A successful brand is one that has a name, symbol or design or combination of, that helps the company's product obtain a sustainable competitive advantage in the marketplace. Some examples of brands that managed to do this are Apple, McDonald's and Google. This competitive advantage will help these brands consistently achieve better profit and market performance than lesser-known brands.

A brand that presents a sustainable competitive advantage is considered an asset. However, this asset will deteriorate without regular investment. For example, Billabong was a prime Australian brand, at one time the biggest brand in the surf-wear market. The company had 560 stores worldwide and annual sales of USD $1.3 billion. In the year 2007, Billabong valued the brand at AUD $3.84 billion (Fickling 2013). Sadly, this value was reduced to zero by August 2013 (Speedy 2013). Billabong lost its cool edge with customers as competing international brands started to enter its markets. Instead of focusing on using the brand's equity with customers to counter these new entrants, Billabong focused on store expansion. This lack of brand investment in the face of increased competition meant that the company lost a 3.84 billion dollar asset.

Customer emotions and brand

A key to a strong brand is the building of an emotional connection between the brand and its customers. Typically, customers will find their feelings for a preferred brand difficult to explain. Consider, for example, the good feelings a customer may feel when driving their Porsche convertible. These values that come from feeling close to a brand (brand intimacy) can be influenced and encouraged by strong, consistent marketing strategies. These strategies seek a unique position for the brand in the consumer's mind. Over time, consumer familiarity with the brand increases as they develop more personal experiences with the brand. Familiarity may also come from having more exposure to the brand. Arguably, this increases the consumer's feelings of closeness with the brand, making them perceive that they know the brand better than other brands. This situation is similar to knowing close friends better than more distant acquaintances. The stronger the emotional connection, the greater the impression the brand has on the consumer. Theory suggests that when customers have a favorable impression of a brand, they are less likely to switch to other brands (Aydin 2005).

A good way to explain how brands appeal to consumers is to observe that people buy things that suit their lifestyle. Most consumers have an idealized lifestyle, this is the image they have in their mind about the way they live, or aspire to live. For many consumers, part of their lifestyle is expressed through the products they use and activities they choose to partake in.

Successful brands seem to fit certain lifestyles especially well. For example, consumers can live a country-club lifestyle, adventurous lifestyle, or a suburban, married-with-children, lifestyle. Marketers have even coined terms like YUPPIE, YUMMIE and DINKS to describe customers with different types of lifestyles (Atwal and Williams 2009). These lifestyles are linked strongly to different types and styles of consumption, a part of the consumption is the brands different customers buy. For example, affluent consumers who perceive themselves to have an active outdoors lifestyle may buy adventure gear from brands like North Face. This is because North Face portrays a rugged, ready, go anywhere, do anything image. This fits with the customer's image of who they are. The company also provides quality products at a premium price. This appeals to the customer's social standing. The branding process carried out by North Face seeks to fit the brand to the perceptions of conscious affluent buyers who view themselves as being adventurous, self-sufficient and capable people. These are people who are attracted to attributes like rugged, capable, ready, go anywhere, quality and premium products. These customers tend to shop at camping, outdoor sport, hiking and adventure shops. With their lifestyle, they may likely drive a utility or sport utility vehicle, perhaps a Jeep, a Land Rover, Range Rover or Toyota Land Cruiser. As such, this group of consumers will buy a whole host of brands that fit their desired lifestyle. There are many other examples. A person who sees themselves as being a "skateboarder" may prefer brands like Vans and Baker. Consumers who have a "luxury" lifestyle may prefer Louis Vuitton, Prada and Chanel. Some consumers who see themselves as weekend motorcycle "warriors" – these are weekend Harley motorcycle riders – who aspire to the bad boy/girl image and the freedom, excitement and camaraderie that comes from living an outlaw motorcycle-rider lifestyle may use Harley Davidson related products. Yet, many of these weekend riders are also responsible and upright citizens with respectable jobs. They buy the Harley Davidson brand of products, and wear them on weekend outings so that they get to live their dream. In short, people buy things to fit the way they think they want to live. If this is the case, what is a brand? What does a brand do?

Brands as handles for memories

As discussed, a brand and its associated trading marks serve as a token or artefact to help consumers quickly and conveniently recall their experiences with a seller's product (Keller 1987) – note that sellers can also be manufacturers, but for the sake of convenience, we refer to the company owning a brand as "sellers". Consumers consist of the brand's buyers and users. Some people may buy a brand but not use the product – e.g., professional buyers of heart attack medicine in hospitals who do not have heart attacks will not consume the product. Some may use but not buy – e.g., young children tend not to make purchases; instead they use the things that are bought for them.

Because brands serve as an identifier, they make it more convenient for consumers to discuss the different brand choices available in a market. Effectively, consumers use brands as familiar "handles" to pull up memories associated with the brand. They act as a kind of "shorthand" that enables consumers to quickly draw upon their brand knowledge to compare different brands. Marketers often depict the results of these comparisons using perceptual maps. These map the relative position of competing brands in a market, usually using two metrics, for example, price versus quality. In this way, a brand acts as a "bookmark" in consumers' minds that facilitates quick access to the associated memories. These placeholders give consumers a system for "sorting" and "filing" different brands in their memories. This helps to make routine purchases easier. After a while, customers with sufficient knowledge simply buy their favorite brand. When this is not available, they go to their next acceptable brand. They no longer need to go through a deliberation and comparison process each time they buy in the familiar product category. Imagine a world without brands, where you have to deliberate every purchase decision afresh – supermarket shopping would be a nightmare for many buyers.

Brands perform an important role as a "mental shortcut"; this helps consumers define a market position for the brands they know. Because consumers tend to encounter many brands, the process to create a clear and memorable market position is extremely important. Only a few brands in a product category will stand out. Standing out makes it more likely for customers to consider buying the brand – the brand becomes a part of a consumer's consideration set for purchase in the product category. For many product categories, there is simply too much choice, making it impossible for consumers to try every alternative available. Nor would most consumers want to try every brand out there. To help them decide which brands to try, consumers will access the collective market knowledge available to them to identify the brands they should avoid. In doing so they also identify the "valuable brands" in the category.

This process of eliminating unfavorable brands and identifying favorable ones is also used by novice buyers. They are the ones who tend to benefit most from the collective knowledge about a brand. This brand knowledge is documented (e.g., product reviews, ratings, blogs), communicated verbally through recommendations and hearsay or via marketing communications (e.g., advertising). This knowledge helps novice buyers reduce the risk of purchase (Johnson 2008). These shared stories are also a way to spread word-of-mouth about a brand and are essential for promoting product diffusion (Lam et al. 2009). This communication and discussion in the marketplace helps to build a brand's positive or negative reputation. Reputation depends on the brand's consistency, attributes and the way these attributes are linked to influence consumers' purchase decisions (Gounaris and Stathakopoulos 2004). For new brands, the ability to build brand knowledge will help diffuse the brand to different consumer groups. This type of information diffusion helps the brand gain space in supply chains and on retail shelves. As brands become more well-known, customers will ask for them, leading shopkeepers to stock the brand. Retailers and suppliers are less likely to carry brands that are not "famous" or in-demand; this means that less well-known brands will have difficulty securing distribution.

Branding process

The branding process works because it seeks to associate a product or product-line with selected desirable attributes. These associations are accomplished by weaving a "story" or narrative that explains the way the brand is linked to these attributes. Normally, this narrative is promoted by the brand's owners. For example, some brands of toothpaste link with the idea that their product is "minty", others promote a "clean crisp taste", yet other toothpastes "fight cavities". Some brands link the products of other companies to negative attributes. Notable campaigns are anti-smoking campaigns that try to promote the knowledge that cigarettes are health risks and will kill consumers. Together with the consumers' experience with a product, these stories form a collective idea in the market about what type of product performance to expect from the items and brands (Fournier 1998). In this way, having a successful and well-known brand sets up consumers' expectations about the way the branded product will perform, and promises a certain level of product performance. For example, Avis promises to "Try Harder" and Visa promises that their cards will be accepted around the world. A brand's promise can incite emotions that can create extremely powerful connections between the consumer and the brand. Many researchers argue that it is these emotions which will ultimately lead to repurchase and brand loyalty (Aaker and Biel 1993). For a company, branding activity must focus on the brand's promise and keep delivering on that promise. Consistency in fulfilling what the brand promises to consumers helps to strengthen the brand's identity. A brand that consistently delivers on its promise builds trust and becomes dependable in the eyes of its customers.

Brands live in consumers' perceptions, experiences and emotions. For example, Nike's mission is "to bring inspiration and innovation to every athlete in the world". Nike believes that "if you have a body, you are an athlete". Nike expresses their mission and suitably aims to influence consumers through the image represented in their logo "Swoosh", their slogan "Just do it" and through the Nike brand name. As a result, some consumers may see the brand to represent performance, strength, athleticism and good health. However, other consumers may view the brand in a different light. Negative public sentiment in recent years about the extramarital affairs of its brand ambassador, Tiger Woods, and the anti-sweatshop movement, may generate negative connotations about the brand. Detractors have coined alternative slogans of "Just do her", and links with exploitation of workers are damaging to the brand's identity. This illustrates how it is very difficult for marketers to control a brand's image in the eyes of the consumer. A brand is what the consumer sees the brand to be, not how the marketer wants them to see it.

Elements of a brand that influence consumer decision-making

Brands offer consumers choice in a marketplace. At their very core, brands seek to differentiate from other brands (Schmalensee 1982). This offers consumers variety. Variety breeds competition. Competition tends to drive prices down and promote innovation in a product category, resulting in better products. For example, consumers can buy different brands of cars that belong to the subcategories of upmarket, family car, sport car, or sport utility vehicle.

For products that have highly subjective qualities like perfume and beer, branding to secure a position in the market is even more important (Pechmann and Ratneshwar 1991). Consumers may choose some brands that provide the desired quality, taste, touch, smell or another attribute. In this way, brands also communicate nuances that differentiate similar products within a category (Keller 1993).

To consumers, brands are more than a name or symbol. A well-designed and executed brand offers consumers many benefits: a brand identity, assurance of quality, trust and a way to imply certain qualities for a product.

Even simply putting the name of a country on a product is a way to brand. Think about the connotations attached to Made in China (affordable, lower quality, fake, imitation, counterfeit), Swiss Made (precision), German engineering (things that work), and Goodness from New Zealand (purity).

Consumers also use brands to signify the quality and type of material used to make the product (Goldemberg and Height 2000). For example, different marks approved by the British Crown are used to indicate the content of gold or silver in jewelry and in ingots. These brands are well understood by people in the trade and used as indicators for the quality of precious metal.

When done well, branding efforts will clearly position a product as belonging within a product category; that is, branding imbues a product with qualities perceived to be similar to other products in that category. In branding, this is called "points of similarity" (Keller 2008). This is an extremely important role that brands play because being identified as belonging to a product category avails the branded product the possibility of being included in consumers' consideration sets (also called choice sets or reference sets). As discussed, consideration sets consist of the brands that consumers will consider when buying from a product category. If a product is not within a choice set, then it has a much lower chance of being purchased by the consumer.

The information and image surrounding a brand also serves to inform consumers about the context/situation when the brand may be suitable for use. For example, a person may use everyday brands from supermarkets for their everyday clothes. However, they may wear more exclusive brands for special occasions. Many companies build "usage" contexts into their advertising as a part of building knowledge about the brand. For example, M&M chocolate advertisements show M&Ms being eaten at parties, in front of the television, at movies, baked into cakes, shared on public transport, as a part of confectionary, added to ice-cream and being given away as gifts. This builds the knowledge that M&M chocolates are a "sharing" chocolate that are suitable for social occasions.

Benefits of a strong brand

Establishing a strong brand is argued to be a key factor for success for most businesses, and the major task of marketing (Kotler and Keller 2009). For example, the performance of the Google brand in the technology sector highlights the true power of a successful brand. Google first joined Interbrand's Best Global Brands Top 100 in 2005 and has achieved consistently strong growth to reach second position in 2013 with a brand value of $93.3 billion (Interbrand 2013). The brand has evolved from a search engine to become a genuine leader of the technology age. Google's success can be attributed to its relentless adaptation to the changing marketplace which attests to the brand's ability to anticipate and continuously fulfil the needs of its consumers. It has fought hard to discover and retain its relevance.

Interbrand lists the most important factor driving brand value across all sectors – financial services, consumer goods, and automotive – is a brand's sustainability. Jez Frampton, Global CEO of Interbrand said, "The key to success, in good times and bad, is understanding how your brand creates value".

Parts of Google's brand success can be attributed to a strong brand management strategy that has helped the company achieve and maintain rapid and sustained growth in a product category (internet search engine websites) where it would appear difficult to establish brand individuality. It also highlights how brand management is of great importance for any company.

Of course brands can also rapidly lose value. Often, a brand's success or failure depends on its potential buyers' perceptions of the brand. Consider the BlackBerry brand, it fell from the Interbrand's Best Global Brands Top 100 in 2013 whilst its main competitors, Apple and Google were number 1 and number 2 respectively. BlackBerry was the market leader in smartphones in 2007 but lost its way with poor performing products and reduced relevance amongst its key business target market. The successful launch of the Apple iPhone and Android smartphones has reduced its market share to around 1% percent in the key markets of the United States, Germany and Spain, with its highest market share being just 3.3% in the United Kingdom (Reed 2013).

Another good example of a brand losing its favorable perceptions and share is the US based Schlitz brand of beer (Fredrix 2008). The Joseph Schlitz brand of beer was founded in the 1850s in Milwaukee (USA). For much of the twentieth century, Schlitz was the top selling brand of beer in the United States. The marketers of Schlitz misinterpreted a classic brand taste test study conducted by an executive of a beer company and a professor at The University of Illinois (Allison and Uhl 1964). That study investigated beer consumers' taste perceptions. They found beer consumers were generally unable to discriminate among major brands, and even unable to distinguish their favorite brand from among other brands when the labels were removed from beer bottles (they used the same bottle for different beers). The Schlitz executives decided that if consumers were unable to discriminate, then why have the expense of a longer than "necessary" brewing period? They shortened the fermenting process and added new ingredients that lowered the manufacturing expense of their brand of beer. Unfortunately, that change ultimately led to the brand going out of business in 1981. Consumers stopped buying Schlitz beer because they could discern a difference.

While consumers may not be good at picking a particular brand of beer in a blind taste test, they still made decisions on how they perceive the brand. A similar situation occurred when Coca-Cola modified the taste of its Coca-Cola branded drink after taste tests showed consumers preferred the taste of its closest rival (Fournier 1999). Consumers stopped buying Coca-Cola, forcing the company to reintroduce the old formula as Coke Classic. The company has since reverted to the original taste.

However it is not all doom and gloom for a brand if it experiences a decline in brand value. There are instances where a successful brand can take a hit in brand value and share but with effective marketing strategies and management the brand can resurrect itself into a brand leader. Case in point is the LEGO brand. LEGO was found in 1932 by Ole Kirk Christiansen and during the 1980s the popularity of LEGOs surged, with profits doubling every five years (Knowledge@Wharton 2012).

In 1993 sales started to stagnate as similar products from China were manufactured and entered the market at a fraction of the cost. LEGO also failed to keep pace with the revolutionary changes in kids' lives with the advent of video and computer games. Children were also getting older faster and thus substituting LEGO products for more sophisticated toys. The LEGO brand was rapidly becoming irrelevant. In 2004 the company experienced a net loss of DKK1.9 billion and was nearly bankrupt but was able to turn this around to a DKK3.7 billion net profit in 2010 (Brands & Rousers 2012). A key success element of this turn around was reconnecting with its core target market, children, by becoming relevant in the digital age. To do so, management secured licensing deals with entertainment brands such as Star Wars, Harry Potter, Lord of the Rings and Toy Story which re-connected the brand with its core target market. In 2012 LEGO became the world's most valuable toy manufacturer with sales of DKK 23.4 billion (Metcalf and LaFranco 2013).

Brand utility and identity

Aaker (1996) defines brand identity as "a unique set of brand associations that the brand strategist aspires to create or maintain. These associations represent what the brand stands for and imply a promise to customers from organization members" (p. 68). Aaker's definition takes on a strategist perspective which emphasizes it is the strategist's role to create a brand's identity. Aaker and Joachminsthaler (2000) add that brand identity "represents what the organization can and will do over time" (p. 13). Aaker's definitions consider brand identity solely from the point of view of the company, an internal focus. This view is not from the perspective of the customer.

A brand's identity is what makes a brand unique. When consumers think of products, most will think of a brand. Consider you want a refreshing alcoholic drink. The majority of people will firstly think of the product class – alcoholic drinks – and then mentally evaluate which brand will most effectively achieve their need. The process of assessing the different options in the category is the process of comparing brand identities. The consumer will continually select the brand identity that most effectively fulfils their needs.

Identification

In contemporary marketing, a brand's first and arguably most important function is to act as a name for a product. In its most basic form, a brand helps identify the producer or seller of a product (Keller et al. 2002). As discussed, brands can be expressed as marks, symbols or names (Shaw 1912). Over time, these marks acquire associations with specific pieces of information. For example, consumers may associate Coca-Cola with a certain bottle-shape and Ferrari with a specific red color. Collectively, these associations form knowledge about the brand in a market.

While this information may be factual, it is the way this information is understood and perceived that gives the brand its identity. Consumers' link different pieces of information that are associated with a brand to form an understanding about the brand, this creates "brand knowledge". For example, Champagne is a brand associated with France; consumers understand that only French sparkling wine made in the geographic area of Champagne in France can be called Champagne. In this case, the Champagne brand describes a product from a particular source or place of origin.

Brands also create value in and of themselves. This has seen the creation of brand-only companies that do not manufacture or sell any products, but lend their brands to other companies. One example is the Hello Kitty brand. Hello Kitty is licensed to many well-known companies and appears on products ranging from jet airliners to cosmetics, from lunch boxes to lingerie, from candy to cushions, from matches to coffee mugs. These are leading edge products made by the leading companies in their respective industries (Melinda 2009). Hello Kitty is a much sought after partner brand for many industry leaders because of the brand's popularity. Worldwide, Hello Kitty has many loyal customers. Licensing and partnering with Hello Kitty gives other brands access to this group of customers who will buy and try their products because it is a "Hello Kitty" product. In this way, the Hello Kitty brand becomes a tool that enables producers of different brands to raise awareness in the market about their latest product offerings.

Brand awareness

Brand awareness is the first component necessary for a consumer "branding" a product (Keller 1993). Establishing brand awareness draws upon the consumers' use of brands to identify a producer or seller in the marketplace. Brand awareness occurs when consumers become conscious that a brand exists. When asked, they may report that they have been exposed to a brand – they report having heard of the brand and that it is vaguely familiar. Consumers with more exposure may report more familiarity and are most likely able to identify the brand on sight, or when it is described (Aaker and Jacobson 2001).

The likelihood that consumers will try the brand increases as brand awareness spreads. Companies often try to increase brand awareness using advertising. As more consumers become knowledgeable about the brand, more buyers will become aware of how the brand can help solve their problems. This prompts trial behavior where consumers begin to buy the brand. To promote trial, brands will use direct promotions like sales, trial packs and product launches to promote purchase. With each new customer buying the brand, the brand's market penetration increases. Technically, *brand penetration* measures the number of customers in a market (e.g., China market, Beijing market, Sydney market) who buy a product category, who also buy the brand – this is counted as the number of consumers that buy the brand in a market during a given period of time (a "counting" period). A brand's "share of the market" (brand share) is calculated as the brand's penetration multiplied by the number of times the product is purchased and repurchased during a period. Effectively, brand share (sometimes also called market share) is the number of items a brand sells in a product category, compared to the overall category sales in the market for a given period of time. This is usually expressed as a percentage.

In a market, collective brand knowledge increases as more consumers buy, use and experience the brand. This first-hand experience mixes with the information spread by the brand's owners (e.g., through paid advertising) and recommendations from other consumers. This information forms a story about the brand. This shared knowledge facilitates discussion where consumers will likely recommend good brands to others, spreading good word-of-mouth about favored brands and warning others to avoid unsatisfactory brands. These recommendations help some brands penetrate the market more (Frank and Talarzyk 1972). At a point in the brand's growth, the recommendations from the first customers to use the brand (the pioneers/early adopters) will be overtaken by those who imitate (imitators) the consumption patterns of these early adopters (Bass and Wilkie 1973). These are normally called the early majority and late majority groups of customers. When majority consumers outnumber early adopters, the brand has achieved mainstream status and is accepted by most consumers in the category (Lee and Edwards 2013).

Brand preference

After trying a brand, consumers will likely repurchase the brand if it lives up to their expectations or if the brand is better than the brand they currently use. Repurchase shows that consumers develop a preference for the brand – of course, this is contingent on there being a choice of brands in a market; it does not work in a monopoly market. In marketing, this is called *brand preference*. Customers express brand preference as a liking for the brand, as feeling that resides in the consumers' hearts and minds.

Brand preference develops from consumers liking a brand. When their liking for a brand reaches a critical point, brand preference eventuates. If affordability and availability do not present barriers to purchase, consumers will seek the brand. As a result, they are willing to pay a price premium for their most preferred brand. A price premium is a purchase price that is higher for a preferred product, compared to similar products.

Of course, customers may not always buy their preferred brand. Most customers will also have one to typically three other brands in a category that they find acceptable as substitutes. Note that a customer's most preferred brand may not be their favorite brand, but the brand that they buy most often. Sometimes, a customer's top preferred brand is selected from the brands that are available – for example, customers will choose a favorite brand of beer from the range of brands that are available for sale in a pub/tavern/bar. Some customers may not be able to afford their favorite brand – for example, many people state their favorite brand of car is Porsche, but they drive a Toyota vehicle.

A portion of customers may feel so strongly that they will insist on a brand, they show loyalty by forgoing consumption if their preferred brand is unavailable – this is called *brand insistence*. When this happens, customers will go to great lengths to search for their preferred brand – this is called *brand search* – going from store to store seeking the brand.

Even stronger brand relationships see a customer becoming a brand evangelist/ promoter, this is when they recommend a brand to others using word-of-mouth (*brand recommendation*); this becomes free and trusted advertising for the brand.

Consumers may also look at a brand negatively. This will have consumers avoid or *reject* a brand. For example, consumers boycotted BP during the Gulf of Mexico oil spill, rejected Exxon products during the Exxon Valdez oil spill in Alaska, boycotted milk powder made by the Three Deer brand in China when the brand's infant formula was contaminated with the industrial glue melamine. This later widened to become a boycott of all brands of infant formula from China (Ingelfinger 2008). When a consumer has a negative perception of a brand, the brand has to work harder to change this perception and it takes time, in some cases many years.

Many smaller brands are in a situation where they do not have adequate levels of brand awareness, most consumers in the market have never heard of the brand. Some weak brands have some recognition, but consumers typically do not know enough about these brands to form an opinion or develop any feelings for the brand. This makes it improbable that the consumer will try the brand. However, sometimes consumers are forced to use a brand they do not know of (*no awareness*), for example, heart attack medicine when they experience a heart attack.

Sometimes, consumers may know about a brand – there is awareness – however, they have no opinion about the brand. This often happens because the brand has failed to make an impression on the customer. These increasing levels of brand preference in a market are portrayed as a continuum in Figure 2.1.

Figure 2.1 shows that when done well, brands can offer a competitive advantage via developing a high level of brand preference. Customers search for, are more loyal to, and will pay more for a preferred branded product. This advantage also works in the product category's value chain because retailers prefer to stock well-known brands as these sell better, command higher prices and have higher sales volume. More volume and profits also means that wholesalers and other intermediaries will pay more attention to promoting these brands. Original equipment manufacturers (OEM) are also more likely to want to make products for well-known brands.

↑ Increasing preference levels	Brand recommendation	I will recommend this brand to my trusted in-groups, my friends and family.
	Brand insistence	This is the only brand I would consider using. I will not use other brands.
	Brand search	I will spend time, money and other resources to search for my preferred brand.
	Brand preference	I have a preference for this brand. I will buy it again even if it is more expensive than other brands.
	Brand acceptance	This is not my most preferred brand, but for this price, it is acceptable.
	No opinion	I have heard of this brand but I do not know enough to form an opinion.
	No awareness	I have never heard or encountered this brand.
	Reject	I have heard or experienced bad things about this brand. I do not want to use it. Sometimes customers will also spread bad word of mouth about the rejected brand.

FIGURE 2.1 Continuum of increasing levels of preference for a brand

Why are some brands more successful?

Many brands find success in the marketplace because marketers undertake planned and proactive campaigns to promote and build their brand. These efforts seek to build an identity and a "story" that is shared between the brand, the product and the customer. The idea is to make the brand and its story relevant to existing and potential customers.

As the branding process unfolds, brands evolve and reposition in the market. In positioning brands to be competitive, the brand's managers must identify the brand with attributes that position a product as belonging to a product category. This means the brand's image, the attributes associated with the brand and its narrative must present/position the brand as being part of a distinct product category. This is called highlighting the brand's *points of parity* (Keller 1993). For example, it is commonly held that a car should have at least four wheels. Bajaj, a large scooter, motorcycle and moped maker has produced a four wheeled vehicle with a body that is similar to a car. It even has a steering wheel. This company is having a difficult time marketing the product as a car because of the Bajaj's brand associations with the motorcycle industry (Saxena 2012).

Universal points of similarity in a product category

Points of parity operate at the product category level and at the sub-market level. They serve to identify the product as belonging to the product category and which part of the market (e.g., luxury or budget) the brand operates in.

At the category level, a brand will seek points of parity that are commonly used to identify the product as belonging to the category. These are attributes that all brands competing in the category must possess. To illustrate, let us discuss the beer product category. For an alcoholic beverage to be considered beer, it needs to have attributes that identify it as a beer. The beer should contain alcohol, have a very specific type of "beer" taste, and be manufactured/ brewed in a specific way using ingredients common to beer like wheat, hops and malt. If these common elements are not fulfilled, consumers may not see a product as a beer – for example, an alcoholic beverage made from fruit is considered cider, not beer. In terms of branding, the brand must have common elements with other brands in the category. Common brand positions for beer are, taste, refreshing, purity, reward and a drink for a working-person/blue collar person.

Meeting the necessary attributes that identify a brand and product as belonging to a category does not mean that consumers will choose your brand. It simply means that buyers are more likely to think that the brand is worth considering for purchase. However, lacking any of these attributes is a "deal breaker" that gives consumers a reason not to choose the brand.

Sub-market/market segment points of parity

The points of parity used by successful brands also identify them to a sub-market of the product category. These identify the brand to service a specific section of the market (e.g., premium, mainstream and low-priced market segments). Each brand competing in a sub-market must have attributes common to the segment. For example, Figure 2.2 identifies the sections of the beer market in China. They are premium, mainstream and low-end segments.

All premium beer brands have the segment point of parity – *The Taste of Success.* Mainstream beers have *Great Taste.* Low-end beers are sold as *Good Beer at Cheap Prices.* Customers use these differences between the segments to distinguish between high, mid and low-end beers. These segment points of parity are similar within a segment, but different between segments. At this level, brand sub-market points of parity operate the same way as the segmentation principle from Market Segmentation Theory (Smith 1956).

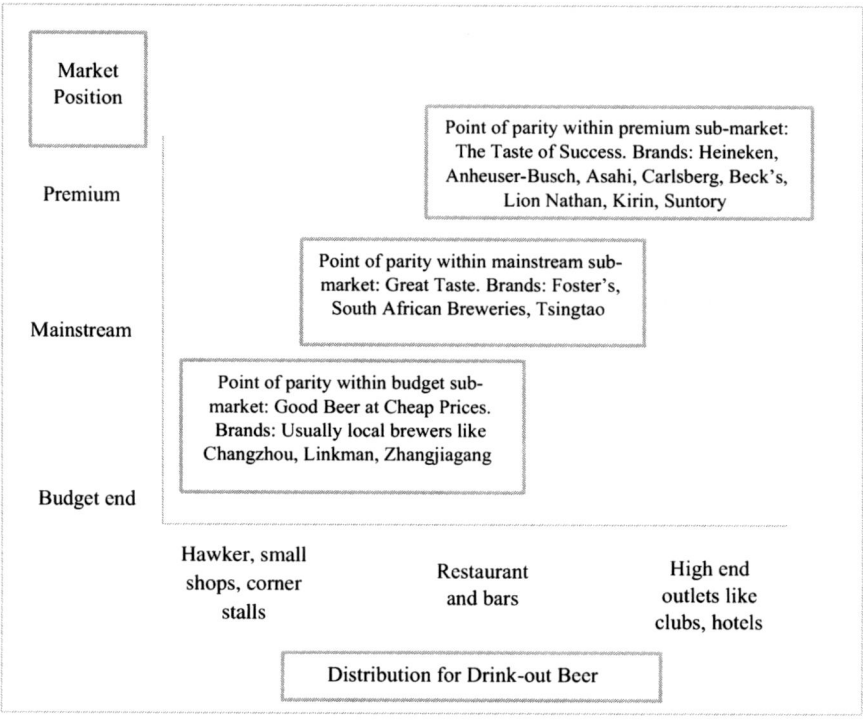

FIGURE 2.2 Points of parity for beers in different market segments in China

Points of difference

For a brand to stand out, managers have to create *points of distinctiveness* (Keller 1993) that resonate with their target buyers. Points of distinctiveness are also referred to as points of difference. These points of difference form attributes that sets the brand apart (distinct) from its most direct competitors. It is important that these points are communicated to consumers.

When these differentiating aspects of the brand become meaningful to customers, they serve as the brand's "unique selling proposition", giving the brand a unique competitive position in the marketplace (Keller 1993). This is a strong advantage for the brand. Note that a brand's unique selling proposition is a position that resides as a perception in consumers' minds. This helps consumers make comparisons when deciding which brand to buy. For example, in the premium beer segment, Asahi, a dry Japanese beer, promotes its dry taste, while Becks distinguishes itself as a German beer brewed under the German "pureness" law that allows the use of four ingredients in making beer.

Marketers often depict brand positions in a market through perceptual maps. Perceptual maps are two dimensional plots of relative brand positions in a market

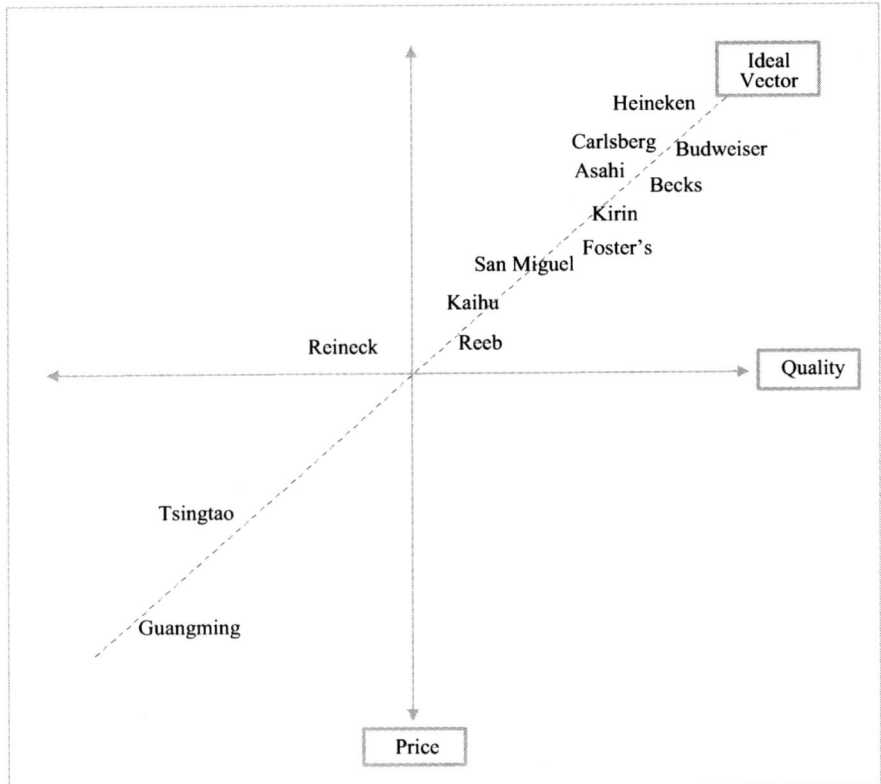

FIGURE 2.3 Perceptual map of market positions for beer brands in China

segment or product category. These positions are determined using two attributes that are the most important to consumers.

Figure 2.3 depicts a perceptual map of beer brands in China. This map is generated using the same data used for Figure 2.2.

Figure 2.3 is a typical two dimensional perceptual map showing the brands positioned along an ideal vector (dashed line). This ideal vector is where successful brands in the category have managed to find equilibrium in terms of quality and price. The separation between brands arranged along the ideal vector shows how each competitor distinguishes themselves from competitors (point of difference). Their position in terms of price and quality signals participation in a specific sub-segment – these signals depend on associating with points of parity for the sub-segment. The brands all have to associate with brand and product elements that signal they compete in the beer market (point of parity – category). Brands that are able to find this equilibrium position along the ideal vector tend to succeed while those that deviate significantly will fail – simply because customers tend to perceive those brands not to offer a good mix of value.

Brands help consumers choose when products are very similar

Many products are very similar. For example, many brands of bottled water are indistinguishable. Yet, some brands are able to command higher prices than others. Some brands are more preferred and others have more sales. Consumers use brands and their attributes to compare between the different offerings in these categories.

There have been many "taste-tests". Hull (1924) found that blindfolded subjects in his cigarette taste tests frequently failed to distinguish between real tobacco smoke, and warm moist air. In a separate study, Husband and Godfrey (1934) reported cigarette smokers could not correctly identify their brands above chance or guessing. This is reinforced by a study on cigarette taste discrimination and identification by Ramond et al. (1950) who found an overall improvement over that reported by Husband and Godfrey in the average correct percentage of cigarette brand identification, but labelled this improvement small in magnitude. Our consulting with confection company M&M/Mars found that more than half of those testing a candy bar could not tell that two pieces of the same bar were the same brand. Clearly, the past research into consumers' ability to correctly identify brands – including their favorite – finds that they are very poor at this task.

Ralph Allison and Kenneth Uhl's classic "blind" taste test on beer brands we have discussed (1964) was conducted by marketing experts that tested a category (beer). Beer is often considered a product where consumers make their buying decisions primarily on the taste of a beer; where a beer's taste drives brand choice. Beer has long been sold on having a personality and on the imagery surrounding a brand. This is a category where significant advertising and sales promotion effort has succeeded in developing many distinct and possibly different brands in the minds of consumers. A few brands of beer like Heineken and Tsingtao have been successfully sold worldwide. This success has been attributed to the way consumers view the brands.

What Allison and Uhl did was to test whether beer drinkers who drink a least three times a week could differentiate between the tastes of six major brands of beer. Today, this level of consumption is what we would consider to be a heavy drinker. A second objective was to see if they could identify their favorite brand of beer. In week one of the experiment, the two researchers tested the sample of beer drinkers by delivering six brands of beer with identifying labels intact.

The participants drank and rated the beer. In week two, the sample received the same beer brands, this time with all their identifying material brushed off. This is what is known as a "blind" taste test. The brands were given an alphabetical identity like "F", "A", "C". When the branding labels were visible, the beer drinking sample provided ratings of the brands' eight taste criteria (e.g., aftertaste, aroma, bitterness – see Figure 2.4). They completed the same rating exercise done previously. The ratings did not differ significantly by brand with the labels removed. The sample also was unable to choose their favorite brand of beer beyond chance.

FIGURE 2.4 Rating tags from Allison and Uhl (1964)

The beer drinkers in the Allison and Uhl sample appeared to distinguish products through their receptiveness to the various firms' marketing efforts, rather than through objective physical product differences (product attributes). They seemed to choose brands on perceptions built through marketing, not on physical sensations like taste; this is because without brand identification, they could not distinguish between the different brands of beer. The perceptions built through marketing may not be about physical aspects of a product, but about how distinctive the brand is in the consumer's mind (Ehrenberg 1972). Contemporary views of Marketing Management view the management of a brand's image as the role of marketing, and propose that favorable or perhaps just distinct imagery can develop into favorable brand knowledge, and lead to consumers developing preference for a brand, and loyalty to that brand over time (Kotler and Keller 2009).

The importance of branding for the international market

It is only relatively recently that academics have begun exploring the relationship between having a strong brand and establishing a strong market position (Court et al. 1997). Brands are an important apparatus in a company's toolbox for international expansion. Typically, a company must first build a strong brand in their home market and leverage the brand's fame, reputation and equity into foreign markets. While companies like Nike and Visa truly undertake global branding, the great majority of companies expand by buying out existing brands in national markets. National brands help a company's international expansion by providing a functioning infrastructure for the company's operation in foreign nations.

Having a strong brand helps a company establish its identity in the new market quickly, especially when the expansion involves buying a foreign national brand. The strength and reputation of the brand goes towards growing customer franchise in the new market (Aaker 1996). Having a strong brand, or a family of strong brands in different countries helps a firm efficiently integrate its marketing strategies internationally. The strong international brand serves to tie together the smaller local brands to give the company scale. Having a strong brand or an umbrella brand for companies like P&G who have a plethora of brands at the product level helps a company consolidate fragmented markets. Typically, these markets have many brands with small scale distribution. This lack of scale means that the brands cannot afford the marketing and advertising investment necessary to build a strong brand image.

That companies undertaking international expansion end-up with many brands is a result of the way large multinationals buy up smaller brands in their efforts to grow. This becomes very evident as a market reaches maturity, where there is little room in the market to build new brands. This is the time when the largest market players resort to acquisition to gain market share. Ironically, this is the stage in the market life-cycle when the strongest brands have the resources to expand (Lee and Edwards 2013), often doing this by acquiring national brands in foreign markets. The company quickly realizes the need to synchronize these acquisitions with their in-house brand. This means linking their in-house brand to the newly acquired brands and to other entities, places, people, things in the foreign market. This requirement for synchronicity adds layers of complexity to the brand building and maintenance process (Roth 1995). Interpreting this linking process involves understanding consumer brand knowledge and how it changes after making new associations, and the acquired brand's relative market position, cultural and linguistic associations. This work to harmonize the company's strong in-house brand with newly acquired foreign national brands is important because entering new countries not only means that the international brand's reputation is brought into the new market, but the way the brand performs in tandem with the acquired brand leaks back out from the new market to affect the brand's international reputation and equity. When branding is not synchronized well in international markets, customers in the "leaky" borders of neighboring markets get confused because they are receiving conflicting signals. For example, when a brand maintains different market positions in neighboring countries, consumers get confused as to which segment the brand serves.

Summary

Building strong brands requires the knowledge offered by the science of branding as well as the judgment needed to make branding an art. A strong brand offers a company many opportunities and becomes an asset the company can use to increase sales, expand to new territories, and to build equity. Brands are now increasingly linked to a company's market position, for consumers' think of market position in terms relative to brands. In order to facilitate the art of branding, we will transition to discussing the science of branding in the next chapter.

Bibliography

Aaker, D. A. and R. Jacobson (2001), "The Value Relevance of Brand Attitude in High-Technology Markets", *Journal of Marketing Research*, 38 (4), 485–94.

Aaker, David A. (1996), *Building Strong Brands*. London: Simon & Schuster, Free Press.

Aaker, David A. and Alexander L. Biel (1993), *Brand Equity & Advertising: Advertising's Role in Building Strong Brands*. Hillsdale, NJ: Lawrence Erlbaum Associates.

Aaker, David A. and Erich Joachminsthaler (2000), *Brand Leadership*. New York: Free Press.

Allison, Ralph I. and Kenneth P. Uhl (1964), "Influences of Beer Brand Identification on Taste Perception", *Journal of Marketing Research*, 1 (3), 36–9.

Atwal, Glyn and Alistair Williams (2009), "Luxury Brand Marketing – The Experience is Everything!" *Journal of Brand Management*, 16 (5), 338–46.

Aydin, S. (2005), "Customer Loyalty and the Effect of Switching Costs as a Moderator Variable", *Marketing Intelligence & Planning*, 23 (1), 89.

Bass, Frank H. and William Wilkie (1973), "A Comparative Analysis of Attitudinal Predictions of Brand Preference", *Journal of Marketing Research*, 10 (3), 262–70.

Brands & Rousers (2012), "Lego Aims to Inspire and Develop the Builders of Tomorrow – Brand & Rousers Case", (accessed May 16, 2014), [available at: www.thinkholisticactpersonal.com/en/?p=314].

Court, David C., Anthony Freeling, Mark C. Lerter and Andrew J. Parsons (1997), "If Nike Can 'Just Do It' Why Can't We?" *McKinsey Quarterly*, 3, 25–34.

Ehrenberg, A. S. C. (1972), *Repeat-Buying: Theory and Applications*. London: Charles Griffin.

Fickling, David (2013), "Billabong Losses Triple as 40-Year-Old Brand Seen Worthless", (accessed November 9, 2014), [available at: www.bloomberg.com/news/2013-08-26/billabong-posts-a-860-million-loss-as-brand-deemed-worthless.html].

Fournier, Susan (1998), "Consumers and Their Brands: Developing Relationship Theory in Consumer Research", *Journal of Consumer Research*, 24 (4), 343–53.

—— (1999), "Introducing New Coke", Boston, MA: Harvard Business School.

Frank, M. Bass and W. Wayne Talarzyk (1972), "An Attitude Model for the Study of Brand Preference", *Journal of Marketing Research (pre-1986)*, 9 (000001), 93.

Fredrix, Emily (2008), "Schlitz Back on Shelves, Drums up Beer Nostalgia", in SFGate.com: Associated Press.

Goldemberg, R. L. and E. R. Height (2000), *Antique Jewelry: A Practical & Passionate Guide.* Lincoln, NE: Crown Publishers.

Gounaris, Spiros and Vlasis Stathakopoulos (2004), "Antecedents and Consequences of Brand Loyalty: An Empirical Study", *The Journal of Brand Management*, 11 (4), 283–306.

Hull, Clark L. (1924), "The Influence of Tobacco Smoking on Mental and Motor Efficiency: An Experimental Investigation", *Psychological Monographs: General and Applied*, 33 (3), i–161.

Husband, Richard W. and Jane Godfrey (1934), "An Experimental Study of Cigarette Identification", *Journal of Applied Psychology*, 18 (2), 220–3.

Ingelfinger, Julie R. (2008), "Melamine and the Global Implications of Food Contamination", *New England Journal of Medicine*, 359 (26), 2745–8.

Interbrand (2013), "Interbrand: Rankings," (accessed April 1, 2014), [available at: www.bestglobalbrands.com/2014/ranking/].

Johnson, Tim (2008), "Chinese Parents in Agony Over Tainted Baby Formula", in McClatchy Newspapers. World ed. Washington DC.

Keller, K. L. (2008), *Strategic Brand Management. Building, Measuring, and Managing Brand Equity* (3rd ed.). Upper Saddle River, NJ: Pearson Prentice-Hall.

Keller, Kevin Lane (1993), "Conceptualizing, Measuring, and Managing Customer-Based Brand Equity", *Journal of Marketing*, 57 (1), 1–22.

———— (1987), "Memory Factors in Advertising: The Effect of Advertising Re", *Journal of Consumer Research*, 14 (3), 316.

Keller, K. L., Brian Sternthal and Alice M. Tybout (2002), "Three Questions You Need to Ask About Your Brand", *Harvard Business Review*, 80 (9), 80.

Knowledge@Wharton (2012), "Innovation Almost Bankrupted LEGO – Until It Rebuilt with a Better Blueprint", (accessed October 20, 2014), [available at: http://knowledge.wharton.upenn.edu/article/innovation-almost-bankrupted-lego-until-it-rebuilt-with-a-better-blueprint/].

Kotler, Philip and Kevin Keller (2009), *Marketing Management.* New Jersey: Prentice-Hall.

Lam, Desmond, Alvin Lee and Richard Mizerski (2009), "The Effects of Cultural Values in Word-of-Mouth Communication", *Journal of International Marketing*, 17 (3), 55–70.

Lee, Alvin and Mark G. Edwards (2013), *Marketing Strategy: A Lifecycle Approach.* Melbourne, Australia: Cambridge University Press.

Melinda, Varley (2009), "Can Hello Kitty Continue to Rule the World?" *Brand Strategy*, Feb (229), 32–6.

Metcalf, Tom and Robert LaFranco (2013), "Lego Builds New Billionaires as Toymaker Topples Mattel", (accessed November 20, 2014), [available at: www.bloomberg.com/news/2013-03-13/lego-builds-new-billionaires-as-toymaker-topples-mattel.html].

Pechmann, Cornelia and Srinivasan Ratneshwar (1991), "The Use of Comparative Advertising for Brand Positioning: Association versus Differentiation", *Journal of Consumer Research*, 145–60.

Ramond, Charles K., L. H. Rachal and Melvin R. Marks (1950), "Brand Discrimination among Cigarette Smokers", *Journal of Applied Psychology*, 34 (4), 282.

Reed, Brad (2013), "Europe is Ground Zero for Windows Phone's Surge", (accessed November 20, 2014), [available at: http://bgr.com/2013/12/02/windows-phone-q3-2013-market-share/].

Roth, Marvin S. (1995), "Effects of Global Market Conditions on Brand Image Customization and Brand Performance", *Journal of Advertising* 32 (May), 163–75.

Saxena, Ruchita (2012), "Bajaj Auto Launches Low Cost Car RE60, Promises 40km per Litre", (accessed November 20, 2014), [available at: http://profit.ndtv.com/news/corporates/article-bajaj-auto-launches-low-cost-car-re-60-promises-40-km-per-litre-295239].

Schmalensee, Richard (1982), "Product Differentiation Advantages of Pioneering Brands", *The American Economic Review*, 72 (3), 349–65.

Shaw, Arch Wilkinson (1912), "Some Problems in Market Distribution", *The Quarterly Journal of Economics*, 26 (4), 703–65.

Smith, W. (1956), "Product Differentiation and Market Segmentation as Alternative Marketing Strategies", *Journal of Marketing*, 21 (1), 3–8.

Speedy, Blair (2013), "Billabong at Brand Zero, Company Posts $860m Loss", in the Business Review section of *The Australian* newspaper, (accessed: November 20, 2014), [available at: http://m.theaustralian.com.au/business/companies/billabong-at-brand-zero-company-posts-860m-loss/story-fn91v9q3-1226705295349?nk=dfa80d26d544ced0e369e657f11 3c6fb].

3

THE SCIENCE OF MEASURING BRAND PERFORMANCE

Science necessarily begins with measurement. How do we measure a brand? What does a brand do? How do people interact with a brand? How do consumers understand a brand? How does a brand affect buyers' decisions? These questions are central to the study of branding. The whole aim of the branding process is to create value for a brand, to make a brand valuable in the eyes of consumers. This value means that the brand can command a preferential position in the market with distributors and with consumers. Brand value translates into demand for the brand. This helps increase consumers' willingness to pay a higher price for well-known brands, ultimately resulting in an increase of sales and profits.

Brand value

A brand's value is traditionally measured as the amount of business a brand can generate in the future. To determine the value of a brand today, the brand's forecast future sales, measured as future cash flows from sales of products carrying the brand name, are discounted to reflect the value of money at today's rates – this uses the concept and computations for calculating net present value from future value commonly utilized in the finance discipline. This value is then compared to the value of a similar but unbranded product.

Stated more formally, brand value represents the net present value of future cash flows from sales of a branded product compared to sales of a similar but unbranded product (Arvidsson 2006; Emmer and Henshall 2002; Schultz 2004), or a product with a little known brand. The resulting difference in sales can be attributed to the effects of brand. This measurement gives shareholders and management an idea of the brand's monetary worth.

While this system of determining a brand's worth is theoretically sensible, it is very difficult to accurately calculate this value. There seems to be no set formula, many different ways have been proposed to help determine this value – e.g., Interbrand, Brand Ten methods.

Using a less mathematical explanation, a brand is worth what consumers are willing to pay for it, compared to what they are willing to pay for an identical but unbranded product. For example, the price Coca-Cola cola is able to charge compared to a non-branded counterpart, what buyers are willing to pay for a pair of Nike sneakers compared to a similar unbranded pair. This way of describing a brand's value, judged by consumers' willingness to pay a higher price, seems positively correlated with the level of favorable knowledge customers have about the brand (Keller 2003). This is knowledge that reflects what the brand stands for, its market position, and promises about how the product will perform. As discussed, these brand qualities provide a meaningful way to make the brand distinct. This distinctiveness helps to create a unique selling proposition.

Brand Equity and Brand Knowledge

Developing an individual's favorable knowledge about a brand is thought to generate a tendency to prefer that brand. When a customer chooses a brand repeatedly, this is a behavioral measure of the brands' equity with that customer (Keller 2001). Over the longer term, sustained purchase loyalty to a brand should increase and reinforce a brand's value or equity (Erdem et al. 1999).

Brand Equity is regarded as an asset that profits from brand awareness, brand loyalty, perceived brand quality and other positive associations with the brand (Aaker 1991). Theoretically, a brand's equity reflects the way consumers think, feel and act concerning the brand; these take into account the brand's price, market share and the profitability of the company that owns the brand (Kotler and Keller 2009). Customer-Based Brand-Equity (CBBE) is often referred to as the differential effect that a consumer's knowledge about a brand exerts on their response to the brand's marketing. While this response is argued to drive their willingness to pay a higher price, it is measured very differently from the monetary measures of a brand's value. A brand's equity is argued to have three key ingredients (Kotler and Keller 2009):

1. the consumer's response (e.g., willing to pay a price premium),
2. the consumer's perceptions of the brand, and
3. their preference for the brand and their brand-related behavior (buy and repurchase, positive word of mouth about the brand).

Brand Knowledge is often defined as a knowledge structure that is stored in a consumer's memory. This is memory that specifies the features and relevant attributes of a brand for a consumer (Casey 2003). Brand knowledge has been viewed as having at least eight components (Keller, 2003) – images, attitudes, attributes, benefits, thoughts, feelings, experiences and awareness concerning the brand.

Since the 1980s, the concept of Brand Equity has been a topic for extensive academic and practitioner interest and research. Part of its popularity is due to the concept's theoretical claim to provide one true measurement of Brand Knowledge (Keller, 2003).

The concept of Brand Knowledge is argued, and anecdotally supported, to be the basis for a brand's equity with the buyer/consumer. As many researchers have argued in the literature, relatively strong and favorable equity towards a brand is believed to increase the customers' preference for the brand at a price premium compared to other brands; and their repurchase loyalty to that brand when tempted with offers from other brands (Keller 2003; Keller et al. 1998). A brand's equity is typically viewed relative to other brands, although the specific comparison varies by consumer. For example, we tried to establish the value premium for several brands of M&M/Mars candy but could not find close approximates for brands like Snickers. This suggests that Snickers occupies a unique place in the market and has no real competitors.

There is a wide range of favorable support for the assumed relationship between Brand Knowledge and Brand Equity in Consumer-Based Brand-Equity (CBBE) theory, but this creates a theoretical and practical problem. How can all of these often quite different models of Brand Equity interact with elements of Brand Knowledge? How is it that they all work in their own way?

Empirical support for Brand Knowledge and Brand Equity

The literature offering empirical tests of brand equity is quite extensive. A number of disciplines outside of marketing have applied this concept to their problems and in the process have tested a wide variety of models in some fashion. That so many very different models and constructs purport to reflect "true" brand equity is confusing for guidance in monitoring and improving a brand's equity.

The vast amount of the empirical research tests whether a proposed model fits the data collected. Only a few studies offer a test of discrimination or prediction, and two (so far) have tested a Brand Knowledge/Brand Equity model for determining the preference and loyalty for users of a product category. It is important to establish support for a model because it may help understand the Brand Equity phenomenon, and its ability to identify and predict the factors of consumers' brand knowledge that would have special interest to marketers. This chapter is focused on the usefulness of knowing consumers' Brand Knowledge in their actual preference and loyalty to a preferred brand.

Testing Brand Knowledge and Equity for two very different markets

We will use the beer category as a context to test our view of brand knowledge and equity. For this category, we want to target the heaviest user groups as they will have more experience with the product category. These heavy beer drinkers can be identified as young adults, in particular college or university students (Creyer et al. 2002). As such, they represent the ideal group with high knowledge of beer, are regular users and would be expected to be sensitive to beer promotion and prices.

We therefore chose university students from Perth Australia and Beijing China as our sample and examine their Brand Knowledge in the beer category. These students were 18+ years old, exceeding the legal age to drink in both countries. Our test of both samples finds that their Brand Knowledge concepts about beer have many similarities. Importantly, there are also some very discernible differences. The test reported in this book finds these Brand Knowledge concepts to predict sample members' preferences between brands very well, taking into account their willingness to pay a premium for a brand.

The first research to report on the importance of subjective perceptions in eliciting consumer preference in brands, studied the beer category (Allison and Uhl 1964). This lends support to using beer to examine our Predictive Brand Choice model (PBC). This is because PBC seeks to predict consumers' preference based on subjective brand based attributes. For the beer category, subjective attributes may include the brand's image, place of manufacture (e.g., German beer) and use contexts (e.g., utilities derived from using beer during gatherings like parties and meals). For a long time, the beer category has built brands and sold products using subjective perceptions. The category continues to operate on subjective perceptions about products (Fredric et al. 1999). Relying on consumer perceptions and experiences is considered to be an effective approach in differentiating brands offering a relatively similar product in the beer category.

In different countries, the beer category is in different stages of the Product Category Life Cycle (PLC). Using our understanding of the Product Life Cycle Theory, a product will move through a series of stages – introduction, growth, maturity and decline – before being removed from the market. A fundamental driver of the movement from one stage to another stage is the level of knowledge about the product in a market (Stark 2011). For example, there would be more market knowledge in a mature market about the product category compared to the level of knowledge in a growing market. The knowledge in the mature market would also be more accurate as it would be based on more consumer past experiences, have had time to develop and be transmitted wider to a market – the market will have more depth and breadth of knowledge. A large part of knowledge in a product market exists in the form of Brand Knowledge. This is because brands form the fundamental unit of comparison between products that are similar or alike in a market.

By testing the PBC model in markets that are at different stages of the Product Life Cycle, we are able to examine the way different levels of market knowledge affect our prediction. This lends a degree of external validity to the model. Testing Brand Knowledge and its link to Brand Equity in different markets may suggest how these constructs evolve over time in a population.

It is also important to add a method to evaluate the effects of more subjective (soft) brand attributes on consumer choice of purchase. Our PBC model adds this dimension to the tests for Brand Knowledge and Brand Equity. This is because of the more imprecise nature of subjective attributes as compared to objective attributes. For example, products with more concrete objective attributes would be easier to compare – e.g., home loans can be compared using interest rates, repayment provisions and length of loan. The subjective attributes used to compare between beer brands are more difficult to capture and link to purchase decisions. The following sections review the literature behind this test and provide the rationale for the theory behind the PBC.

Effects of Brand Knowledge

As we have discussed, Ralph Allison and Kenneth Uhl (1964) wanted to know whether their subject's knowledge of beer brands (brand knowledge) affected the way they thought different brands of beer tasted. This test was done in the United States with males who drank beer at least three times a week; this qualified these subjects as regular beer drinkers. Today, this group would be considered heavy users.

Allison and Uhl conducted a blind taste test of six brands of beer. For this test, they proposed that beer drinkers would not be able to distinguish taste differences between major brands of unlabeled beer. They chose to test the subjects' perceived after-taste, aroma, bitterness, body, carbonation, foam, strength and sweetness as characteristics of the taste of beer.

After conducting their test, Allison and Uhl reported that the beer drinkers in their sample were unable to distinguish between different brands of beer when the beverage was presented in unlabeled bottles. As discussed in Chapter 1, in the blind test most of the respondents could not correctly identify "their" regularly consumed brands. These findings show that most beer drinkers, at least in the Allison and Uhl sample, are unable to distinguish between the tastes of different unlabeled brands of beer, even when they were drinking their "regular" brand. This is surprising as regular beer drinkers would be expected be more accurate in identifying the taste components of their regularly used brand, especially if they were heavy users of that brand of product.

When the taste test was not blind, when the respondents were provided brand labeled beer, they were then able to provide significantly different perceptions of the taste between different brands. This result shows that the respondents primarily relied on brand identification to generate "similar" perceptions about the subjective attributes of each brand of beer. They appear not to use the brands' objective performance to distinguish between brands of beers on taste. At least with this beer drinking sample, brand identification is more important than actual physical product differences (e.g., product attributes) in determining reported taste. This result appears to suggest that the branding process conditions the beer drinker to think different beers have unique tastes. The authors presumed there would be similar effects in their sample's brand preference and loyalty. However, Allison and Uhl did not test loyalty. Our PBC model extends this work to predict a customer's loyalty from their knowledge of the brand. In our examination, we also build in a price-based premium for the subject's most preferred brand of beer. This tests for brand equity.

Allison and Uhl did not measure all the components that make up beer brand knowledge, nor did they link Brand Knowledge to Brand Equity – perhaps because these concepts were not yet formalized in academy in 1964. However, many researchers have replicated the finding that the perceptual nature of taste, other salient attributes and antecedents of preference are similar for many different products (Pham et al. 2009). Other researchers have worked to develop models that explain how buyers' brand preference and loyalty decisions are influenced by what they "know" about brands.

Brand Equity and Brand Knowledge

Brand Equity, as a construct, appears to have been originally theorized and named by Aaker (1991). Aaker's theory describes Brand Equity as the value a brand has over other competing brands. He further explains that brand equity comprises a set of assets that are associated with the brand. These are assets that add value to the brand. This value or equity can facilitate the brand obtaining a higher price premium over products from competitor brands.

Brand equity can also help leverage the brand name into other categories. This is especially valuable when the brand's owners seek to undertake unrelated diversification strategies. For example, the Virgin group has managed to leverage the Virgin brand name into industries that include airlines, mobile phone contracts, insurance, travel agencies, music distribution, radio, gymnasiums and space-flight (Virgin 2014).

Within the same category, Brand equity can help the brand obtain greater distribution and command more consumer loyalty to the brand. Aaker also noted that a brand's equity is associated with consumers' awareness of the brand, their favorable brand associations (brand imagery) and their favorable feelings toward the brand (brand affect). Brand equity may also make consumers new to the category more willing to try the brand – novice consumers tend to want to try the more famous brands.

Following Aaker's conceptual definition, Keller (1993) later developed the Brand Knowledge construct. This focuses on consumers' memory of the brand, as measured by the way consumers view and remember a brand. In Keller's operation of the Brand Knowledge concept, memory comprises two constructs. The first is consumer awareness of the brand. The second is the imagery consumers' associate with the brand. Imagery refers to the mental associations that consumers develop between the brand and other constructs and ideas. For example, a consumer may associate a Volkswagen with the ideas of Germany, a Daisy flower and Beetle. Keller's Brand Knowledge construct appears to share several aspects with Aaker's Brand Equity. Aaker also noted the importance of Brand Awareness and Brand Associations in his model.

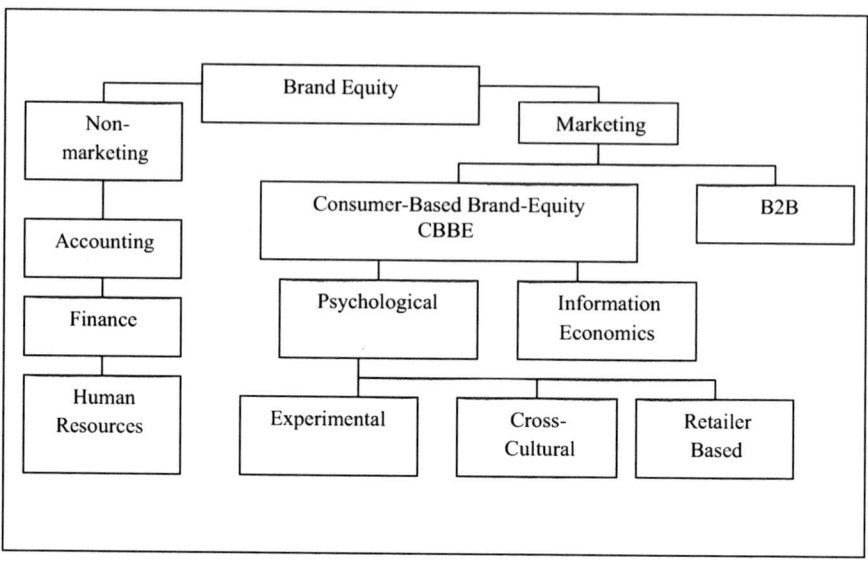

FIGURE 3.1 Brand Equity research literature

There has been extensive theorizing and empirical testing of what a brand's equity comprises of, and the brand knowledge potential consumers have about a brand. Many researchers propose and test a relationship between the two constructs, but the measures used and the nature of the relationships are often quite different between tests. A number of theoretical approaches and ways to test these models have been published and will be discussed shortly in more detail.

To potentially complicate the nature of the constructs and their relationships, the construct of Brand Equity has been used in a wide variety of applications with very different outcomes (see Figure 3.1). The Human Resources, Accounting and Finance areas have adopted the Brand Equity construct for their respective applications.

Accounting and Finance

Accounting and Finance view a brand's equity as the premium at which investors are willing to purchase a company's stock compared to the shares of a company with a less well-known brand. In Accounting and Finance, the informing measure for Brand Equity seems to be an updated valuation of "good will" toward the firm marketing the brand (Kapferer 2008).

This view of Brand Equity adopted by Accounting and Finance appears to place the value of the brand at the corporation level. This is a universal measure of a company's stable of brands, for many corporations have more than one brand. It is not suitable for use in marketing because of the operational need to measure, strategize and implement branding actions at the level of individual brands.

Human resources – Industrial Relations

The Industrial Relations (IR) application also views Brand Equity at the firm level. The IR definition is the influence of the company's reputation (brand) on the firm's ability to recruit and retain employees (Koçak et al. 2007). This reputation depends on the positive associations (images) staff and potential employees have developed with the company over time. This view of Brand Equity lends more weight to measuring equity as reputation, which is different from Accounting and Finance's view of Brand Equity as goodwill.

While these models have similar factors like awareness, associations and imagery, the outcomes theorized and tested have little relevance to marketing. Another major difference, the Accounting and Finance and IR focus is at the firm level and not at the brand level. Therefore, this literature will not be further reviewed.

Marketing and branding

Business to Business

Marketing studies of Brand Equity can be categorized as those adopting a Business to Business (B2B) based focus (Taylor et al. 2004) and those using a consumer based approach (Keller 1993). The models for B2B are similar in concept (e.g., brand knowledge) but quite different in terms of the associations made (see Figure 3.2)

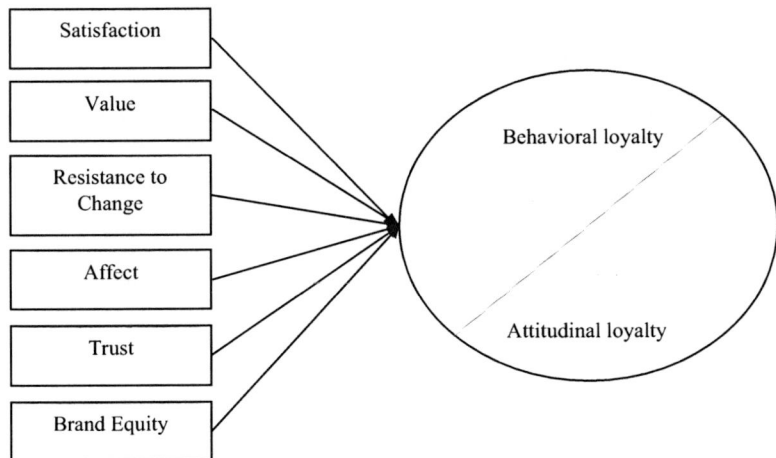

FIGURE 3.2 Adapted from Taylor, Celuch and Goodwin's (2004) B2B Brand Equity model

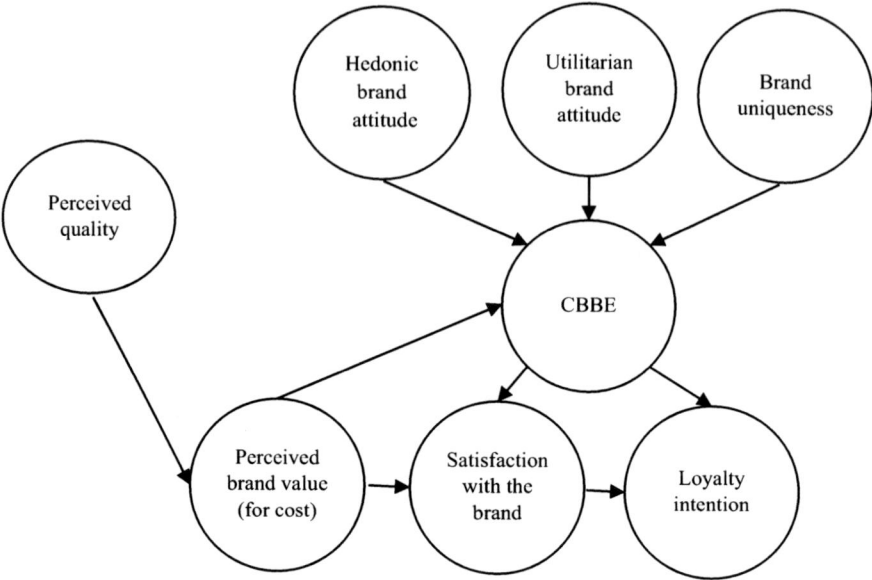

FIGURE 3.3 Adapted from Taylor, Hunter and Linberg's (2007) B2B Brand Equity model

and the respondents sampled. The B2B studies use managers and marketers of firms to provide self-reports on their awareness, perceptions and affect. These are conducted in industries like waste management (Kuhn et al. 2008; Taylor et al. 2004), financial services (Taylor et al. 2007) and heavy equipment (Taylor et al. 2004). Taylor et al.'s (2004) model is also less relevant as it looks at Brand Equity as an antecedent to loyalty.

In the B2B studies reviewed in this book, Brand Equity is measured with "global" values like trust or the use of results from open-end qualitative methods (Kuhn & Alpert, 2004). These values are based on elements defined in Keller's (2003) CBBE-based model as respondent perceptions of Brand Equity. Given this study's interest in end-users' (drinkers') beer brand knowledge and its relationships to beer brand equity, these two studies describing B2B applications are not directly relevant (see Figures 3.2 and 3.3). Here, we question the relevance of branding elements in the B2B perspective given the type of products tested – waste management systems and financial services – where subjective evaluations would most likely be less influential for purchase.

Consumer-Based Brand-Equity

Referring to Figure 3.1, the CBBE literature can be further devolved into the "psychological" and Information Economics paradigms. Although both of these paradigms attribute much of their theoretical arguments to Aaker's Brand Equity (Aaker 1991) and Keller's Brand Knowledge (Keller 1993) concepts, the views of each paradigm are quite different in terms of the constructs, and the measures used to capture these constructs. Unlike research in B2B, the vast majority of studies on CBBE use student samples.

Signaling Theory and Information Economics

Erdem and Swait (1998) incorporate a test of consumer perceptions of brands into their brand equity model in Signaling Theory. Signaling Theory originates in Spence's (1974) work in the information economics area. This theory specifically addresses the effects of the "imperfect" and asymmetric information in the market. These imperfections were first theorized by Stigler (1961).

According to Erdem and Swait, consumers' certainty about the salient attributes of a brand can be affected by the signals sent out by the brand's marketing efforts. Indications of a consumer's certainty or uncertainty of purchase can be measured as signals that result from the consumer's strength of belief about a brand. These indications are affected by marketing signals that convey a brand's position and its quality. The indications also encompass other consumers' perceptions of the brand, and the buyer's own perceived risk when purchasing the brand. Erdem and Swait also include consumers' perceived costs for obtaining the desired information about the brand in their model – these can come from the media, word of mouth communications or personal experience with the brand. Erdem and Swait posited that effective and favorable signaling by a brand using its marketing actions is positively correlated with the way consumers perceive the brand's quality. Appropriate signals also decrease the consumer's perceived risk of purchasing the brand and lowers the information costs associated with the search and selection of the brand in the purchase process.

Erdem and Swait report their Brand Equity model (see Figure 3.4) to satisfactorily fit the data provided by undergraduate students. These students responded to questions about jeans garments and concentrated orange juice.

Wang, Wei and Yu (2008) argue Signaling Theory to be superior to the psychological view of Brand Knowledge. This is because Signaling Theory can capture the effects of imperfect and asymmetric information in "real markets" (Figure 3.5). The vast majority of the product categories Wang, Wei and Yu tested tended to be for products like financial services (credit cards, loans), personal computers and high-price athletic shoes. These are products where objective criteria would appear to be more readily available and predominantly relied upon by the consumer when developing brand knowledge. Beer would be a category where the users' judgments of a brand's attributes are subjective and do not appear to be highly based on objective criteria (Allison and Uhl 1964).

In an earlier article, Wang et al. (2007) also note that in Signaling Theory, antecedents of Brand Equity are reductions in the consumers' perceived risk and the information costs attributable to a brand. They argue that Keller (1993) views those reductions as consequences of Brand Equity – that is, they are an output after a company has achieved Brand Equity. However, neither the early (1993) nor later

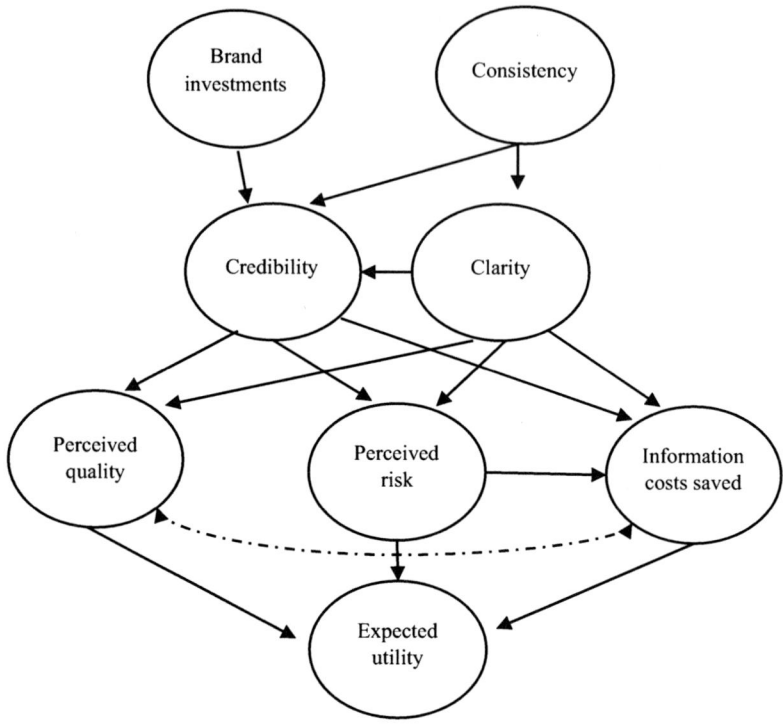

FIGURE 3.4 Adapted from Erdem and Swait's (1998) Brand Equity model

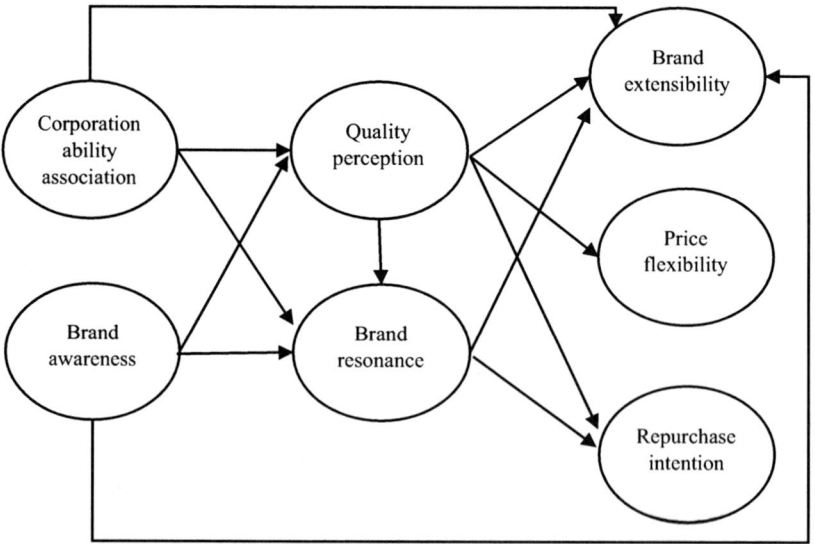

FIGURE 3.5 Adapted from Wang et al.'s (2008) Brand Equity model

Keller (2008) articles appear to agree with Wang et al.'s (2007) portrayal. Finally, Erdem and Swait (1998) see loyalty to a brand as a result of the brand having developed Brand Equity. However, Wang et al. (2007) suggest that Aaker views brand loyalty as one of the many assets or outcomes of Brand Equity. As you can see in this discussion, there is much disagreement about the reflective and formative nature of Brand Equity in relation to the different "assets" argued to be attributable to the Brand Equity construct.

The Information Economics paradigm has several replications (Erdem et al. 2006) and extensions of the Brand Equity construct (Erdem et al. 2002; Erdem et al. 2004; Wang et al. 2007). This paradigm appears to provide a more systematic program of research than the psychological-based CBBE paradigm. Wang et al. (2007) have also provided one of the few pieces of empirical research that tests the external validity of the sampling model for predicting brand choice. Using a discrete choice experiment tied to measures for Signaling Theory, they found the model was correct for identifying consumer choice for between 55% (Equity Loans) to 65% (Charge Cards) of the respondents across four financial service subcategories.

A substantial number of studies have validated and extended the "Brands as Signals" idea in Information Economics. Remember that this model is based on the way elements discussed by Keller and Aaker are expected to link to Brand Equity – where it is posited that Brand Knowledge is an antecedent that drives Brand Equity. However, these models use measures that quantify Brand Knowledge elements that would appear relatively more "reasoned" (objective) and are less about a "subjective" experience; such as you would expect to have with a brand of beer. The Brand Knowledge elements regularly measured in Information Economics Signaling Theory models include perceived risk, perceived information costs and perceived quality.

The products chosen by the Information Economics studies also tend to be subject to more complex cognitive processes. For example, questions in Wang et al. (2007) asked, "I have trouble figuring out what image this brand is trying to create", and, "I know what this brand stands for" (p. 143). These questions require complex reasoning. Normally, questions about brand perception would ask a respondent to what degree they agree that a brand had a good image, or that the brand is popular, or cheap; these are all straightforward comparison questions that can be used to position a brand relative to other brands in the respondent's mind. Nonetheless, the Signaling Theory of Information Economics appears to be the most discriminating model, being able to explain up to 65% of why consumers choose a particular brand. However, the categories and measures seem to favor more reasoned decisions about products.

Although the signaling perspective has been applied to a wide variety of categories – for example, frozen orange juice concentrate, jeans, athletic shoes, personal computers, shampoo and financial services – none of these appear to be products where the decision-making is based on subjective perceptions of attributes that are not based on experience. Further, none of the signaling studies have tested the beer product category.

Psychological paradigm

Keller (1993) may be the first author to formally discuss and define the construct of Brand Knowledge. The Keller view defines Brand Knowledge as a structure about a brand. This structure is stored in consumers' memory and provides information about the brand's features, imagery and affect towards a brand (Casey 2003).

Keller (2003) portrays brand knowledge to have eight components (see Figure 3.6): brand images, attitudes about the brand, brand attributes, brand benefits, thoughts about the brand, feelings associated with the brand, experiences with the brand, and awareness of the brand.

Keller (2003) also discusses important secondary sources of Brand Knowledge, such as the sources of information that lead to the development of brand knowledge. He notes that information about a brand can come from other people (employees of the company, endorsers of the brand), places (country of origin, channels), things (events, causes, third-party endorsements), and other brands in the consumer's portfolio (alliances, ingredients, company and extensions).

A limitation of Keller's work is that he provides very little discussion about how a consumer's knowledge of other brands are likely to affect the consumer's choice of their favorite brand. Keller seems to focus predominantly on consumers' knowledge of one brand. This distinction of having knowledge of other brands in tandem with knowledge of a focal brand can be very important for some markets. Lambert (2008) reports the lack of brand knowledge as a key effect in three to four year old children's preference and loyalty to a fast-food brand. In this case, the fast food brand the child preferred the most was the brand they knew the most about (highest level of brand knowledge), rather than simply having brand knowledge of a brand. Another study that highlights the effect of knowledge of multiple brands studies adult buyers. Capraro, Broniarczyk and Srivastava (2003) reports a lack of brand information as a main factor influencing customer defection from a health plan.

Park and Srinivasan (1994) developed and tested a multi-attribute preference model of Brand Equity that is based on individual consumer responses. This research seems to be the first research using the psychological view of Brand Knowledge; predating Erdem and Swait (1998) by four years. Park and Srinivasan divided Brand Equity into attribute and non-attribute–based perceptions; for example, likeable ads versus more expressive ads. They tested their model with brands of toothpaste

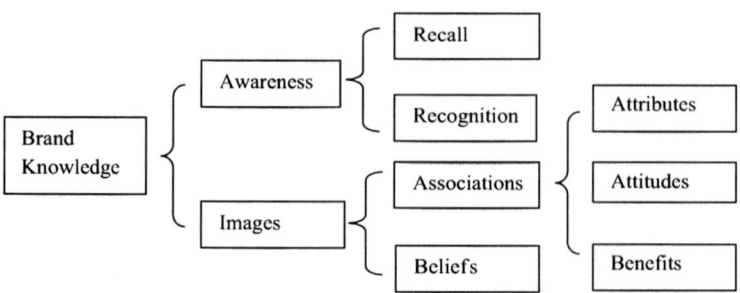

FIGURE 3.6 Adapted from Keller's model of Brand Knowledge (2003)

and mouthwash. These products are usually referred to as examples of fast moving consumer goods (FMCG).

Using their Brand Equity model, Park and Srinivasan find non-attribute perceptions to be more dominant than attribute-based perceptions of the brand. This finding lends weight to measuring the subjective elements of brand knowledge in affecting consumer choice. The responses used in Park and Srinivasan's model return a significant but modest association (simple r = 0.35, p < 0.001) with their sample's reported purchasing of the tested toothpaste and mouthwash brands.

In another study that measured the effects of knowledge about several brands, Lassar, Mittal, and Sharma (1995) measured university students' perceptions of several brands of television monitors (TV sets) and wrist watches. They attempted to capture the respondents' perceptions of how the brands would affect their social image. They also measured the relative value of the different brands used in their study. This included the brand's trustworthiness and the degree to which the respondent formed a personal attachment with each brand. These areas can be seen as elements of Brand Knowledge.

Using Structural Equation Model (SEM) analysis, Lassar et al.'s (1995) model fit their data (CFI = 0.87) to a construct called Brand Equity. Their Brand Equity construct has five underlying dimensions: performance, value, social image, trustworthiness and commitment. However, Lassar et al. did not report a test of this Brand Equity construct with a possible outcome like brand preference or brand loyalty. The products (TV sets and watches) are relatively high in expenditure, infrequent in repurchase and would have few similarities to beer.

Yoo, Donthu and Lee (2000) report on a model using a psychologically based Brand Knowledge construct that uses factors of brand awareness and brand associations (see Figure 3.7). Surprisingly, Yoo et al. (2000) fails to note the Erdem and

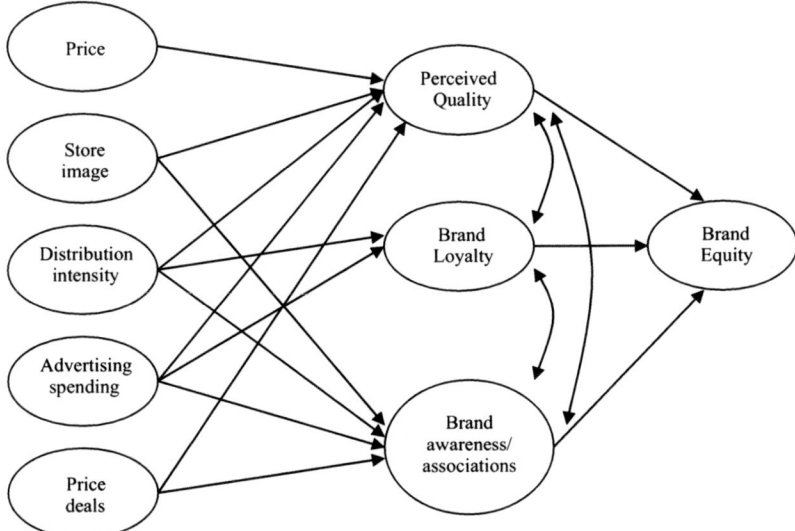

FIGURE 3.7 Adapted from Yoo et al.'s (2000) structural model of marketing mix elements and Brand Equity

Swait (1998) study and their test of the information economics model but cite Keller (1993), Keller et al. (1998) and Aaker (1992) when building the theoretical foundations for their model. This is unusual given Yoo et al.'s (2000) model has similarities with Erdem and Swait (1998), both models including a construct called perceived quality.

Yoo et al. (2000) combine the Keller and Aaker constructs of Brand Awareness and Brand Associations as one construct and use this to measure brand imagery. In this construct, they ask respondents to rate the statement, "I have no difficulty in imagining (brand name) in my mind". This measure is problematic as it is unclear. The question can be perceived as measuring the imagery of a brand, or the ability of the perceiver in imagining the brand. To answer the question, imagery may not even have to be involved. This approach is certainly different than asking whether the rater can perceive a specific image.

In the Yoo et al. (2000) study, Brand Equity is measured using responses from a sample of university undergraduate respondents. These students rated statements that compare a named brand to its unbranded counterpart. Presumably, the unbranded option has little or no Brand Equity. This study was conducted before more recent work (e.g., Pham et al. 2009) that reports "unbranded" private label products tend to be rated very favorably against national brands by their users.

Yoo et al. (2000) used three product categories as contexts to test their model – athletic shoes, camera film and color television sets. These products belong to categories that offer a lot more objective criteria as compared to beer. They also require a much larger economic commitment than a drink of beer. This means that consumers may evaluate the products very differently because of the cost and longevity of the purchase.

Investigators in the Yoo et al. (2000) study chose brands that represent high and low shares of the categories, explaining that these matched actual market shares. However, this way of setting up a test would provide a much easier array for the researchers to explain or predict Brand Equity. This is as compared to the reality of most categories where a few brands dominate with closer brand shares; for example, consumers will only consider closely related brands (e.g., in premium segment) and are unlikely to consider brands from different segments simultaneously (e.g., compare premium with budget segment for purchase). Most categories like beer have only a few brands with large shares, and predicting these share situations would require a much more rigorous test of discrimination or prediction.

Using SEM, Yoo et al. (2000) report that their data fit their model. The constructs of brand loyalty, perceived quality and brand awareness/associations are positively related to multiple statements like, "Even if another brand has the same features as (insert brand name), I would prefer to buy (insert brand name)". This statement is a self-reported hypothetical preference under specific conditions. This type of statement may not represent scenarios relevant to most respondents. Yoo et al. offers no further tests to establish the discriminating or predictive ability of their model.

Vázquez, Río and Iglesias (2002) attempt to separate the contributions of different "utilities" in a brand's equity. They propose that a brand's equity is partially a function of the category in which the brand operates. The authors feel that much of a brand's equity is associated with the category in which the brand is purchased. The brand and category effects are conceptualized as providing either functional or symbolic utilities to the consumer who is accessing their view of a brand's equity.

Using responses from 1,054 respondents from three cities in northern Spain and Structural Equation Modeling analyses, Vázquez, Río and Iglesias (2002) report that the data fit their model. Their final model has significant relationships of both the category and the brand. While they reported tests of the overall discriminate validity for their model, they do not test the model's accuracy in predicting or discriminating a purchase outcome. This limits their model to describing a relationship between brand and category.

Netemeyer et al. (2004) develop and test the Brand Equity model depicted in Figure 3.8, purifying this model using four related studies. This model features a reflective construct, where perceived quality (PQ) and perceived value for the cost (PVC) reflect the respondents' willingness to pay a price premium for a brand (Brand Equity). The authors use two items to measure purchase intent. They also measure the share of a respondent's past purchases by brand through two questions. The responses Netemeyer et al. collect fit their model. These data contain responses about cola beverages, jeans garments and athletic shoes from a sample of university students.

In a final study, Netemeyer et al. (2004) uses the model developed in studies one to three to predict reported brand share percentages for three fast-food restaurants. They calculate the self-report measures of purchase in an additive fashion – each brand receives one point for each of the five weeks it is patronized. They find they can predict brand choice. However, this method will probably not reflect the true distribution of use of the different brands (Ehrenberg 1972). This is due to the well-known distribution of purchase occasion and frequency developed in the Negative Binomial Theory (NBD). The NBD is used in marketing to predict the brand share

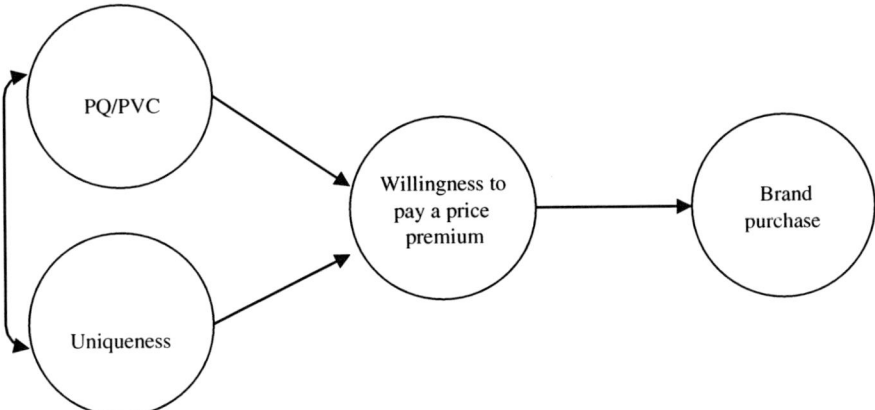

FIGURE 3.8 Adapted from Netemeyer et al.'s (2004) core/primary CBBE facets and brand purchase model

and purchases of frequently bought product categories – we will discuss this theory at length in a later section of this book. The fast-food category and cola category that Netemeyer et al. (2004) studies would be similar to beer in terms of purchase frequency. These categories would also rely on the use of subjective perceptions to evaluate products and brands and would be relatively low expenditure purchases.

Punj and Hillyer (2004) offer their cognitive model that is based on Keller's CBBE (see Figure 3.9). They disaggregate the construct into four structural components: global brand attitude, brand heuristic, brand knowledge and strength of

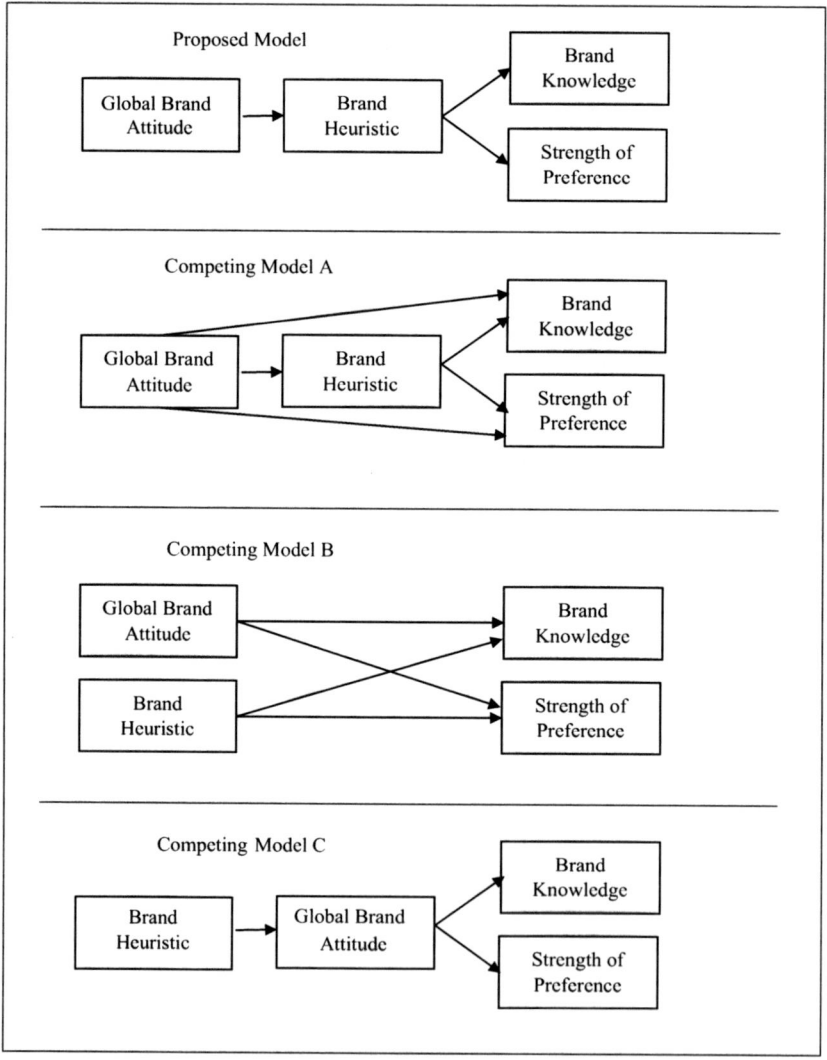

FIGURE 3.9 Adapted from Punj and Hillyer's (2004) cognitive model of Brand Equity "components"

preference. The research is positioned as CBBE for frequently purchased products where Punj and Hillyer test their theory on the hand-soap and toothpaste product categories. For a theory that is based on CBBE, placed in the Information Economics area, and sharing many constructs with Yoo et al. (2000), it is worrying that they fail to refer to Yoo et al. (2000), or to the number of information economics studies done in this area, nor the use of frequently purchased products like orange juice in previous studies in Information Economics. Toothpaste and hand soap are also fast-moving consumer-goods like orange juice. Punj and Hillyer argue that authors like Keller (1993) and Aaker (1991) are considered as the dominant view in CBBE, and that the Brand Equity model is composed of attitudinal loyalty.

Punj and Hillyer have a unique interpretation and measurement for their Brand Knowledge construct. While Keller and Aaker discuss Brand Knowledge as comprised of constructs like images, affect and awareness, Punj and Hillyer argue that Brand Knowledge should be, ". . . tested as a behavioral construct because our model presumes relatively stable purchase behavior" (p. 127). They further assume that brand knowledge will, ". . . more closely resemble actual consumption" (p. 127). Instead of measuring Brand Knowledge as a mental construct, Punj and Hillyer appear to propose Brand Knowledge as a behavioral construct. This is a significant departure from the existing understanding and measurement of what is regarded as Brand Knowledge in branding studies.

Measuring Brand Knowledge with two questions, the first Punj and Hillyer question asks the respondent for the percentage a brand represents of their total purchases in the category for the last month – for example, Brand A represented 17.5% of my total purchases in the Cola beverage category last month. They follow by asking the respondent about the number of "non-most-preferred" brands they bought in the last eight months. These questions are not reasonable as respondents will be not be able to accurately account for these statistics. Besides being difficult to impossible to accurately answer, Punj and Hillyer provide no validation or report of validation of these measures.

Using the dubious data they collected from US university undergraduate students, Punj and Hillyer (2004) report the data to fit three configurations of "brand equity components" – Figure 3.9, proposed and competing models A and B. However, the link between the "global brand attitude" and the "strength of preference" constructs is reported as not significant for all brands of soap or toothpaste. This indicates that their models cannot make the link between a consumer's attitude towards a brand and the consumer's preference for the brand. This does not fit with the fundamental assumption that Brand Knowledge links to Brand Equity. Although the three models all fit the data, the authors offer no attempt to predict brand preference using Brand Knowledge. From the insignificant link, these models are unable to predict brand preference by Brand Knowledge, or estimate how Brand Knowledge would link to Brand Equity. This is because Punj and Hillyer argue that Brand Knowledge and "strength of preference" are outcomes of a process they label as Brand Equity.

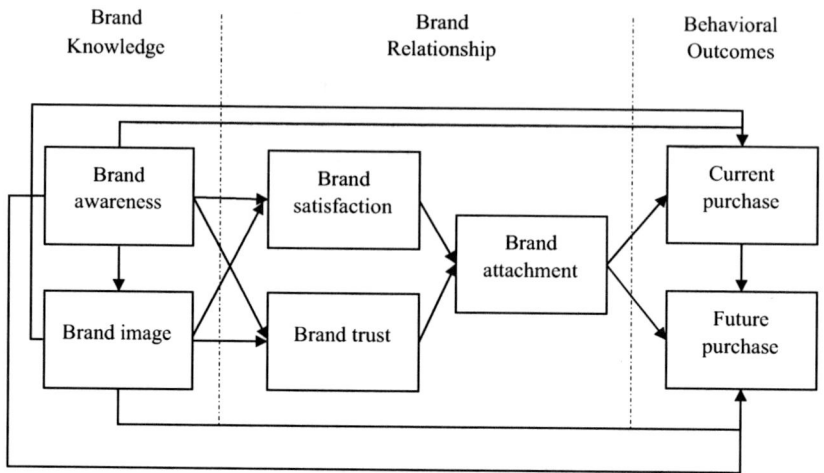

FIGURE 3.10 Adapted from Esch, Langner, Schmitt and Geus's (2006, p. 53) CBBE model

Esch, Langner, Schmitt and Geus (2006) report an extremely complex Brand Equity model. This complexity exists to test whether perceived brand relationships should be added to improve the model (Figure 3.10). The authors argue brand awareness and brand image as antecedents to brand satisfaction and brand trust. Ultimately, satisfaction and trust give the long-term outcome of customers forming a strong attachment to the brand.

The authors collect responses from a sample of European university business students about athletic shoes and chocolates and use a Structural Equation Model to establish the data fit their Brand Equity/Brand Attachment propositions. The data include self-reports of current and past purchases. The researchers report that the data fit their model. Esch et al.'s (2006) model finds brand image and perceived brand relationships as factors that affect present and future (intended) purchase. The authors report a total effect that comprises of different constructs on present and intended purchase from 0.31 to 0.63. However, this is neither an r^2 statistic nor does this effect gauge the model's success at discrimination or prediction.

In the Esch et al. model, while brand image and perceived relationships are predictors, surprisingly, several factors do not return significant effects. These are brand awareness, brand satisfaction and brand trust. This suggests that a relationship with the brand (i.e., brand intimacy) does not play a functional role in predicting future purchases. This finding does not support the CBBE assertion that familiarity with a brand and developing a relationship with a brand are antecedents to preference and purchase.

Kayaman and Arasli (2007) applies the Brand Equity concept to a hospitality service context. They are particularly interested in testing the theory that ". . . memories of their experiences" (p. 93) is the major equity building activity for brands in the category. Proposing that having a strong brand with high perceived

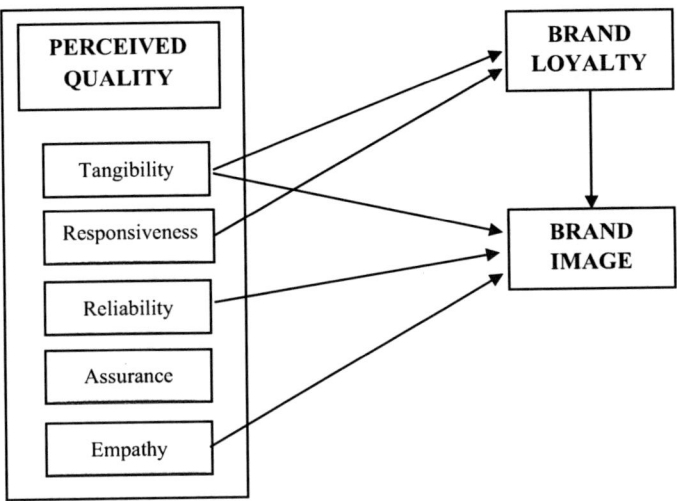

FIGURE 3.11 Adapted from Kayaman and Arasli's (2007) Brand Equity model

equity enables customers to mentally visualize and comprehend what they term as "tangiblizing the intangible hotel experience" (p. 93).

Kayaman and Arasli's conceptual model (see Figure 3.11) uses theory and constructs from services marketing and tries to capture respondents' perceptions towards five aspects of Brand Equity. These include the respondents' "perceived quality" of the service in terms of tangibility of the service encounter (e.g., using tangible signs of quality), "responsiveness" of service personnel, "reliability" of the service, "assurance" (i.e., knowledge and politeness of employees and capacity to convey trust and confidence) and "empathy" (i.e., the level of care and individualized attention service personnel demonstrate during the service episode). These researchers propose the effects of these dimensions to be linked to the respondents' ratings of loyalty towards, and awareness of, the brand of hotel.

Kayaman and Arasli (2007) hypothesize 15 effects. However, only six return significant associations between the hypothesized constructs. Surprisingly, awareness of the brand is not a significant effect in their modeled data. This goes against the brand building continuum, where consumers need to have basic awareness of a brand before a brand can build more significant relationships with consumers. This means that in Kayaman and Arasli's model brand awareness does not predict, and therefore, it is not a significant factor that affects their version of Brand Equity.

The authors report a significant discriminate validity of the total final model, with modest R-values for significant effects (0.59 to 0.77). The construct of tangibility of the experience may have some similarities with the beer category. However, it is debatable whether respondents' perceptions are based on experience and not largely subjective like they would be in the beer category. Additionally, the applicability of the constructs of the brand's "responsiveness" and "empathy" appear questionable for an application to the beer category.

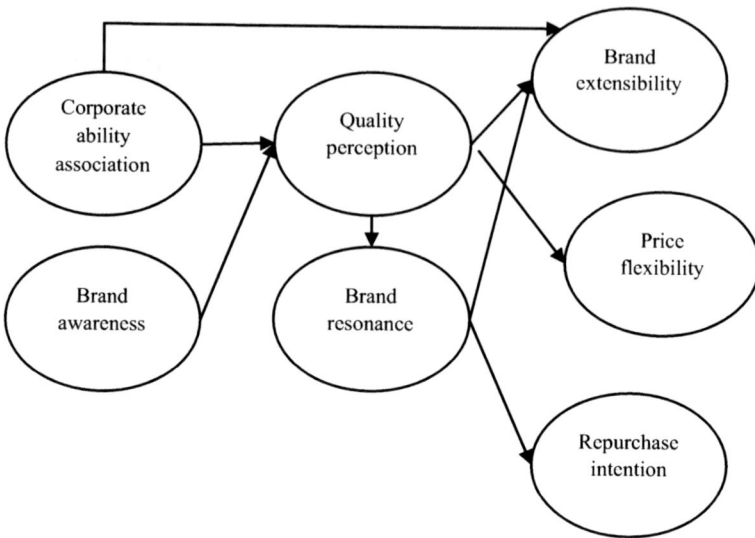

FIGURE 3.12 Adapted from Wang et al.'s (2008) CBBE model

Using aspects of Aaker and Keller's work in Brand Knowledge and Brand Equity, Wang et al. (2008) develop and test a model of building brand equity that is based on a theory called Corporation Ability Association (CAA).

Wang tests the model shown in Figure 3.12 with a select number of large international brands. They do this by showing the test-brands to a sample of two thousand respondents from three major cities of China. These respondents are current users of products from the categories and brands featured in the test. The brands in the study are seven established international brands, in one of three product categories. These categories are hair shampoos, color televisions and personal computers. The use of the personal computer category is supposed to represent an example of a high technology product in China in the year 2005. The respondents answer questions about how they perceive the seven brands and how they will behave toward these brands under different scenarios such as a price rise.

Wang et al. (2008) specifically collect responses to questions about the associations consumers may have with the brand, their awareness of the brand (e.g., "The brand is very famous" – this appears to be something beyond awareness), their perceptions of the brand's quality (e.g., "I think this brand is capable of upgrading" – another questionable choice), the brand's "resonance" (e.g., "This brand would be my first choice"), the brand's "extensibility" (e.g., "The extension by this brand must be popular"), "price flexibility" (e.g., "When this brand increases in price, it must have justified reasons") and the respondent's "repurchase intentions" toward the brand ("What is the probability of you purchasing this brand next time you need to purchase it?").

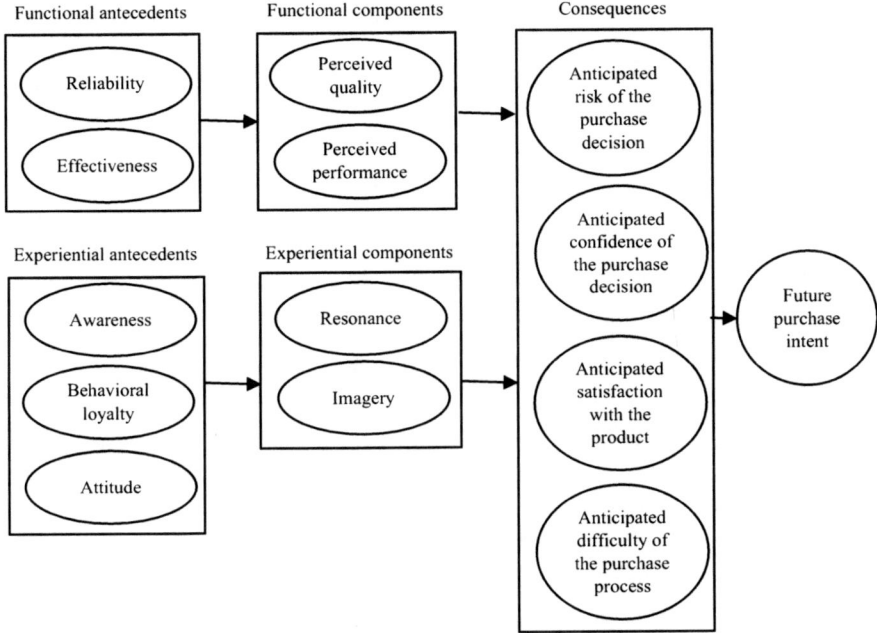

FIGURE 3.13 Adapted from Broyles, Schumann and Leingpibul's (2009) initial brand equity antecedent/consequence model

The data fit their model and Wang et al. (2008) argue for the discriminative validity of their model. However, as with most studies in this area, they fail to provide information about their model's ability to discriminate between respondents that intend to purchase, and those without intentions to buy.

In Wang et al.'s research, the shampoo category they use for their test may contain largely subjective criteria and perceptions about different brands. However, the measures in their survey do not seem to capture these attributes well. An explanation may be that the study is conducted in China, perhaps many of these differences are culturally based – the Chinese may have a different way for evaluating and describing these subjective attributes. An additional note is that none of the attributes they ask about are hedonic like beer (e.g., taste). The closest hedonic reference concerns whether the brand is "very innovative".

Broyles, Schumann and Leingpibul (2009) examine antecedents and outcomes for Brand Equity (Figure 3.13) in an attempt to improve the measurements for the nuances inherent in elements of Brand Knowledge. For example, what the difference between "Crispy" and "Tender and Juicy" results in when referring to KFC Chicken. They also test their model on the Coca-Cola brand.

Broyles et al. (2009) uses US undergraduate university students as subjects to answer their survey, and Structural Equation Model analyses to fit the resulting data to a model. This study attempts to see if the data they collect for the future purchase intent of KFC and Coca-Cola brands will converge with the Brand Knowledge antecedents they specify in their model.

The authors note their most important finding as the substantial direct effect the "experiential antecedent" respondents' report with the product and brand. This experiential antecedent affects their intentions to purchase the brand. Although experiential refers to some experience with a brand, Broyles et al. (2009) use the respondent's attitude toward the brand and his or her imagery about the brand to measure experience. The blending of the two as experiential has little rationale and may be interpreted as reflecting other constructs like affect. Nonetheless, the experiential nature and subjective perceptions of beer would appear to have similarities with this study.

Summary

This chapter has reviewed some mono-cultural studies that have specified and tested different constructs that their authors called Brand Knowledge and Brand Equity. From this review, it is very obvious that there is no singular definition for either construct. There is also no specific way that the constructs "hang" together, or relate, to specify the relationship between the antecedent Brand Knowledge and the outcome Brand Equity.

That there are so many variations, and so many ways to specify these two constructs suggest that researchers have not yet arrived at the "truth" concerning the relationship between Brand Knowledge and Brand Equity. That the predictive values between the antecedent and outcome constructs range between 0.3 and 0.65 also indicates that there is much improvement to be made. Note that many of the studies use SEM to fit the data to the proposed models. This may partially contribute to the problem of finding low predictive power. Many of these studies do not seem able to fulfil the data to prediction ratio requirements of SEM. SEM is not a true way to predict as it is variable and not stochastic. The prediction of stochastic behavior should best be done with stochastic behavioral modeling like Negative Binomial Distribution. We will discuss this further in following chapters.

A major limitation of the studies reviewed in this chapter is their overwhelmingly mono-cultural context. Most of the studies reviewed in this chapter were conducted in the United States of America, with one study in China and another in Spain. As discussed in Chapters 1 and 2, brands are very important in multi-country contexts. The next chapter reviews cross-cultural studies that seek to predict the link between Brand Knowledge and Brand Equity.

Bibliography

Aaker, D. A. (1992), "Managing the Most Important Asset: Brand Equity", *Planning Review*, 20 (5), 56–59.

Aaker, David A. (1991), *Managing Brand Equity: Capitalizing on the Value of a Brand Name*. New York: Free Press.

Allison, Ralph I. and Kenneth P. Uhl (1964), "Influences of Beer Brand Identification on Taste Perception", *Journal of Marketing Research*, 1 (3), 36–39.

Arvidsson, Adam (2006), "Brand Value", *Journal of Brand Management*, 13 (3), 188–93.

Broyles, Allen S., David W. Schumann and Thaweephan Leingpibul (2009), "Examining Brand Equity Antecedent/Consequence Relationships", *Journal of Marketing Theory and Practice*, 17 (2), 145–62.

Capraro, Anthony J., Susan Broniarczyk and Rajendra K. Srivastava (2003), "Factors Influencing the Likelihood of Customer Defection: The Role of Consumer Knowledge", *Journal of Academy of Marketing Science*, 31 (2), 164–75.

Casey, R. A. (2003), "The Effect of Brand Equity on Brand Knowledge: An Empirical and Comparative Analysis". Unpublished D.B.A., Nova South-eastern University, United States – Florida.

Creyer, Elizabeth, H., John C. Kozup and Scot Burton (2002), "An Experimental Assessment of the Effects of Two Alcoholic Beverage Health Warnings Across Countries and Binge-Drinking Status", *The Journal of Consumer Affairs*, 36 (2), 171.

Ehrenberg, A. S. C. (1972), *Repeat-Buying: Theory and Applications*. London: Charles Griffin.

Emmer, Maurice and John Henshall (2002), "Building and Maintaining Brand Value", *International Tax Review*, 41–49.

Erdem, Tulin, Joffre Swait, Susan Broniarczyk, Dipankar Chakravarti, Jean-Noel Kapferer, Michael Keane, John Roberts, Jan-Benedict E. M. Steenkamp and Florian Zettelmeyer (1999), "Brand Equity, Consumer Learning and Choice", *Marketing Letters*, 10 (3), 301–19.

Erdem, Tülin, Ying Zhao and Ana Valenzuela (2004), "Performance of Store Brands: A Cross-Country Analysis of Consumer Store-Brand Preferences, Perceptions, and Risk", *Journal of Marketing Research*, 41 (1), 86.

Erdem, Tulin and Joffre Swait (1998), "Brand Equity as a Signaling Phenomenon", *Journal of Consumer Psychology*, 7 (2), 131–57.

Erdem, Tulin, Joffre Swait and Jordan Louviere (2002), "The Impact of Brand Credibility on Consumer Price Sensitivity", *International Journal of Research in Marketing*, 19 (1), 1.

Erdem, Tulin, Joffre Swait and Ana Valenzuela (2006), "Brands as Signals: A Cross-Country Validation Study", *Journal of Marketing*, 70 (1), 34.

Esch, Franz-Rudolf, Tobias Langner, Bernd H. Schmitt and Patrick Geus (2006), "Are Brands Forever? How Brand Knowledge and Relationships Affect Current and Future Purchases", *The Journal of Product and Brand Management*, 15 (2), 98–107.

Fredric, Kropp, M. Lavack Anne and J. S. Holden Stephen (1999), "Smokers and Beer Drinkers: Values and Consumer Susceptibility to Interpersonal Influence", *The Journal of Consumer Marketing*, 16 (6), 536.

Kapferer, Jean-Noel (2008), *The New Strategic Brand Management: Creating and Sustaining Brand Equity Long Term*. Philadelphia: Kogan Page.

Kayaman, Ruchan and Huseyin Arasli (2007), "Customer Based Brand Equity: Evidence from the Hotel Industry", *Managing Service Quality*, 17 (1), 92–109.

Keller, K. L. (2001), "Building Customer-Based Brand Equity", *Marketing Management*, 10 (2), 14.

Keller, K. L. (2008), *Strategic Brand Management. Building, Measuring, and Managing Brand Equity* (3rd ed.). Upper Saddle River, NJ: Pearson Prentice-Hall.

Keller, Kevin Lane (2003), "Brand Synthesis: The Multidimensionality of Brand Knowledge", *Journal of Consumer Research*, 29 (4), 595–600.

———— (1993), "Conceptualizing, Measuring, and Managing Customer-Based Brand Equity", *Journal of Marketing*, 57 (1), 1–22.

Keller, Kevin Lane, Susan E. Heckler and Michael J. Houston (1998), "The Effects of Brand Name Suggestiveness on Advertising Recall", *Journal of Marketing*, 62 (1), 48–57.

Koçak, Akin, Temi Abimbola and Alper Özer (2007), "Consumer Brand Equity in a Cross-cultural Replication: An Evaluation of a Scale", *Journal of Marketing Management*, 23 (1), 157–73.

Kotler, Philip and K. L. Keller (2009), *A Framework for Marketing Management* (4th ed.). Upper Saddle River, NJ: Pearson/Prentice Hall.

Kuhn, Kerri-Ann and F. Alpert (2004), "Applying Keller's Brand Equity Model in a B2B Context: Limitations and an Empirical Test", The Australian and New Zealand Marketing Academy (ANZMAC).

Kuhn, Kerry-Ann L., Frank Alpert and Nigel K Li Pope (2008), "An Application of Keller's Brand Equity Model in a B2B context", *Qualitative Market Research*, 11 (1), 40.

Lambert, Claire (2008), "Young Children's Fast Food Brand Knowledge, Preference and Equity", The University of Western Australia.

Lassar, Walfried, Banwari Mittal and Arun Sharma (1995), "Measuring Customer-Based Brand Equity", *The Journal of Consumer Marketing*, 12 (4), 11.

Netemeyer, Richard G., Balaji Krishnan, Chris Pullig, Guangping Wang, Mehmet Yagci, Dwane Dean, Joe Ricks and Writh Ferdinand (2004), "Developing and Validating Measures of Facets of Customer-Based Brand Equity", *Journal of Business Research*, 57 (2), 209–24.

Park, Chan Su and V. Srinivasan (1994), "A Survey-Based Method for Measuring and Understanding Brand", *Journal of Marketing Research*, 31 (2), 271–89.

Pham, Thang, Katherine Mizerski, Saalem Sadeque and Richard Mizerski (2009), "The Effect of Product Familiarity in Perceptions and Preferences of Private Label and National Brands", in ANZMAC. Melbourne: Australia New-Zealand Marketing Educators Association.

Punj, Girish N. and Clayton L. Hillyer (2004), "A Cognitive Model of Customer-Based Brand Equity for Frequently Purchased Products: Conceptual Framework and Empirical Results", *Journal of Consumer Psychology*, 14 (1), 124.

Schultz, Don E. (2004), "Understanding Total Brand Value", *Marketing Management*, 13 (2), 10.

Spence, M. (1974), *Market Signaling: Informational Transfer in Hiring and Related Screening Processes*. Cambridge, MA: Harvard University Press.

Stark, John (2011), *Product Lifecycle Management*. London: Springer.

Stigler, G. D. (1961), "The Economics of Information", *Journal of Political Economy*, 69, 13–26.

Taylor, Steven A., Kevin Celuch and Stephen Goodwin (2004), "The Importance of Brand Equity to Customer Loyalty", *The Journal of Product and Brand Management*, 13 (4), 217.

Taylor, Steven A., Gary L. Hunter and Deborah L. Linberg (2007), "Understanding (Customer-Based) Brand Equity in Financial Services", *The Journal of Services Marketing*, 21 (4), 241.

Vázquez, Rodolfo, A. Belén del Río and Víctor Iglesias (2002), "Consumer-Based Brand Equity: Development and Validation of a Measurement Instrument", *Journal of Marketing Management*, 18 (1), 27–48.

Virgin (2014), "Find a Virgin Company", (accessed July 1, 2014), [available at www.virgin.com/company].

Wang, Haizhong, Yujie Wei and Chunling Yu (2008), "Global Brand Equity Model: Combining Customer-Based with Product-Market Outcome Approaches", *Journal of Product & Brand Management*, 17 (5), 305–16.

Wang, Paul, Constantinos Menictas and Jordan Louviere (2007), "Comparing Structural Equation Models with Discrete Choice Experiments for Modelling Brand Equity and Predicting Brand Choices", *Australian Marketing Journal*, 15 (2), 12–25.

Yoo, Boonghee, Naveen Donthu and Sungho Lee (2000), "An Examination of Selected Marketing Mix Elements and Brand Equity", *Academy of Marketing Science Journal*, 28 (2), 195–212.

4

CROSS-CULTURAL STUDIES, LOYALTY, CHOICE, EXPERIMENTS AND HYPOTHESES

Maintaining brand consistency across different market segments, markets, cultures and countries is challenging. Globalization is not necessarily globalization in branding. There are very few brands that manage to develop identical knowledge, attributes and mental links in consumers' minds from different markets and countries. At the time of writing, only a handful of truly global brands exist (Knowledge@Wharton 2014). This is because changing the knowledge behind a brand to suit local preferences seems to be the best way forward. This is compounded by the reality (as discussed in Chapter 2), that many companies expand into new markets by acquiring local brands. As a result, it is necessary to merge the company's international brand with local brands.

What has research into the measurement of brands across cultures revealed? This chapter will review past research relating to Brand Equity measurement models which have embraced a cross-cultural perspective in their analysis and model development.

Yoo and Donthu (2002) extend work from their earlier Yoo et al. (2000) article. This time they test the same model's fit across samples from two populations comprising of South Korean and US university students. The addition of a sample from a different country leads Yoo and Donthu to discover additional constructs. These include constructs pertaining to brand and category experiences (Brand Experience and Category Experience), overall attitudinal loyalty to a brand (Brand Loyalty), and the respondents' judgment of a brand's overall excellence. The respective data fit the models for each country (Figure 4.1). However, Yoo and Donthu do not report any prediction or discrimination tests.

Koçak et al. (2007) duplicate Vázquez, Río and Iglesias's (2002) Consumer-Based Brand-Equity study in a "cross-cultural" setting, using responses from a sample of university students in Turkey to test the model. These students are from a different cultural background to the Spanish sample Vázquez, Río and Iglesias (2002)

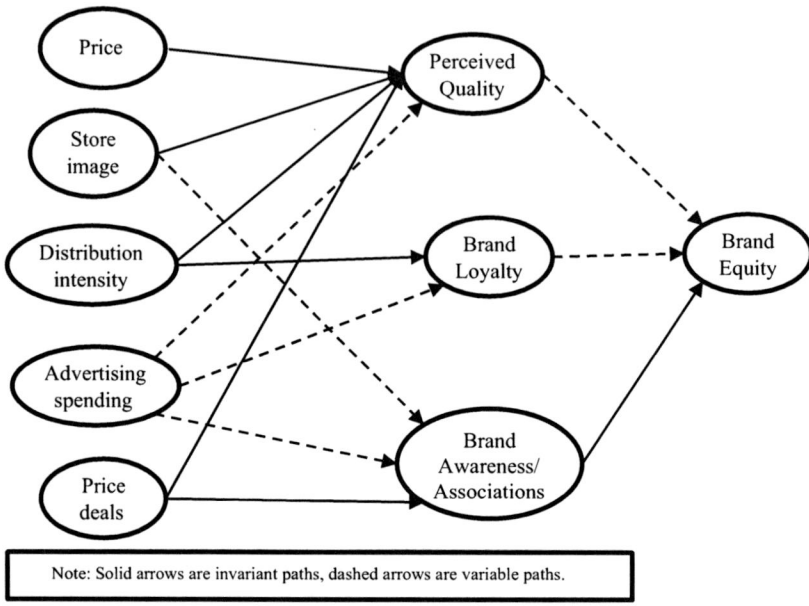

FIGURE 4.1 Adapted from Yoo and Donthu's (2002) CBBE model

uses. What Koçak et al. find is that they have to modify the scales in order to fit the way Turkish students look at brands. After conducting exploratory and confirmatory factor analysis, they find the Turkey sample's responses do not fit the model. They adjust the scales for cultural sensitivities and the model fit. Going back to Koçak et al. (2007), this study indicates that different cultural environments will guide consumers to different evaluations of brands.

Their model appears to blend the perspectives of the Information Economics' Signaling Theory and the Keller's psychological Customer-Based Brand-Equity (CBBE) view (Keller 2003; Keller 2008). Koçak et al.'s Brand Equity measure is based on the utilities a brand will provide over its competitive brands (Vázquez et al. 2002). The authors use sport-shoes as the branded category for their test which was consistent with the product category used by Vázquez et al. (2002). This makes it easier to account for the influence of cultural effects in the replication study.

Koçak et al. (2007) uses questions that count the functional and symbolic utilities of the product category and of the brand. These are incorporated into their Brand Equity model as "product functional utility", "product symbolic utility", "brand name functional utility" and "brand name symbolic utility". For example, to measure "product functional utility" respondents rate a brand of sport-shoes on flexibility and grip. These were part of the "functionality" construct. Respondents also rate the sport-shoes on things like the number of color options. The survey does not ask about the output of Brand Equity – e.g., brand preference or intention to buy a brand. As such, the researchers cannot conduct discriminatory or predictive tests.

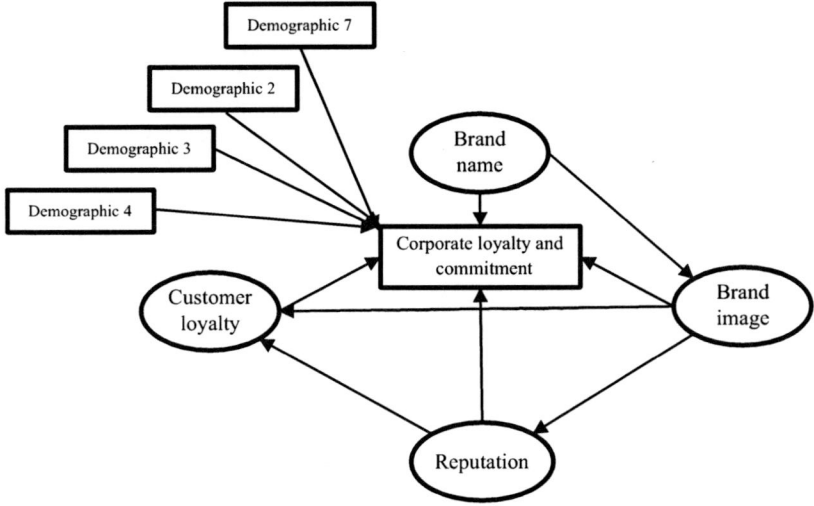

FIGURE 4.2 Adapted from Souiden, Kassim and Hong's (2006) CBBE model

As mentioned, the data collected from the students in Turkey fit the Vázquez's et al. (2002) model, but not before modifications to the scales. Compared to Yoo and Donthu's results from the United States and Korea samples who also rated sport-shoes (athletic shoes), Koçak et al. interpret many attributes differently. Given the lack of an outcome measure for Brand Equity – e.g., buying or intent to buy, it is difficult to support Koçak et al.'s model as predictive or discriminating.

A study that supports the finding that consumers from different countries will evaluate the same brands differently is Souiden, Kassim and Hong (2006). This is another study with a cross-cultural aspect using Aaker and Keller's work. However, this look at Aaker and Keller's vies that corporate brands influence consumers' evaluation of brands. This is distinct from consumers' evaluation of brands as proposed by the CBBE concept. We discuss this study because it provides a comparison of brand perceptions from samples from different countries.

The Souiden, Kassim and Hong model views the Brand Equity of an automobile brand as comprising of consumer perceptions of the brand's name, image, reputation and loyalty. They test this model (Figure 4.2) with a convenience sample of people in the United States and in Japan. These respondents responded on a mail-back survey. The authors have problems providing an adequate Structural Equation Model analysis because of the small sample size against the number of constructs being measured. They also have about half of their hypothesized relationships rejected. They report the effects of corporate name and corporate reputation to be supported in terms of their link to a construct they call Corporate Loyalty/Commitment. This is for both the United States and Japan. However, there are no attempts to test the discrimination or prediction of the model in terms of Brand Equity outputs like loyalty to brands.

Retailer brands

Retailer brands, especially those that are sold online, have the ability to have a presence in different countries. As such, it is useful to review research that tries to map the Brand Equity of these brands that are sold through online retailers.

Chen and He (2003) specify a conceptual model to understand consumers' intentions to adopt an online retailer brand. The model is based on brand theory, risk theory and information theory. This seeks to understand consumers' intentions to purchase from a particular online retailer by exploring their use of Brand Knowledge. They hypothesize that Brand knowledge is negatively related to "Perceived Risk", and positively related to "Intention to Adopt". Further, Perceived Risk is negatively related to the action of "Information Search Online". Information Search Online is where the buyer searches for information about competing retailers. This search seems to act to decrease the amount of Perceived Risk related to the purchase (see Figure 4.3). In other words, searching for information increases the risks encountered by an online retailer as it expands the consumer's chances of finding more favorable choices, thus possibly lowering their intention to adopt the existing retailer. Search behavior also reduces the risk of purchase for the customer because it increases their choice, making it more likely that they will get a better deal.

After testing with a Structural Equation Model analysis, the data is reported to fit the model; "Brand Knowledge" is a direct and positive effect in "Intention to Adopt" an online retailer and is strongly mediated by "Perceived Risk". Further, Perceived Risk is positively related to "Information Search Online", supporting the hypothesis that searching for information increases the risks for an online retailer as increases buyers' chances of finding better deals with competing online merchants.

Although the authors investigate a dimension of Brand Equity – Brand Knowledge, they do not provide any tests of determination or prediction for the Brand Equity construct. Although the study uses an online sample, this may include respondents from different countries and cultures, the authors only commented on the gender and age demographics of the sample; no cultural effects are investigated.

Pappu and Quester (2006) examine the effect of consumers' satisfaction with "bricks and mortar" retailers and the equity they associate with a retailer's brand.

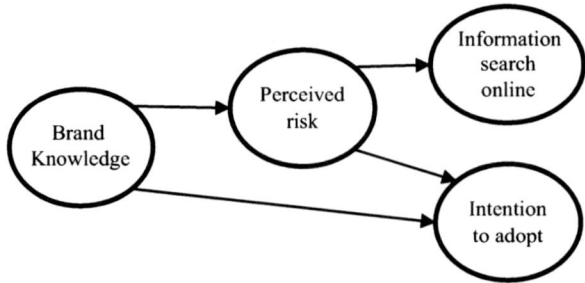

FIGURE 4.3 Adapted from Chen and He's (2003) model to interpret consumers' intentions to choose from an online retailer

They argue that a retailer's Brand Equity in the two retail subcategories – department store and specialty stores – will vary considerably as a function of consumer satisfaction with the retailer. More specifically, the researchers expect that retailer awareness, associations and perceived quality will vary significantly as a function of customer satisfaction. The relationship between customer satisfaction and retailer loyalty is also expected to vary depending on the type of retailer (see Figure 4.4).

Pappu et al. (2006) find CBBE to vary significantly for both department stores and specialty stores, with these variations correlating to the amount of reported satisfaction with the retailer. For department stores, all predictive dimensions in the model vary with levels of consumer satisfaction with the retailer. However, only three predictors are significant for specialty stores (retailer awareness, associations and perceived quality are significant). This suggests that the way consumer satisfaction affects consumers' loyalty to retailers may be specific to different retail-categories.

Although Pappu et al. (2006) report some interesting findings, their model return only moderate results, with only modest levels of association between the constructs. Also their model does not provide any output measures for the brands' equities or information about the way the model discriminates between the different brands tested. This means the model cannot predict their respondents' choice of brands.

Martenson (2007) investigates retail brands, focusing on the impact of the corporate store image on customer satisfaction and loyalty to the store. This is in the grocery retailing setting. Although Martenson (2007) does not refer to Keller's work (Keller 1993; 2003), she discusses retail store loyalty as a function of a component

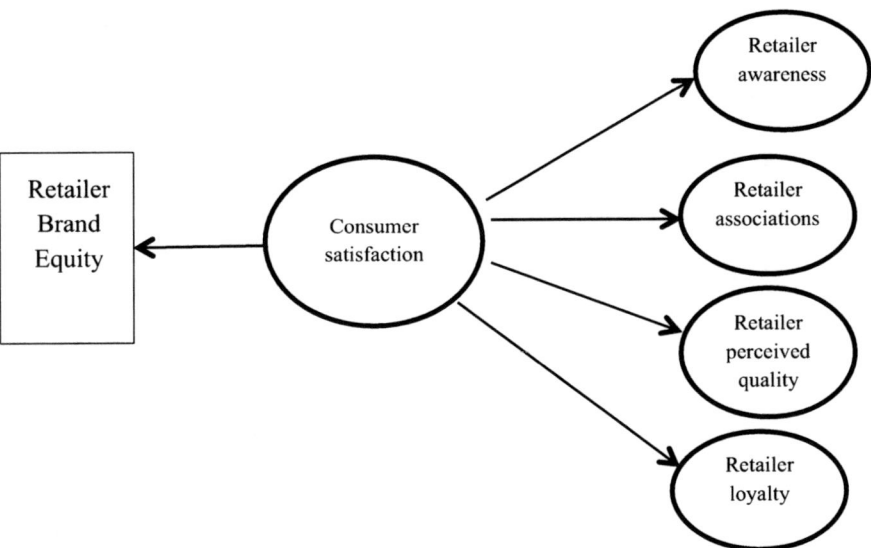

FIGURE 4.4 Adapted from Pappu and Quester's (2006) model for testing the impact of consumer satisfaction on retailer brand equity

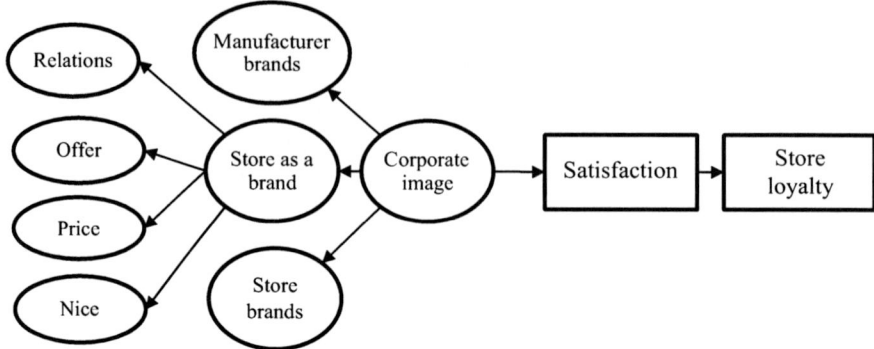

FIGURE 4.5 Adapted from Martenson's (2007) model for the role of store image for satisfaction and loyalty

of Brand Knowledge – image, specifically corporate (store) image. Martenson puts forth that corporate image is a prerequisite for brand equity to develop. The author finds that store brand image and the buyer's satisfaction with the store affect the customer's self-reported loyalty to store and to private brands and manufacturer brands (Figure 4.5). This gives the unremarkable insight that satisfied customers will be more loyal.

Not surprisingly, the data collected through surveys sent to a nationally representative sample of large purchasers of groceries is consistent with the model Martensen proposes. Although no tests of determination or prediction are offered, the author notes only a weak relationship between satisfaction and loyalty ($r^2 = 0.2$). Although this study tests a wide variety of categories (e.g., gourmet food, detergent and vacuum cleaners), this test uses only hypothetical "manufacturer's brands" and not real manufacturer's brands. The study is restricted to a sample from one country – Sweden, and therefore does not really address cultural implications. Although it tests satisfaction – which can be seen as an outcome of brand knowledge, and it tests loyalty, overall, this study does not provide a good basis for examining the beer category.

Subscription market

Subscription markets are markets where subscribers buy products and pay a monthly fee. Examples include mobile phone and internet access, magazines and insurance products. These product categories are dominated by many international brands. For example, *Vogue* magazine was founded in the United States but is published in many countries and in many languages. Mobile phone subscribers can subscribe to Virgin, Vodafone and Orange services in many countries. The international nature of many subscription markets warrants a review of the literature that examines the brands operating in this market.

Aydin and Ozer (2005) look at the constructs that can be measured as Brand Knowledge (e.g., Corporate Image, Perceived Quality). More specifically, they

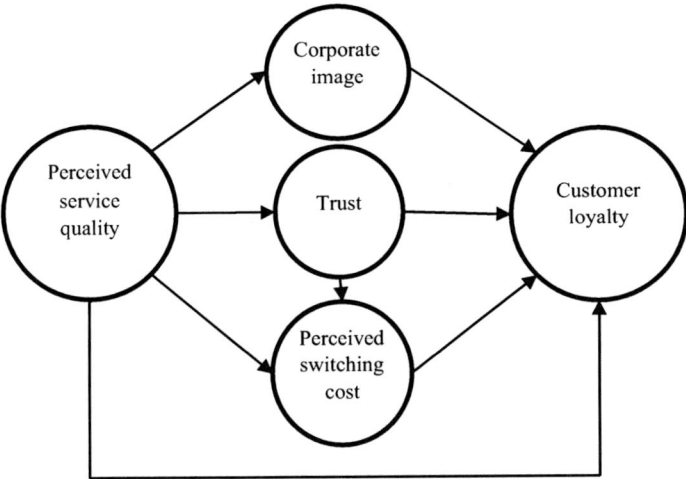

FIGURE 4.6 Adapted from Aydin and Ozer's (2005) customer loyalty model

examined the relationship between "Corporate Image", "Perceived Service Quality", "Trust and Customer Switching Costs" with "Customer Loyalty" (see Figure 4.6). The researchers perceive these Brand Knowledge constructs as antecedents to "Customer Loyalty" in a subscription market called the Turkish Global System for Mobile Communications (GSM). In this market, switching is only allowed after a long period of time because of "tie in" contractual arrangements.

They hypothesize that "Perceived Service Quality", "Corporate Image", "Trust and Perceived Switching Costs" will demonstrate a positive effect on "Customer Loyalty". The measures of Customer Loyalty consist of repurchase intention (next-use), resistance to switching to a superior competitor product, and willingness to recommend the preferred vendor's product. Aydin and Ozer's data from mobile telephone users in Turkey fit their model, with all factors in the model having positive effects on Customer Loyalty. Trust is reported to be the most significant determinant of Customer Loyalty. While Perceived Service Quality is a necessary factor to predict Customer Loyalty, it is a mediating factor that cannot predict Customer Loyalty by itself. This means perceptions of good quality is insufficient by itself to affect and develop customer loyalty.

Consistent with prior research, Aydin and Ozer also report "Corporate Image", "Perceived Service Quality" and particularly "Trust" to be important factors predicting Customer Loyalty. These factors seem to be crucial to any strategies to address and develop loyalty to a brand.

Unfortunately, the researchers do not report any test of their model's discrimination between brands or the ability to predict loyalty. Given that beer purchase take place in a repertoire market (frequent repurchase), not a subscription market, this model may not be applicable. A repertoire market is where there is more than one brand in the market and the same consumer is likely to use more than one brand.

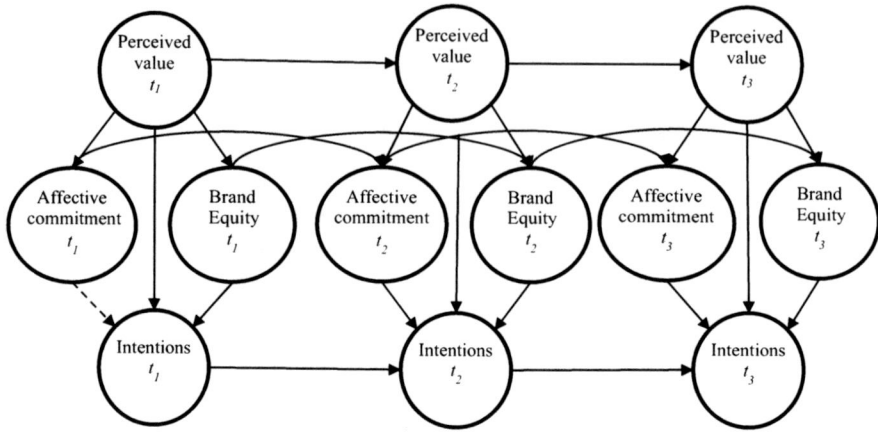

FIGURE 4.7 Adapted from Johnson Herrmann and Huber's (2006) loyalty intentions model

Note: Dotted line is not significant at 0.05 level.

The nature of the Brand Knowledge factors tested would also appear less subjectively based than those for beer.

Johnson, Herrmann and Huber (2006) examine the drivers of loyalty intentions for a panel of loyal customers who purchased and used a new-to-market offering (cellular phone) through the introduction and growth stages of the Product Life-Cycle. They incorporated two particular attitudes not previously studied in this line of research: the affective commitment toward maintaining a relationship with a company, and Brand Equity. The researchers track these loyal users over a four-year period that coincide with the introduction and growth stages of the product's Life-Cycle. This tracking study seeks to test how "Perceived Value" may change in its influence on "Loyalty Intentions" over the Life-Cycle of a product. It is expected that Perceived Value will have a more direct effect in the early stage of the Life-Cycle. However, as the Life-Cycle evolves, more affective attitudes – affective commitment and brand equity – should have greater influence on Loyalty Intentions. Furthermore, these two constructs should mediate the effect of Perceived Value on Loyalty Intentions (see Figure 4.7). Focusing on a developing market also allows for an understanding of how loyalty drivers will grow and change as competition increases.

The authors report that in their sample, respondents' perceptions of the overall value of a brand tend to drive the early diffusion of cell phones. Later on in the product adoption stage, affective factors become more important in respondents' reported loyalty to a brand. The constructs are measured using multiple items, including intent to be loyal. For example, respondents are asked, "Next time I will definitely buy this cell phone (or its successor) again".

Actual or self-reports of their behavior are not collected or used in the analyses. Additionally, the study focuses on a subscription product market (cellular phones), not a repertoire market like beer. Nonetheless, a potentially important finding is that the composition and relationship of the Perceived Value, Affective Commitment and Brand Equity constructs may change over time in regards to their influence on Loyalty Intentions. As expected they find Perceived Value – a cognitive perception – drives Loyalty Intentions in the early stages of the Life-Cycle. However, as the market grows and consumers become more experienced, Affective Commitment and Brand Equity become strong drivers of Loyalty Intentions. The model however is unclear about whether consumers' having Affective Commitment towards a brand leads to Brand Equity and the outputs of Brand Equity. The study is also restricted to one country – Germany.

Capraro et al. (2003) focuses on furthering the understanding of customer defection. Their study concentrates on repurchase decisions that require an evaluation of alternative brands by the respondent. These evaluations are based on information the respondent has about the brands being tested.

This investigation by Capraro et al. tests the relationship between the customer's level of knowledge about objective (e.g., product features) and subjective (what they perceive they know) about alternatives. The answers to questions on these dimensions is then used to predict their likelihood of defection to other brands. A control variable Capraro et al. use is respondents' satisfaction level with the brand.

In order to test for the interrelationships between knowledge and satisfaction dimensions to affect respondents' self-stated likelihood of defection to another brand, Crapraro et al. specified the model shown in Figure 4.8, Model 1A). Figure 4.8, Model 2 shows their attempt to validate whether the influence of knowledge is moderated by satisfaction level. Figure 4.8, Model 3 tests whether a mediating effect is evident between knowledge and satisfaction level on likelihood of defection.

Capraro et al. (2003) collect their survey with university staff members. These respondents are given scenarios to select health insurance plans, the survey provides a situation where respondents have to seek more information about alternatives before deciding on their plan. Only one of the relationships proposed is significant – the level of objective and subjective knowledge about alternatives exert a direct effect on the respondents' likelihood to defect to other brands of insurance, above and beyond the respondents' satisfaction level. Respondents' knowledge about alternative brands do not mediate the relationship between satisfaction and the likelihood to switch to another plan. There was also no interaction effect between satisfaction with the current plan and the respondents' level of knowledge about alternatives.

The context of the Capraro et al. study is a subscription market (insurance). This is similar to the mobile telephone study by Aydin and Ozer (2005). However, subscription markets are not readily applicable for beer brands. Further, the requirement to seek additional information about alternatives is also not typically relevant for the beer market.

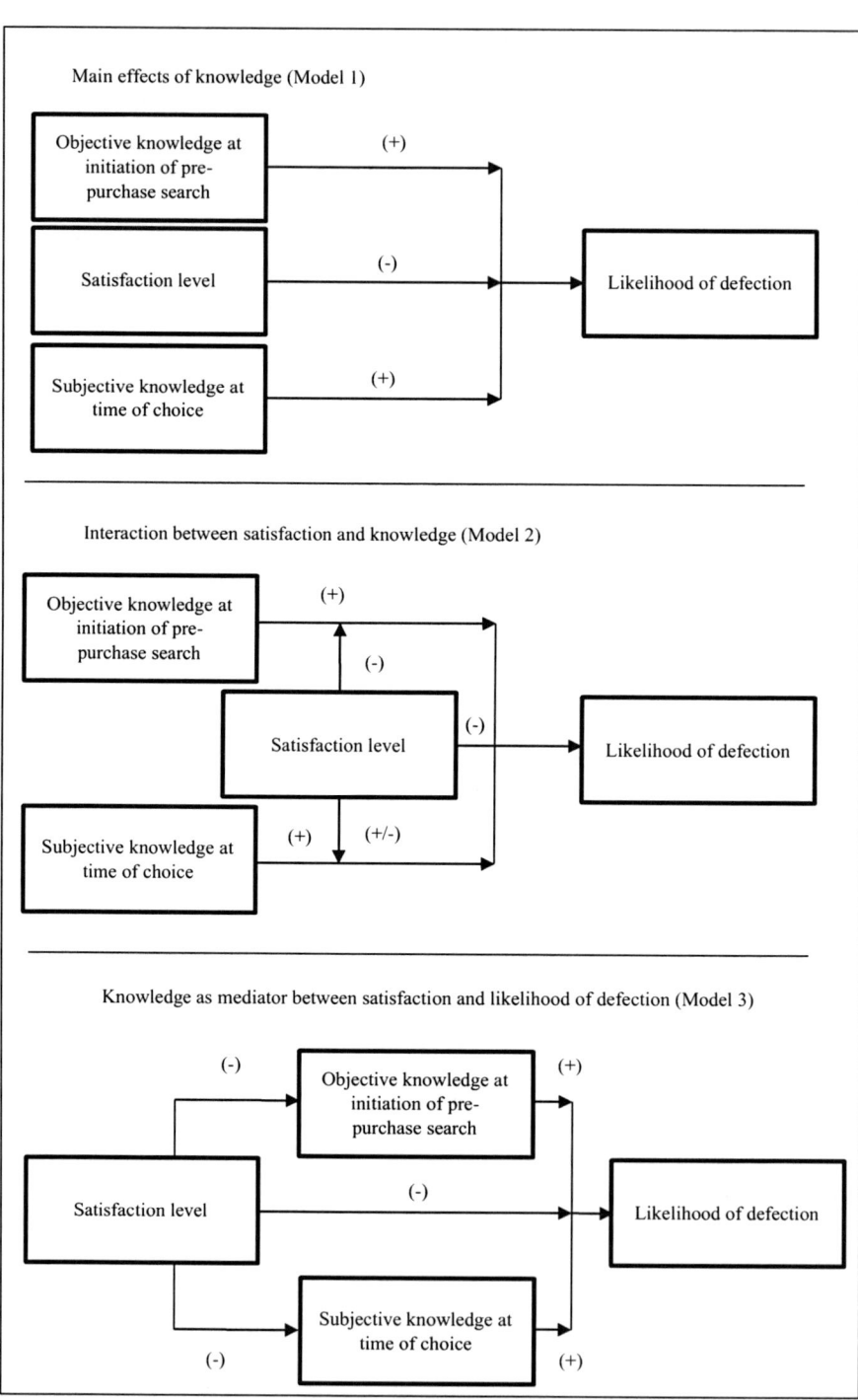

FIGURE 4.8 Adapted from Capraro et al.'s (2003) relationship between consumer knowledge, satisfaction level and likelihood-of-defection

Sports

Bauer, Sauer and Schmitt (2005) apply the Brand Equity concept to a sports context, studying the German Soccer League of 18 teams. They base their model's theoretical underpinnings on Keller's CBBE concept. These researchers calculate a Brand Knowledge construct from the responses of visitors to a sports website. From this, they model Brand Equity with two determinant dimensions, brand awareness and brand image. The brand image dimension appears to be entirely subjective in nature – much like beer taste is subjective. For example, they measure fan identification with the teams and the fans' feelings of nostalgia and escape when viewing their team perform.

Using their model, Bauer et al. report no evidence that Brand Awareness affects Brand Equity. They argue that their respondents have a high level of awareness about the soccer teams – these are fans who follow the league closely. As such, awareness of the 18 brands in their self-selecting sample is not useful as a factor to discriminate between brands. This is also likely to be the case for our beer drinking sample to test our Predictive Brand Choice model – where universal or near-universal awareness of the brands being tested will negate the usefulness of brand awareness as a predictor variable. However, there are also many studies that are conducted using non-fan based contexts like fast-moving-consumer goods that awareness of brands are effective in predicting brand equity. For example, between very well-known brands of beer in the Allison and Uhl (1964) study and other studies that replicated their work.

Bauer et al. (2005) also test another element of Brand Knowledge. This is their respondents' perceptions whether a team is "a strong brand". This factor reports a strong link to Brand Equity; this is measured as the number of spectators the team had over the year. The authors explain that they also perform a test of discriminate validity. However, they do not write about how well this test discriminates on the output variable. The only result they report on the Brand Knowledge to Brand Equity link is that more than 50% of the variance is explained ($R^2 = 0.50$) for their construct of Brand Equity. Consequently, this model does not provide a discriminative test. The Bauer et al. captures data online. This may result in capturing responses from soccer fans from different countries. However, the study does not report discrimination prediction by culture or country.

Experimental studies in Brand Knowledge/Brand Equity

Agarwal and Rao (1996) compares Brand Equity constructs largely developed with single item measures against with multiple items in the construct. Unsurprisingly, Agarwal and Rao report finding that multiple measures of the Brand Equity construct should do better than the single items tested. This is a common finding, increasing the number of relevant questions in a construct will improve the construct's predictive value, up to a point. Although this research uses "actual lab purchases", these lab purchases appear to be quite removed from consumers' actual decision-making. At most, the respondents choose a free item among a few other items in a product category that are displayed in a laboratory setting.

Broniarczyk and Gershoff (2003) manipulate attributes of a hypothetical down jacket and test these on a sample of undergraduate university students – the students read a description of the jacket but do not have an actual jacket to look at. These researchers study how potential buyers may differentially perceive the use of trivial attributes, depending if these attributes are used by brands with high or low equity. They report that the use of a known (by consumers') trivial attribute hurts a low equity brand; the same attribute has no effect in evaluations of high equity brands. This study does not screen respondents for potential purchase, and the report does not provide any tests of discrimination or prediction. This study appears to have little relevance to the task of modeling the Brand Knowledge link to the Brand Equity of beer, except that they support a link between Brand Knowledge and Brand Equity.

An article by Korchia (2006) reports on an experiment that evaluates the influence of valence (favorable vs. unfavorable) and uniqueness of brand associations on Brand Equity. Not surprisingly, unique favorable associations are linked to high brand equity. This experiment measures Brand Equity with four items; three items ask respondents about their preference for the brand under different comparisons, the fourth question asks about how reasonable it is to buy the brand, ". . . even if they (both brands) look the same" (p. 11).

The Korchia experiment obtained its sample by the internet, although it is not clear if this experiment is conducted individually or as a group in a computer lab. Korchia tests the product category of "garments" using a fictitious brand. As with the other study using an experiment by Broniarczyk and Gershoff (2003), the findings offer little relevance to the task of modeling the link between Brand Knowledge and Brand Equity except more support for associations of the constructs of Brand Knowledge and Brand Equity.

Beer brands

Two studies apply theories of Brand Equity to the beer category. Krishnan (1996) collects respondents' perceptions of two brands in each of eight product categories studied. These categories are beer, fast food restaurants, pizza retailer, television sets, shampoos, cola, toothpaste and athletic shoes – almost all of these product categories have been studied by researchers. Krishnan evaluates the respondents' perceptions for their unaided recall of brands, their perceptions of the brand's familiarity, the number of associations the respondents can provide in an open-ended format, the valence of these associations and the respondents' judgment about the origin of the associations – whether the respondents' form the associations through exposure to advertising, experience or word-of-mouth communication. Krishnan also tests the "uniqueness" of the association (compared to the product category). The measures Krishnan uses are novel.

Krishnan finds differences between brands in a category, these differences are consistent with the estimates of each brand's relative equity. Krishnan reports the differences between the perceived sources of associations by category. However, the parametric properties of these constructs are questionable, as is the ability of the respondents to make meaningful judgments on the origin of associations (Nesbett and Wilson 1977). Most of the time, respondents will exhibit "faulty memory" when asked to recall things that happened a long time ago, especially insignificant events like where they first heard about a brand and the subsequent encounters with the same brand. Most respondents simply would not be able to recount this information with any level of accuracy.

Rajh, Vranesevic and Tolic (2003) study a sample of Croatian consumers to test a Brand Equity measure. This measure tests five product categories that includes beer, plus coffee, chocolate, milk and carbonated soft drinks. They use the responses to two questions: "Which brand did you buy last time?" and "If that brand had not been available, what would you have done?" to specify a construct they call "sustainability". Sustainability is used to classify respondents into one of six segments, the authors' argue these segments indicate a consumer's propensity to repeat purchase or their loyalty to a brand. Rajh et al. (2003) propose positive relationships between a brand's repeat purchase rate, its equity and its marketing profitability. To test this proposition, they evaluate the equity of brands in each category with a mechanism they call the "repeat rate ratio". For beer, one brand reports twice the market share and repeat rate than the second brand. This finding that a brand's share in the market and its rate of repeat purchase is linked is not new. The Stochastic paradigm that Ehrenberg (1972) calls the NBD – Negative Binomial Distribution – is cited for this assumption by the authors. However, the authors do not provide any NBD analysis beyond discussing relative brand share/equity. They also do not offer any test of the model. Consequently, this limits their study's relevance for the modeling of Brand Equity in the beer category.

Lambert's Brand Equity/Brand Knowledge model

In a more recent application, Lambert (2008; Lambert et al. 2009) develop and test a model that links Brand Knowledge to Brand Equity. Lambert tests her model using fast-food brands with a sample of three- to four-year-old children in Perth, Australia. Similar to Keller and Aaker's conceptualization, Lambert positions Brand Knowledge as an antecedent to Brand Equity.

Lambert proposes that Brand Equity is represented as the child respondent's first brand preference. The respondent's loyalty to their top ranked preferred brand is tested when the child is offered a toy that is included in their second preferred fast-food brand "kids meal" (see Figure 4.9). Alternatively if they choose their first preferred brand's meal, they do not get a toy to go with the meal – as such, they will pay a premium (Brand Equity) to choose their first preferred brand meal.

Although Lambert uses Keller's perspective of imagery in regards to who shopped, counter service, toys, benefits etc., she is limited to using binary responses of yes/no, like/dislike, because of her young subjects' limited ability to respond to questions. Nonetheless, she is able to correctly identify the very young sample's

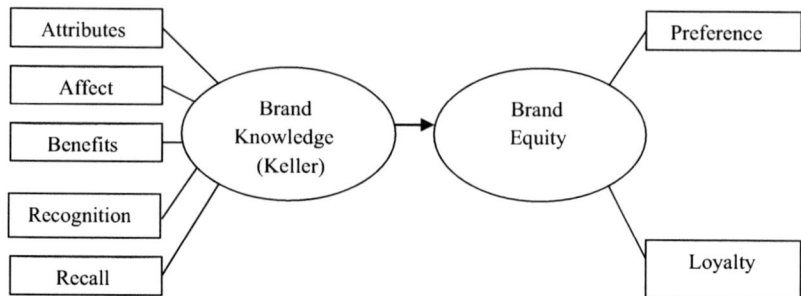

FIGURE 4.9 Adapted from Lambert (2008) CBBE model

preference among three top brands of fast-food. Lambert achieves the highest prediction ability of brand preference, achieving an 85% overall "hit-rate" with her model and method.

Lambert's identification and discrimination model for preference uses a function of four elements of Keller's (1993) Brand Knowledge construct. Her data show the factors to discriminate between different brands, at least for her sample of young children, are a lack of awareness towards the competitor's trade character, recognizing their favorite brand, disliking the brand's competition and imagery. The statistics for discrimination between different brands are far higher than the best previous attempt (Wang et al. 2008), while constrained by having to use limited (binary) response scales because of her sample's young age. However, caution must be exercised when comparing Lambert's findings with those reported by other authors, owing to the large differences in method and sample.

Lambert's thinking seems the most suited for our purposes of testing beer Brand Knowledge and linking this to Brand Equity. Lambert's Brand Knowledge to Brand Equity design appears to be a more accurate portrayal of the link between Brand Knowledge and Brand Equity for more experiential and hedonic responses. Her method uses Brand Knowledge statements about specific Feelings, Images and Affect. These relate to consumers' preferred brands. To the children, these are influential Brand Knowledge factors that predict their Brand Preferences and loyalty to a preferred brand.

Hypotheses

Most of the psychological-based CBBE models that test where Brand Knowledge and Brand Equity are linked appear to capture basic Brand Knowledge elements like experiences and attributes in a form discussed by Keller. While the research and theory of Information Economics provides support of Brand Knowledge leading to Brand Equity, the method in these studies favor products where more reasoned decisions can be made. This is when compared to the almost total subjective and experiential aspects of the beer decision. The review of the literature in the first four chapters of this book leads to proposing the following hypotheses.

These propositions drive our test of the link between our Brand Knowledge and Brand Equity constructs, using beer as an experiential and subjectively based product where brands play a very strong role in consumers' preference. These hypotheses also form the focal point that drives the methodology and modeling processes of our Predictive Brand Choice model.

Our discussion and critique of the literature suggests several hypotheses concerning the relationship between Brand Knowledge and Brand Equity. It appears logical that a Brand Knowledge construct will exist for the beer product category. This Brand Knowledge construct should influence whether a beer drinker prefers a brand among competing brands. We also expect Brand Knowledge to influence whether a consumer will be Loyal to a brand.

Brand Preference and Brand Loyalty are likely to be key outcomes of a Brand's Equity. In some ways, this conceptualization of the link between Brand Knowledge and Brand Equity has similarities to a simplified Theory of Planned Behavior (Ajzen 1991). The beliefs are the probabilities that the brand has Awareness or Imagery, but there are no subjective weights applied to the belief values for Brand Knowledge and Brand Equity.

Keller's CBBE model proposes that Brand Knowledge is a function of a person's awareness of the brand, and their Images associated with the brand – the way they see the brand. Brand images can be positive, negative, or a mix of positive and negative views. The situation Keller describes is not the case in the two beer markets to be studied. Further, all respondents to our field experiment, whether beer drinkers or non-drinkers, are found to be aware of the brands studied. Similar to the way Bauer et al. (2005) and Lambert (2008) conduct their studies, we will not test brand awareness in our model because all respondents are aware of the brands studied. Therefore, this construct cannot provide data for discrimination between brands in our sample.

Keller's 2003 Brand Knowledge model separates the Brand Images construct into two sub-constructs – associations and beliefs. This differentiation between association and beliefs can be difficult for respondents to quantify and may be unnecessary. It is arguable that perceived associations are beliefs, or a perceived likelihood that the association exists (Ajzen 1991). Keller positions attributes, attitudes and benefits as the outputs of associations. However, it may be useful to look at the possibility that each is a separate construct as acknowledged by most studies in the Brand Knowledge – Brand Equity literature. Typically, an individual's beliefs about a brand's attributes, their affect toward the brand, and the benefits they perceive the brand delivers, are related but are also different constructs and measures. This brings us to the point where we formally specify the hypotheses that will drive our field experiment.

> H1: Respondents' favorable Images about a brand will be a significant effect in their Brand Knowledge, their Brand preference and their Loyalty to their preferred brand.
> H2: Respondents' favorable Affect toward a brand will be a significant effect in their Brand Knowledge, their Brand Preference and their Loyalty to the brand.

H3: Respondents' favorable perceptions of a brand's Attributes will be a significant effect in their Brand Knowledge, their Brand Preference and their Loyalty to the preferred brand.

H4: Respondents' favorable perceptions of a brand's benefits will be a significant effect in their Brand Knowledge, their Brand Preference and their Loyalty to the preferred brand.

Summary

Several studies have looked at samples from different countries. These studies indicate many of the Brand Knowledge – Brand Equity models tested can be applied to measure Brand Knowledge and Equity with consumers from other countries and cultures (Erdem et al. 2006; Souiden et al. 2006). These studies have found differences in the perception of the constructs in different countries. However, they have not managed to offer an acceptable explanation for these differences from the angle of differentiating between different brands or predicting preference. It is arguable that these outcomes are the crucial reason for studying and measuring Brand Knowledge and Brand Equity. Despite the many studies in the area, they have not been very good at predicting brand choice. We understand little more than that the Brand Knowledge and Brand Equity constructs are linked. There are many reasons for country differences that have not yet been explored.

A plausible explanation for the differences between countries in terms of Brand Knowledge and Brand Equity could be the countries are at different stages of the product category's Life-Cycle. Remember that Johnson et al. (2006) tracked a sample's Brand Knowledge/Brand Equity through time for a subscription product (cellular/mobile telephone service) and found differences in the constructs as the market matured. It would be useful to assess whether the Brand Knowledge-Equity constructs are different in countries at different stages of the PLC – Product Life-Cycle – for a product in a repertoire market.

This assessment would be exploratory because of the inevitable confounding of cultural and PLC effects on the Brand Knowledge and Brand Equity constructs and how they relate to one another. Therefore, hypotheses specific to the differences between the constructs in the two samples are not proposed. The next chapter will outline our research method and discuss the possible cultural effects of the two samples, the Australia and the China samples.

Bibliography

Agarwal, Manoj K. and Vithala R. Rao (1996), "An Empirical Comparison of Consumer-based Measures of Brand Equity", *Marketing Letters*, 7 (2), 237–47.

Ajzen, Icek (1991), "The Theory of Planned Behavior", *Organizational Behavior and Human Decision Processes*, 50 (2), 179.

Allison, Ralph I. and Kenneth P. Uhl (1964), "Influences of Beer Brand Identification on Taste Perception", *Journal of Marketing Research*, 1 (3), 36–9.

Aydin, Serkan and Gokhan Ozer (2005), "The Analysis of Antecedents of Customer Loyalty in the Turkish Mobile Telecommunication Market", *European Journal of Marketing*, 39 (7/8), 910.

Bauer, Hans H., Nicola E. Sauer and Philipp Schmitt (2005), "Customer-Based Brand Equity in the Team Sport Industry: Operationalization and Impact on the Economic Success of Sport Teams", *European Journal of Marketing*, 39 (5/6), 496–516.

Broniarczyk, Susan M. and Andrew D. Gershoff (2003), "The Reciprocal Effects of Brand Equity and Trivial Attributes", *Journal of Marketing Research*, 40 (2), 161–75.

Capraro, Anthony J., Susan Broniarczyk and Rajendra K. Srivastava (2003), "Factors Influencing the Likelihood of Customer Defection: The Role of Consumer Knowledge", *Journal of Academy of Marketing Science*, 31 (2), 164–75.

Chen, Rong and Feng He (2003), "Examination of Brand Knowledge, Perceived Risk and Consumers' Intention to Adopt an Online Retailer", *Total Quality Management & Business Excellence*, 14 (6), 677.

Ehrenberg, A. S. C. (1972), *Repeat-Buying: Theory and Applications*. London: Charles Griffin.

Erdem, Tulin, Joffre Swait and Ana Valenzuela (2006), "Brands as Signals: A Cross-Country Validation Study", *Journal of Marketing*, 70 (1), 34.

Johnson, Michael D., Andreas Herrmann and Frank Huber (2006), "The Evolution of Loyalty Intentions", *Journal of Marketing*, 70 (2), 122.

Keller, K. L. (2008), *Strategic Brand Management. Building, Measuring, and Managing Brand Equity* (3rd ed.). Upper Saddle River, NJ: Pearson Prentice-Hall.

Keller, Kevin Lane (1993), "Conceptualizing, Measuring, and Managing Customer-Based Brand Equity", *Journal of Marketing*, 57 (1), 1–22.

——— (2003), "Brand Synthesis: The Multidimensionality of Brand Knowledge", *Journal of Consumer Research*, 29 (4), 595–600.

Knowledge@Wharton (2014), "Managing Brands in Global Markets: One Size Doesn't Fit All", (accessed July 3, 2014), [available at http://knowledge.wharton.upenn.edu/article/managing-brands-in-global-markets-one-size-doesnt-fit-all/].

Koçak, Akin, Temi Abimbola and Alper Özer (2007), "Consumer Brand Equity in a Cross-cultural Replication: An Evaluation of a Scale", *Journal of Marketing Management*, 23 (1), 157–73.

Korchia, Michael (2006), *The Effects of Brand Associations on Brand Equity, Subjective Knowledge and Brand Interest*. Bordeaux, France: Bordeaux Ecole de Management.

Krishnan, Shanker H. (1996), "Characteristics of Memory Associations: A Consumer-Based Brand Equity Perspective", *International Journal of Research in Marketing*, 13 (4), 389.

Lambert, Claire (2008), "Young Children's Fast Food Brand Knowledge, Preference and Equity", The University of Western Australia.

Lambert, Claire, Dick Mizerski and Doina Olaru (2009), "Young Children's Fast Food Knowledge and Preference", in Society for Marketing Advances 2009 Conference. New Orleans.

Martenson, Rita (2007), "Corporate Brand Image, Satisfaction and Store Loyalty: A Study of the Store as a Brand, Store Brands and Manufacturer Brands", *International Journal of Retail & Distribution Management*, 35 (7), 544.

Nesbett, Richard E. and Timothy DeCamp Wilson (1977), "The Halo Effect: Evidence for Unconscious Alteration of Judgments", *Journal of Personality and Social Psychology*, 35 (4), 250–6.

Pappu, Ravi and Pascale Quester (2006), "Does Customer Satisfaction Lead to Improved Brand Equity? An Empirical Examination of Two Categories of Retail Brands", *The Journal of Product and Brand Management*, 15 (1), 4.

Rajh, Edo, Tihomir Vranesevic and Davor Tolic (2003), "Croatian Food Industry-Brand Equity in Selected Product Categories", *British Food Journal*, 105 (4/5), 263.

Souiden, Nizar, Norizan M. Kassim and Heung-Ja Hong (2006), "The Effect of Corporate Branding Dimensions on Consumers' Product Evaluation", *European Journal of Marketing*, 40 (7/8), 825.

Vázquez, Rodolfo, A. Belén del Río and Víctor Iglesias (2002), "Consumer-Based Brand Equity: Development and Validation of a Measurement Instrument", *Journal of Marketing Management*, 18 (1), 27–48.

Wang, Haizhong, Yujie Wei and Chunling Yu (2008), "Global Brand Equity Model: Combining Customer-Based with Product-Market Outcome Approaches", *Journal of Product & Brand Management*, 17 (5), 305–16.

Yoo, Boonghee and Naveen Donthu (2002), "Testing Cross-Cultural Invariance of the Brand Equity Creation Process", *The Journal of Product and Brand Management*, 11 (6/7), 380–99.

Yoo, Boonghee, Naveen Donthu and Sungho Lee (2000), "An Examination of Selected Marketing Mix Elements and Brand Equity", *Academy of Marketing Science Journal*, 28 (2), 195–212.

5

RESEARCH METHOD

This chapter presents the research method to collect the data to test our Predictive Brand Choice (PBC) model. We also highlight the brands we use to test PBC – three draught beers in Australia and three bottled beers in China – and the selection process for the venues and samples in Australia and China. Further, we discuss and link Keller's eight dimensions Brand Knowledge in their application to the beer category. Using a ground-up method to build our measures, we purify the questions to collect data on these dimensions through four pre-tests with university students. Finally, we outline the way we administer our field-experiment to collect the data to test PBC.

Product

Allison and Uhl's (1964) article appears to be the first to study consumers' subjective perception of brands and how this perception affects consumers' when they choose a brand. Although there is earlier research from the 1930s on cigarette decision-making that establish brand preference can be based on subjective perceptions rather than objective feedback, Allison and Uhl are the first to explore this in the beer category. This category continues to be dominated by advertising and promotions that feature imagery and messages conveying perceptions about the benefits of the advertised brand (Fredric et al. 1999). These perceptions are expected to form the elements of the knowledge structure consumers that consumers tend to develop for the brands in the beer category.

After repeated exposure, one would expect beer drinkers would be expected to develop knowledge about the brands in their choice set, and that this (brand) knowledge to be associated with their preferences and decision to switch (or not) from their preference (preferred beer). Both preferences for a brand and the potential loyalty to the preferred brand, as measured by not switching, would indicate Brand Equity. In other words, Brand Equity can be measured as Brand Preference and Brand Loyalty for the consumer's preferred brand.

Previous Brand Knowledge-Brand Equity research tends to use survey-based self-reports. These surveys attempt to measure respondents' intended behaviors, often by testing two or more product categories. However, three of four cross-cultural studies we have reviewed use only one category, as do all the retail, sports, experimental, subscription markets, and the Lambert study from which we adopt some theory and methodology. Given this study's complexity of collecting typical purchase data in two venues (Australia and China), and the unique use of an actual behavioral test of loyalty, our research will use only one category, beer. We deem it more important to establish internal consistency of our PBC model. As such, this test forges a degree of complexity that may improve the model's external validity.

Samples

Testing for the existence and effects of beer brand knowledge requires a sample of experienced product users. Around the world, the heaviest users of beer are typically students enrolled in university (Toner-Schrader and Mizerski 1997). These beer drinkers are in the stage of further developing their subjective-based brand knowledge as they consume beer brands with others. This may include trying and evaluating different brands of beer.

Unlike with many products tested in previous Brand Equity studies that use university students as the research sample (e.g. color televisions), university students are the most relevant sample for this study because a larger proportion of them tend be heavy users of beer. The use of university students as a sample can also control for some of the potential effects of education and socio-economic status, as these elements are typically constant amongst the sample. However, the findings may not be generalizable to other groups in the population.

Australia sample

The country Australia ranks among the top countries in per-capita consumption of beer (83.3 liters per capita, per annum (Kirin 2014). A very strong culture of beer consumption has developed (Pettigrew 1999), and binge drinking among young adults is a big problem in Australian society. While per-capita alcohol use remains steady, the percent of the population that drinks beer has been decreasing for the last 15 years. Consumption of beer in Australia peaked in the mid-1970s and now it has more than halved, reaching its lowest level since 1945–1946. However, beer still continues to be the greatest amount of all pure alcohol consumed in Australia (ABS 2014). The decline of beer use in Australia appears similar to that experienced in the UK, US and German markets.

Culture effects

The statistics on drinking volume per-capita show that Australians are certainly not adverse to drinking beer. In fact, there is little doubt that alcohol forms an important part of Australian culture. Through the famous Fosters ads of the '80s and early '90s, Australia even promotes itself to the rest of the world as a beer drinking nation. There are two common drinking customs in Australia that traditionally involve the consumption of beer. One is "shouting" which requires each person in a party to take turns buying a round of drinks for the whole group. The other is "work and bust"; this results after working long and hard in the bush (outback). After all the hard work, workers will partake in a lengthy and extremely drunken period of "relaxing". This second custom is now commonly called "binge drinking" and is a common activity among young Australians. The consumption of alcohol is customary to celebrate events and special occasions. For example, the end of a football season is celebrated by "Mad Monday" celebrations where football players consume a significant amount of alcohol with their team mates.

Many University students in Australia drink beer to socialize with friends, celebrate occasions or as a way of relaxing and enjoying the nightlife. Here, beer and other alcohol give what is colloquially referred to as "giving them Dutch courage" (the courage achieved from being intoxicated with alcohol) to meet a special someone, a potential boyfriend or girlfriend.

Australian venue for data collection

The University of Western Australia (UWA) is a public Australian university in the city of Perth in Western Australia. The University has a tavern that offers many brands of bottled beer, three draught beers on tap, wine and some food. The tavern's clientele are comprised almost exclusively of young adults (18+ years old), with majority being students who attend the university. The legal age to drink in the tavern is 18 years old (Australia-wide alcohol laws). This tavern will serve as the venue to collect the Australian sample. There is no other venue available for student consumption of alcohol at the UWA, except for infrequent special functions like graduation. The most popular option for consuming beer by university students in the Tavern is via a "middie" of tap beer (served in a glass, not bottled). The university tavern location offers convenience in data collection, responsibility for alcohol control and represents a venue where this cohort typically consumes beer socially.

China sample

China is the market of the world's largest aggregate consumption of beer. While per-capita beer consumption is relatively low, consumption of this category is rapidly growing in China. Among the new users, university students are among the largest segment and are also believed to be a strong influence on adoption. Unlike

Australia where there is a well-documented drinking culture on what some may consider to border on alcohol abuse, there is little coverage of youth abusing alcohol at this point in its Product Life-Cycle in China.

Where Australia and other Western markets are in the decline stage of the beer (PLC), China is in the growth stage of the PLC. The collection of data from two samples at different stages of the PLC will provide an effective comparison of the effects of brand knowledge on brand preference and the way brand equity develops in a market. It is expected that beer drinkers' brand knowledge is influenced by the PLC stage the product is experiencing in that market. In comparison to China's drinkers, Australia's drinkers would have longer experience with beer use, advertising and promotion. Due to the PLC stage the China market is in for the product category, China's drinkers will have less experience with these socialization agents. As a result, it is expected that the components of brand knowledge, and their association with preference and loyalty to a brand, will differ for markets in different stages of the PLC.

Culture effects

Culture and other potential factors can also significantly affect a consumer's brand choice. The Chinese idiom says "无酒不成席 – It's not a banquet without alcohol". This phrase means that to welcome friends one should have good alcohol with the best food. While this Chinese idiom reflects contemporary culture in China, it likely has its roots in the Confucianism teachings on hospitality.

The Chinese philosopher Confucius (551–449 BC) said "有朋自远方来，不亦乐乎?" This means, "How delightful it is to have a friend visiting from far away?" This saying represents the core of how the Han race in China believe guests should be treated. This age old tradition for being hospitable has given rise to the Western understanding of "saving face". Chinese societal norms dictates that friends and guests are welcomed with hospitality, the best food and alcohol. It is normal practice for the Chinese hosts to go into debt to provide the level of entertainment, food and drink they perceive as worthy and that befits their visitor's "rank" and importance. Society will judge the host negatively if they fail to do this, looking down upon the host as "cheap". If the visitor is very important (e.g., an official), failure to provide an appropriately high level and quality of food, drink and entertainment may bring shame to the host and their family.

Many Chinese university students drink beer with classmates as a way to socialize, relax and have fun. For the majority of students, these outings are special, often happening only during celebrations because of their limited discretionary spending power. As such, this makes these occasions even more special and important. Because of the social pressure to provide the best for their guests, many students will try to spend more so as to offer their friends and guests a better brand of food and drink. As such, the price of a product may be substituted for brand image. The more expensive the beer, the better it is perceived to be. When drinking alone, the same student may choose a cheaper brand because they do not have to "save face". Of course, there may be similar phenomenon in the Australia or other market samples (Allison and Uhl 1964). For example, many Australian university students in the authors' classes remark that they drink "cardboard" wine (carton wine) when at home but more expensive bottled and branded wine when going to restaurants for meals with friends, especially if it is for a special occasion. The more special the occasion, the more they are willing to spend on a good brand of wine.

To test for differences in the measurement and effects of Brand Knowledge on Brand Preference and Loyalty, we access a sample of young Chinese university students. To match the data collection venues in both countries, interviews are conducted with students (young adults 18+ years of age) enrolled in the China Agricultural University (CAU) in Beijing China. Both the UWA and the CAU are ranked in the top 10 universities of their respective countries. We recognize factors beyond the PLC and cultural effects may influence the findings using these samples, where possible, we have put in controls to minimize the differences between the two samples we will study.

Chinese venue for data collection

China's universities do not typically offer on-campus taverns for alcohol consumption, so an identical venue to the tavern at the UWA is not available at the CAU. At CAU, beer and other alcohol products are purchased and consumed in several restaurants spread around the campus. We selected the most popular restaurant on campus as the venue to collect our data. This restaurant has seating facilities similar to the UWA tavern. As with the UWA tavern, students at CAU use the restaurant to socialize with other students. Beer can be purchased without purchasing food, draught beer is not available in the CAU restaurant, but bottled beer sold.

Personal observation of Chinese students' drinking behavior suggests that in China, bottled beer tends to be preferred over draught beer on tap. One reason for this is because Chinese consumers' have a higher level of health concerns and of food safety. Chinese consumers prefer the bottle to be opened (uncapped) in front of them. In China, there have been many cases of food and beverage poisoning, and consequently, many consumers believe bottled beer is safer, and less prone to counterfeit (fake beer). It must be noted that top national or international brands do offer draught in central venues like leading restaurants, clubs and hotels. The top brands and imports are generally viewed as "more healthy", or less likely to make you sick in comparison to smaller brands.

The alcohol content of Chinese beer tends to be lower than Australian light beer, so the "middie" used by the Australian sample is about the same potency as one 330 ml bottle of the top three beers offered at the CAU restaurant.

Research objectives and overall procedure

The first task is to identify whether beer consumers/buyers have a mental construct that may be called Brand Knowledge about beer. Once a concept of beer Brand Knowledge is established, tests will then be conducted for the association between Brand Knowledge elements (e.g., imagery, affect) and the respondents' equity toward their preferred beer. Finally, respondents' loyalty to their preferred brand will be tested – whether they stay with their preferred brand when tempted by a price-discount off their second preferred brand of beer. The respondent's initial brand preference and their decision to stay or switch (loyalty) will be considered as indicators of a brand's equity (Aaker 2003). Actual beer (via the provision of a voucher) will be used as an incentive for the beer drinker's co-operation to participate in the study.

Lambert (2008) has a way to elicit Brand Knowledge, Preference and Loyalty information from very young children. This method is also reported and used in Lambert, Mizerski, and Olaru (2009). Lambert et al.'s (2009) Brand Knowledge construct is developed based on the individual's perceptions of brands using the factors of brand awareness, brand images and affect. Respondents' rated questions measuring components within these constructs that were relevant to the product category studied.

To identify the relevant factors for the beer product category, this study will use samples of respondents with similar attributes to those that will form the samples for the final survey and choice experiment. Using a respondent's personal preference for the brands of beer available in the venue, the participants in both samples will be asked to rate their top three favorite brands from the range of beer brands available for purchase in each venue. After providing their first and second preference, respondents answer questions about their Brand Knowledge of their top two preferred brand of beer. They are asked to rate their top brand first.

At the end of the survey for their top preferred brand, the respondent is told they can either have a 200 ml glass (a "middie" in Australia) or a bottle of beer (in China) of their second preferred brand for free, or pay a small fee (50% of the regular price of beer at each location) and get their top preferred brand ("middie" for Australia and bottle for China). The respondents are informed the beer is a "thank you" for their cooperation. This latter measure tests their loyalty in a situation where they would have to pay a premium to stay with their top preferred brand (Netemeyer et al. 2004). This willingness to pay a premium is an important aspect of brand equity (Aaker 1991; Lambert 2008).

Pre-testing

Pre-tests are used to collect information to establish dimensions of Brand Knowledge about beer. For this study, four pre-tests are required to collect the necessary information to formulate the final questionnaire. The first pre-test collects responses from 38 UWA tavern customers using an open-ended questionnaire. The questions will seek to determine the respondents' most popular beer brands and the possible associations that the sample may have towards these brands, as well as their preference and equity.

The second pre-test collects 75 survey-based interviews. This test has questions to find the best words to explain images and benefits for the students purchasing and consuming beers.

The third pre-test collects data from 30 students to test the phrasing of questions about possible images and attitudes towards consuming beer at the tavern. Finally the fourth pre-test pilots the final questionnaire with 38 respondents at the UWA tavern. The same process using four pre-tests are also undertaken at the CAU restaurant on students similar to the sample planned for the main experiment.

Initial pre-test

The researcher personally interviewed 38 university students drinking beer at the UWA tavern. The key question was, "Please tell me three beer brands you most like". The researcher also interviewed the tavern's general manager about the top three selling beer brands from his sales records. The respondents' answers closely reflected the three top selling beers from the sales records. The top three selling brands at the UWA tavern were Tooheys New, Amber Ale and Swan Draft. Together these brands accounted for approximately 80% of total beer sales.

The same pre-test was conducted at the CAU. There, the top three selling beer brands in the restaurant venue were Tsingtao, Yanjing and Snow beers. The manager of the restaurant estimated that these top three brands accounted for about 85% of beer sales at the venue.

Keller (2003) identifies Brand Knowledge to have eight different components. These are awareness, images, attitudes, attributes, benefits, feelings, thoughts and experiences. Our respondents are asked about their two most preferred beer brands. Because pretests show that all respondents know the name of the three top brands at each respective test venue, we do not collect any further data for awareness. The fact that everyone we asked knows the top three brands available means that brand awareness does not have power to discriminate between brand choice, preference or equity.

The interviewer requested respondents' feelings, thoughts and past experiences with beer brands. However, few respondents were able to provide this information. These factors also do not appear relevant to the respondents' decision-making on which brand of beer to buy or which brand to stay with (keep buying). This may reflect the more utilitarian comparisons for beer that may feature in buyers in the later stages of the PLC in Australia. This is when there is ample knowledge of the product, the product is widely used and the product begins to assume a more utilitarian role. Through this interview process, we identified that the factors of images, attitudes, attributes and benefits appeared to be relevant to respondents in this qualitative research. We retained these factors for further testing.

Second pre-test

We carried out the second pre-test with a convenience sample of 18+ year old students from an undergraduate Marketing unit at the UWA. This sample was chosen for the convenience it offered in allowing respondents to provide well considered answers to our questions, without the distraction of the social setting and noise the Tavern would have provided. The second pre-test seeks to find the appropriate terms that can describe the benefits and images of beer. We asked respondents about their beer consumption, analyzing only the responses of those who said they had consumed beer in the last four weeks. The interview also asked beer drinkers to write down the images and the benefits they derived from buying and consuming beer. Eligible responses were summarized to describe the images and benefits reported by this sample of marketing students.

The results yielded more than 20 different words to explain images. Beer image was described by the respondents using words like cool, sweet, crisp, attention grabbing image, lower-class beer, exciting, boring, boy or girl's beer and for pubs or bars. Some of the words were very similar in meaning. Respondents also used 26 different words to explain benefits. These were taste good, cheap, for party, get drunk, refined beer, delicious, make friends, feel relaxed, reduce stress, easy sleep, good for health, socializing, and feel cool.

Third pre-test

The third pre-test was conducted at the UWA and comprised of 38 respondents from an undergraduate Marketing class, all of which were 18+ years of age. This test sought to refine the phrasing of questions referring to beer benefits and attributes. In the interim, our review of the literature also yielded additional words to describe benefits, images and attributes related to beer. These additional words were also included in this test.

Pre-test of the final questionnaire

The final questionnaire was constructed from the results of the three earlier pre-tests. For the top two preferred brands, the questionnaire required the respondent to answer five image and four attitude items. There were 15 questions asking respondents' for their perceptions regarding the attributes of their top two preferred beers and 12 questions concerning their perceptions about the potential benefits from drinking their top two preferred brands of beer. These questions used a 5-point response scale for respondents to indicate their answers.

The questionnaire also requests for demographic information – age, gender, disposable income and country of permanent residency. Additionally, we requested respondents to indicate the amount of beer they consumed in the last seven days, frequency of visits to the beer-drinking venue and the respondent's perceived loyalty to their preferred brand (see Appendix 10 and 11 for the final questionnaire).

Measures of the Brand Knowledge construct

Keller initially collected the Brand Knowledge items he discusses in his series of journal articles through personal interviews and pre-tests. We have adopted the same methodology in our test. In our series of tests, it became clear as additional tests were conducted that our sample of beer drinkers did not notice some dimensions of Keller's (2003) Brand Knowledge construct. For example, we had little success in trying to obtain the respondents' "thoughts" about a brand. The following section describes and discusses each of the eight dimensions of Keller's Brand Knowledge construct that we tested.

Brand awareness

Brand awareness occurs when consumers become conscious that a brand exists. Even though the awareness of the three brands of beer in our experiment was universal and therefore, will not be used as a factor to discriminate between the choices of brands for our sample, we do acknowledge the link of awareness to images.

Brand Awareness with strong mental associations of the imagery that is related to a brand, and the brand name, helps consumers to form an image of a brand. Aaker (1991) defines Brand Associations as "anything linked in memory to a brand" and Brand Image as "a set of brand associations, usually in some meaningful way" (p. 109). Brand associations are complicated and connected to one another. They can consist of multiple ideas, episodes, instances and facts that establish a solid network of brand knowledge.

Brand image

Keller (2003; 2008) specified that brand image should be defined as the perceptions about a brand as reflected by the brand associations held in a consumer's memory. Consequently, brand associations are also informational nodes connected to the node that holds information about the brand in the consumer's memory. When connected, the information in memory combines to help the consumer create meaning for the brand. Associations come in a variety of forms and can reveal characteristics of the product. They may even relate to features that are separate from the product itself. For example, a beer brand may have the association of boy or girl's beer attributed to it, this is a link that appears to be separate from the beer product itself.

Brand Associations become stronger when they are based on many experiences with the brand, and/or frequent exposures to the brand's communications (Aaker 1991). Brand associations may also be related to product attributes – for example, relative price or some other aspects of the brand like its image. Brand Associations are argued to be positively correlated with Brand Awareness, this is where higher levels of Brand Awareness will be associated with higher levels of Brand Associations. These constructs are believed to be positively related to Brand Equity because they can serve as a signal of the brand's quality and commitment. In turn, quality and commitment encourages a buyer to consider the brand at the point of purchase. They can also lead consumers to choose to stay with the brand – staying with a brand is considered to be brand loyalty (Yoo et al. 2000).

The following measures of brand images are used in the study:

Please indicate the extent to which you agree or disagree with the following statements by circling the answer that best describes your opinion.

Statements about my top preferred brand:

Imageries:

	Strongly disagree				Strongly agree
1) I feel prestigious.	1	2	3	4	5
2) I feel cheerful.	1	2	3	4	5
3) I feel elegant.	1	2	3	4	5
4) I feel charming.	1	2	3	4	5
5) I feel trendy.	1	2	3	4	5

Respondents also fill out these same measures again for their nominated second preferred brand.

Benefits

A benefit is a construct representing the personal value and meaning that consumers attach to a brand. There are three types of benefits; functional, symbolic, and experiential. These benefits are viewed as consequences from the brand's purchase or consumption (Keller 2003; Keller 1993; Park et al. 1986). That is, consumers realize the benefits of the brand when they buy or use a brand's product.

Functional benefits are the more intrinsic advantages that come from consuming a good or service; for example, a mobile telephone that also has an alarm clock. Functional benefits usually correspond to the product-related attributes. These benefits are often linked to fairly basic motivations such as physiological and safety needs (Maslow 1970), and may involve a consumer having the desire to avoid or remove a problem that they face (Fennell 1978; Rossiter and Percy 1987). They solve their problems by using the product's functions – for example, a person who has trouble waking up uses the alarm clock function on their mobile telephone.

Experiential benefits relate to what it feels like to use the product or service. These experience benefits often correspond to attributes related to the product. For example, consumers may perceive that a package with a lighter color to be "lighter" in weight than the identical package in a darker color. Similarly, lighter packages indicate that a product is "mild", darker packages tend to indicate "full-flavor". Other experiential benefits that consumers seek through brands may include sensory pleasure, variety and cognitive stimulation (Keller 1993). For example, the experience of spaceflight for private citizens is a promise made by the Virgin Galactic brand. Some beers promise a clean, crisp taste.

Symbolic benefits come from the more extrinsic advantages that a consumer can get from consuming a good or service. The brand then becomes a symbol that prompts consumption. This means that these symbolic benefits usually correspond to non–product-related attributes. Symbolic benefits are more likely to appeal to an individual's underlying needs for social approval or personal expression. For example, consumers may value the prestige, exclusivity, or fashion of a brand because of how it improves their self-concept (Solomon 1983). Symbolic benefits should be especially relevant for socially visible, or "badge" products (Keller 1993) like beer, wine, handbags and watches.

The following benefit questions are asked of the respondents in regards to their top preferred brand. The question set is repeated again for their second preferred brand during the interview process:

Please indicate the extent to which you agree or disagree with the following statements by circling the answer that best describes your opinion.

Benefits:

	Strongly disagree				*Strongly agree*
25) It makes me happier.	1	2	3	4	5
26) It makes me feel cool.	1	2	3	4	5
27) It reduces my stress.	1	2	3	4	5
28) It makes me enjoyable and satisfactory.	1	2	3	4	5
29) It gives me energy and courage.	1	2	3	4	5
30) It improves my status.	1	2	3	4	5
31) It makes me sociable and lets me make friends easier.	1	2	3	4	5
32) It's getting attention from others.	1	2	3	4	5
33) It can warmly welcome my guests.	1	2	3	4	5
34) It's good for health.	1	2	3	4	5
35) It's not getting me fat.	1	2	3	4	5
36) It's interesting and exciting.	1	2	3	4	5

Thoughts

A thought about a brand is the personal cognitive response to any brand-related information (Keller 2003). Zajonc (1980) assembles evidence showing that thought and feeling are initially processed independently. The feeling aspect of thinking (affect) is processed faster than the knowledge component, and the processing mechanisms are different (Zajonc, 1980). As such, it may be that consumers must first like a brand before they evaluate other attributes of the brand. Thus, attraction to the brand/product is necessary before wanting to learn more about the branded product. The pre-tests for this research establish that our respondents are not able to provide information relating to their thoughts about beer brands. Thoughts are also found not to be important in regards to the respondents' decision making regarding which brand of beer to buy or which brand to stay with (keep buying). Therefore, the personally administered questionnaire does not include questions relating to the respondent's thoughts.

Attitudes

Keller (2003) highlights attitudes as another brand knowledge dimension and refers to them as "summary judgments and overall evaluations to any brand-related information". Thus, when a consumer evaluates a brand, they may form a positive or negative attitude towards this brand based on their consumption experience. A good consumption experience may lead to a positive attitude (affect toward the brand) developing towards the brand.

Fishbein and Ajzen (1975) have discussed affect towards the brand as a type of evaluative judgment that a consumer has for a brand. This may be explained as a feeling of like/dislike (or other feeling) toward the attitude object. An attitude object may be something like a brand of beer. They proposed the Theory of Reasoned Action where a buyer's beliefs towards a brand's salient attributes would increase the buyer's chances of developing affect toward the brand. If these feelings are favorable, the buyer will more likely choose the brand over other brands they like less.

Feelings

Feelings are classified as another type of affect. Feelings are argued to be more experiential in nature than the like/dislike evaluation of the affect in Ajzen's (1991) Theory of Planned Behavior. A feeling is said to comprise of personal affective responses to any brand-related information (Keller, 2003). Feelings and emotions are two prevalent aspects of consumption that have been said to influence brand perceptions and purchasing behavior (Hirschman and Holbrook 1982).

Gardner (1985) explains about feelings as "a feeling state . . . which will be used to refer to an affective state that is general and pervasive". Further, "These states can be contrasted with feelings directed toward specific objects, e.g., the affective component of brand attitude". Whilst moods is "phenomenological property of an individual's subjectively perceived affective state". Further, "Mood will refer to feeling states that arc transient; such states are particularized to specific times and situation". So take feelings as an "affective state that is general and pervasive". Feelings have been found to uniquely contribute to attitude toward the brand, beliefs about a brand's attributes, and can influence brand perceptions (O'Cass and Frost 2002).

Kahle, Poulos and Sukhdial (1988) point out six types of feelings that are related to brand building. These are warmth, fun, excitement, security, social approval and self-respect. Both China and Australia sample respondents in the pretests for our study have problems providing information about their feelings towards the different brands of beer. Because of this, we do not test for feelings in our final questionnaire.

Experiences

Keller (2003) considers experience as another dimension of brand knowledge, representing the "purchase and consumption behaviors and any other brand-related episodes". For example, Whelan and Wohlfeil (2006) find that event marketing engages customers with the brand through dialogues and personal-behavior-based brand experiences. Experiences with purchasing and consumption of a beer brand, and any other brand-related episodes to behaviors (Keller, 2003) are explored with our pre-test samples. While some sample members in our pre-test are able to recall some events and functions where brands promoted their beers, generally they are unable to recount much more than that there was a promotion and some pro-moters. As a result, experiences are not included as part of the brand knowledge construct that we test in the final questionnaire.

The brand preference measure

Preferences are primarily affectively based behaviors. Zajonc and Markus (1982 p. 128) define preference to be, "a behavioral tendency that exhibits itself not so much in what the individual thinks or says about the object, but how s/he acts towards it. Do they take it, do they approach it, do they buy it, do they marry it?" (p. 128). This definition considers brand preference to have a behavioral element and looks further than the cognitive element of liking. Thus, brand preference is more than just a consumer liking a brand, rather it looks at the possible behavioral outcome that results from this liking. For example, a consumer may like more than one brand of beer at any given time. Brand preference in this situation will be evident through the behavioral outcome of the consumer choosing one brand over another.

Zajonc and Markus (1982) also argue that a preference for X over Y is the ten-dency of the organism to approach X more often and more vigorously than Y. For a measure of beer brand preference, we ask our Australia sample this question:

> If I offered you a middie size (200 ml) glass of beer now, please rate these three brands in terms of your preference. Write down number 1 for your first preferred brand, and number 2 for your second preferred brand.

The Chinese sample are asked the same question. However, we substitute, "If I offered you a 330 ml bottle . . ." to reflect the measure of beer in that market.

The brand loyalty measure

One view of brand loyalty is the degree to which a buying unit, such as a house-hold, concentrates its purchases over time on a particular brand within a product category (Schoell and Guiltinan, 1990) – that is, how long does the household buy the brand, how much of the brand do they buy compared to other brands for the same product category?

To measure brand loyalty, testing a price premium is one of the most impor-tant indicators of brand equity. A price premium is the extra price a consumer is willing to pay for a well-branded product or service, compared to an identical less "branded" or generic version of the same product/service (Aaker and Biel 1993). In our experiment, pre-testing establishes the discount necessary for about half of the members in our samples to switch (Australia and China samples). We use this approximate discount as a promotion in the questionnaire for both the Australia and China samples.

The last question on the survey captures loyalty and states:

> To thank you for your time, I would like to offer (you) either of the following based on the answer you gave earlier,
> You pay only 1 dollar (normally $2.00) for a middie of your first preferred brand of beer, or- you pay nothing for a middie of your second preferred beer.

All respondents are asked to choose one of the options – to stay with their top preferred brand, or switch to second most preferred brand. For the China sample, we adjust the proportion of the price to reflect the price of the beer in the restaurant. Respondents who chose to stay with their top preferred brand are given a voucher for their choice. They can redeem this with the bartender or waiter for that brand of beer – we write the brand down on the voucher. This redemption practice ensures that the ethical responsibility for serving the respondent remains with the management of the tavern. The respondent can immediately redeemed the beer (if not intoxicated) or bring the voucher in at a later time. Finally, we thank the respondent for their participation.

Data-collection procedure

Personally administered questionnaires

For the personally administered questionnaires, we divide the tavern seating area (Australia sample) and restaurant (China sample) into four sections. One interviewer personally administers the questionnaires and interviews the respondents. The interviewer starts in a different section of the venue for each interviewing session. Five sessions at different times of the week are planned for each venue. Once the interviewer arrives at the center of the section, they select the closest patron as the first respondent. This selection technique limits possible selection bias. If the patron refuses the interview, the interviewer simply moves to the next patron on their right.

Because we will attempt to survey all patrons that are present at each interview session, we will approach the potential respondent and ask, "I'd like your opinion on brands of beer". If they agree to be interviewed, the interviewer hands them a four page questionnaire to fill out. The first question asks for their brand preference among the three draught beers on tap (Australia sample) or top three bottled beers sold in the restaurant (China sample).

The respondents are then asked to rate their top preferred brand of beer on 36 statements. These statements ask respondents about the brand's image, their affect toward the brand, the brand's attributes, and the benefits that they receive from drinking that brand of beer. The questionnaire then asks the respondents for their age, gender, country of permanent residence and, "How much is your pocket money per month?" Pocket money is Australian slang for disposable income. This phrase is translated into the equivalent term in Chinese for our interviews in China.

Next, we ask respondents, "How many mid-sized ("middies") beers have you drunk during the last seven days?", or "bottles of beer" for the China sample. Only those respondents who report drinking in the last seven days will be included in our working sample. The responses from this group will be analyzed for brand knowledge, preference and loyalty. This is because we consider these respondents to be recent consumers of beer. As such, they will best be able to recall the information to answer the survey more accurately.

The use of a personally administered questionnaire to collect the data is necessary if respondents are to be interviewed in their natural beer drinking environment. We choose not to collect data during periods of live entertainment, the usual ambient discussion and/or background music level in the tavern and restaurant will be too loud to conduct personal interviews. The researcher will sit near (usually next to or across from) the respondent as they complete the questionnaire. This enables clarification if there are questions from the respondent. Being present also allows for a higher response rate and completion of questionnaires. When patrons gather in groups of more than one, the interviewer will ask the group to fill out the questionnaire individually without discussion between respondents.

Summary

This chapter introduces the method used to identify constructs of Brand Knowledge that uses a series of pre-tests. This is similar to the procedure used by Keller (2003) in identifying his Brand Knowledge construct. We also describe how we sampled and executed the field experiment. The next chapter will provide details about the analysis and results from the data collected.

Bibliography

Aaker, D. A. (2003), "The Power of the Branded Differentiator", *MIT Sloan Management Review*, 45 (1), 83–7.

Aaker, David A. (1991), *Managing Brand Equity: Capitalizing on the Value of a Brand Name*. New York: Free Press.

Aaker, David A. and Alexander L. Biel (1993), *Brand Equity & Advertising: Advertising's Role in Building Strong Brands*. Hillsdale, NJ: Lawrence Erlbaum Associates.

ABS (2014), "Aussies Drinking Less Alcohol", Australian Bureau of Statistics.

Ajzen, Icek (1991), "The Theory of Planned Behavior", *Organizational Behavior and Human Decision Processes*, 50 (2), 179.

Allison, Ralph I. and Kenneth P. Uhl (1964), "Influences of Beer Brand Identification on Taste Perception", *Journal of Marketing Research*, 1 (3), 36–9.

Fennell, Geraldine (1978), "Consumer's Perceptions of the Product-Use Situation", *Journal of Marketing*, 42, 38–47.

Fishbein, Martin and Icek Ajzen (1975), *Belief, Attitude, Intention and Behaviour: An Introduction to the Theory and Research*. Reading, MA: Addison-Wesley.

Fredric, Kropp, M. Lavack Anne and J. S. Holden Stephen (1999), "Smokers and beer drinkers: values and consumer susceptibility to interpersonal influence," *The Journal of Consumer Marketing*, 16 (6), 536.

Gardner, Meryl Paula (1985), "Mood States and Consumer Behavior: A Critical Review", *Journal of Consumer Research*, 12 (3), 281–300.

Hirschman, Elizabeth C. and Morris B. Holbrook (1982), "Hedonic Consumption: Emerging Concepts, Methods and Propositions", *The Journal of Marketing*, 46 (3), 92–101.

Kahle, Lynn, Basil Poulos and Ajay Sukhdial (1988), "Changes in Social Values in the United States During the Past Decade", *Journal of Advertising Research*, 28 (1), 35–41.

Keller, K. L. (2008), *Strategic Brand Management. Building, Measuring, and Managing Brand Equity* (3rd ed.). New Jersey: Prentice Hall.

Keller, Kevin Lane (1993), "Conceptualizing, Measuring, and Managing Customer-Based Brand Equity", *Journal of Marketing*, 57 (1), 1–22.

——— (2003), "Brand Synthesis: The Multidimensionality of Brand Knowledge", *Journal of Consumer Research*, 29 (4), 595–600.

Kirin (2014), "Kirin Beer University Report: Global Beer Consumption by Country 2012". Tokyo, Japan: Kirin Holdings.

Lambert, Claire (2008), "Young Children's Fast Food Brand Knowledge, Preference and Equity", The University of Western Australia.

Lambert, Claire, Dick Mizerski and Doina Olaru (2009), "Young Children's Fast Food Knowledge and Preference", in Society for Marketing Advances 2009 Conference. New Orleans.

Maslow, Abraham H. (1970), *Motivation and Personality*. New York: Harper & Row Publishers, Inc.

Netemeyer, Richard G., Balaji Krishnan, Chris Pullig, Guangping Wang, Mehmet Yagci, Dwane Dean, Joe Ricks and Writh Ferdinand (2004), "Developing and Validating Measures of Facets of Customer-Based Brand Equity", *Journal of Business Research*, 57 (2), 209–24.

O'Cass, Aron and Hmily Frost (2002), "Status Brands: Examining the Effects of Non-Product-Related Brand Associations on Status and Conspicuous Consumption", *Journal of Product and Brand Management*, 11 (2/3), 67–87.

Park, C. Whan, Bernard J. Jaworski and Deborah J. MacInnis (1986), "Strategic Brand Concept-Image Management", *Journal of Marketing*, 50 (4), 135–45.

Pettigrew, S. (1999), "Culture and Consumption – A study of beer Consumption in Australia".

Rossiter, John R. and Larry Percy (1987), *Advertising and Promotion Management*. New York: McGraw-Hill Book Company.

Schoell, W. F. and J. P. Guiltinan (1990), *Marketing: Contemporary Concepts and Practices*. Boston: Allyn and Bacon.

Solomon, Michael R. (1983), "The Role of Products as Social Stimuli: A Symbolic Interactionism Perspective", *Journal of Consumer Research*, 10 (December) (3), 319–29.

Toner-Schrader, Julie and Richard Mizerski (1997), "An Investigation of the Relationship Between Need for Affect and Responses to Alcohol Public Service Announcements", *Journal of Nonprofit & Public Sector Marketing*, 5 (3), 41.

Whelan, Susan and Markus Wohlfeil (2006), "Communicating Brands through Engagement with 'Lived' Experiences", *Journal of Brand Management*, 13 (4/5), 313–30.

Yoo, Boonghee, Naveen Donthu and Sungho Lee (2000), "An Examination of Selected Marketing Mix Elements and Brand Equity", *Academy of Marketing Science Journal*, 28 (2), 195–212.

Zajonc, R. B. (1980), "Feeling and Thinking: Preference Need No Inference", *American Psychologist*, 35, 151–75.

Zajonc, Robert B. and Hazel Markus (1982), "Affective and Cognitive Factors in Preferences", *Journal of Consumer Research* 9(2), 123–32.

6

RESULTS

Sample comparability and Brand Knowledge constructs

This research sought to find the factors that may constitute beer drinkers' Brand Knowledge, and how these factors associate with the beer drinker's reported preferences and their loyalty (stay or switch to another brand when offered an incentive) to their most preferred brand. After conducting a field experiment, we analyzed the data collected using descriptive analyses, exploratory factor analyses, multivariate discriminate analyses (MDA), multinomial logistic regressions (MLR) and binary logistic regression analyses (BLR). These sought to unravel the drivers of Brand Preference and Brand Loyalty towards the beer brands tested with each of our samples.

Samples

We expect current drinkers and non-drinkers or past-drinkers to have different perceptions and behaviors towards beer. Because we cannot link non-drinkers' beer Brand Knowledge to their Brand Preference or Loyalty, we do not analyze data collected from these respondents. As such, we retain only the data from current beer drinkers for their Brand Preference and Loyalty. As discussed in our methods chapter, current beer drinkers are those who have consumed at least one 200 ml glass of beer (Australia) or 330 ml bottle (China) in the last seven days. This restriction means that we will not study infrequent or past-drinkers for Brand Knowledge, Preference or Loyalty.

Current (last seven days) drinkers account for the majority of respondents from both samples. The interviewers in Australia managed to conduct the experiment with 329 respondents. Of these, 283 (86% of 329) reported themselves to be current beer drinkers. The interviewers managed to interview 296 respondents in China. From this group of students in China, 161 (54%) reported drinking at least one bottle in the last seven days, making them current beer drinkers.

For ease of comparison, we report participants' income using Australian dollars. The income reported here is for each month – that is, monthly pay. The exchange rate of the Australian dollar to the Chinese renbinmi (RMB) was about $1 = 6.5 RMB at the time of the interviews. Although we are able to make currency conversions, respondent income is not easily comparable between the samples. This is due to the disparity of the cost of living between the countries. Australia is a developed country where the gross domestic product (GDP) per capita is $50,860 Australian dollars (Pink 2010). The mean income per capita in Australia is about $37,500 Australian dollars. This is difficult to compare with China, which is a developing country where the GDP per capita is approximately $1500 Australian dollars (Statistics China 2010) and the reported average annual income per capita approaches $500 Australian dollars. The students who attend China Agricultural University whom we interviewed for our China sample are from the provinces of China. China Agricultural University statistics, made available to one of the authors, show that many students attending this university originate from areas where agriculture is the main industry. This likely means that their average income is considerably lower than the national average – the average and disposable income of people from areas where farming is the main industry is well below the averages provided by the Chinese Government (that we report).

Following our selection requirements that respondents selected consume 200 ml glasses of beer (Australia) or 330 ml bottles (China) in the last seven days, Table 6.1 reports the demographic breakdown of our sample by country of interview, current drinker status and the number of glasses of beer consumed in the last seven days. We converted the Chinese measure of 330 ml bottles to 220 ml glasses to facilitate a comparison of the beer consumed in the last seven days. Table 6.1 also reports the average number of visits to the venue in the last seven days.

TABLE 6.1 Demographic and product use comparison of the Australia and China samples

	Samples			
	Australia (n = 329)		*China (n = 296)*	
	Current Drinkers n = 283 (86%)	*Non-current Drinkers n = 46 (14%)*	*Current Drinkers n = 161 (54.4%)*	*Non-current Drinkers n = 135 (45.6%)*
Age (years)	19.7	19.4	20.9	20.8
Gender (%) Male	65.7%	48.8 %	72.8%	70.1%
Female	34.3%	51.2%	27.2%	29.9%
Disposable income per year in AUD ($)	$780.22	$335.90	$68.42	$56.60
Amount (200 ml glasses consumed last seven days)	13.9	0	5.5	0
Visits to drinking venue (times last seven days)	2.3	1.7	1.7	0

Differences between the two samples

Age and gender

An independent-sample t-test found a significant difference (p = 0.001) in the average age of the Australia (19.7 years) and China samples (20.9 years). However, this may be due to the large sample size which tends to increase the sensitivity of t-tests, leading to false-positive type 1 errors (Hair et al. 2010). The mean difference in age is a little more than one year (19.7 v. 20.9 years). The age standard deviation is also very similar (China = 1.3, Australia = 1.6). Although there were more male drinkers in the Chinese sample (72.8% China vs. 65.7% Australia), the proportions of beer drinkers by gender are not significantly different between the Australian and Chinese samples (χ^2 = 2.41, df = 1, p = 0.12). These results suggest that the samples are similar demographically. This is a positive point for carrying out further analysis and comparison.

Income

Our sample of beer drinkers interviewed in Australia report a mean disposable income of $780.22 Australian dollars per month, while the Chinese beer drinkers' indicate their mean disposable income is $68.42 Australian dollars per month. This appears to make the average disposable income of our Australian respondents 11 times higher than that of the Chinese sample. However, the Australian cost of living is six times higher than in China (Statistics China 2010). Accounting for the difference between these statistics, the roughly adjusted disposable income of the Australian sample is about twice that of the Chinese sample – that is, our Australia sample respondents have twice as much money to spend compared to our respondents in China.

The Australia sample reports spending 8.2% of their total disposable income on beer, the China sample spends 4.1% of their disposable income on beer. The formula to calculate this statistic can be found in Appendix 1.

Beer consumed

There is a difference in the amount of beer consumed (glasses or bottles in the last seven days) between the two countries. Our Australia sample reports drinking an average (mean) of 13.9 glasses per week, while the China sample reports drinking 5.5 glasses per week. This difference is significant, a t-test shows the Australia sample to have significantly higher consumption of beer than the China sample (t = 6.44, df = 1, p = .001). This seems to be expected given the Australia sample spends roughly twice the amount of disposable income on beer compared to the China sample.

Frequency of visits to the drinking venues

We asked our respondents for their frequency of past visits to the drinking venue. This is to see if their visiting behaviors are stable and if we can compare visiting behavior between the Australia and China samples.

The respondents in the samples report different visiting frequencies. The mean number of visits to the tavern for our Australia sample is 2.3 times in the last seven days, while the China sample visited an average of 1.7 times in the last seven days. An independent sample t-test to compare group differences (see Appendix 2) finds the members of the Australia sample to visit significantly more frequently than the China sample (t = 4.09, df = 1, p = 0.001). This seems to fit the general trend where members of our Australia sample report drinking more. This statistic adds to the picture, members of the Australia sample also visit their drinking venue more often.

Australia sample pattern of visits to venue

In markets where customers have a relatively high rate of repeat purchase, for example the beer market, the pattern of product use often fits an NBD pattern (East 1997). This pattern is used to identify a stable market, with several research studies suggesting the NBD pattern reflects a relatively high level of habitual responses (East 1997).

Figure 6.1 shows the Australian sample's reported visits to the tavern, and the NBD expected visits using the East (1997) NBD software (see Appendix 3). The pattern of reported actual and predicted (expected) visits appears very similar to each other. By applying a linear regression analysis to test the association, the actual reported visits are significantly and highly associated with the NBD expected results (r = 0.98), showing almost perfect predictive ability. This finding is highly indicative that that the reported visits to the tavern made by the Australia sample members reflects a pattern of consumption found in "stable" markets. Market stability, where there are strong habitual purchases are linked to markets experiencing the mature stage of the Product Life-Cycle (Bennett and Rundle-Thiele 2005; Golder and Tellis 2004; Lee and Edwards 2013; Polli and Cook 1969; Thietart and Vivas 1984).

China sample pattern of visits to venue

Of those who are regular drinkers, 54.7% of the China sample report visiting the restaurant in the China Agricultural University in the last seven days. On average,

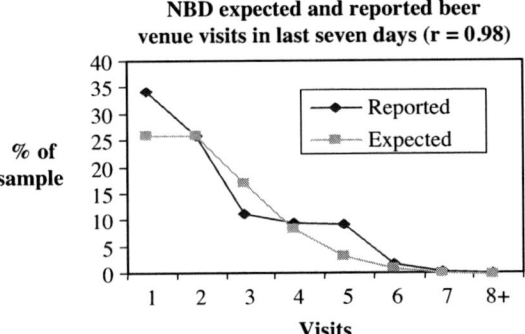

FIGURE 6.1 Australia sample NBD expected and reported tavern visits in last seven days

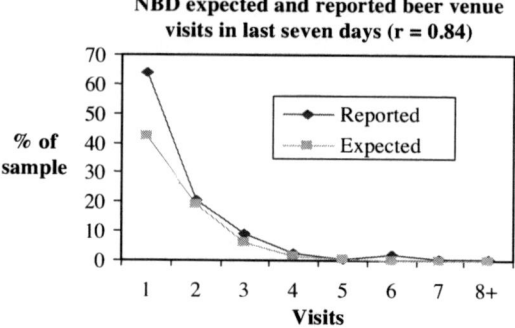

FIGURE 6.2 China sample NBD expected and reported restaurant visits in last seven days

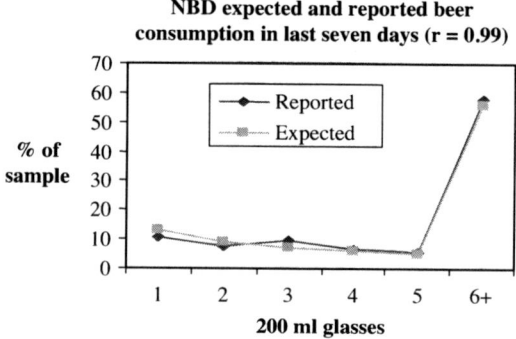

FIGURE 6.3 Australia sample NBD expected and reported amounts of beer consumed in last seven days

sample members visited 1.7 times (mean). East's (1997) NBD software shows that the NBD expected visits and actual visits to be quite similar (see Figure 6.2).

Applying a linear regression to the two distributions finds the actual visits to be highly (r = 0.84) and significantly (p < 0.05) associated with the predicted visit pattern. This suggests the visits to the restaurant in the China Agricultural University exhibits a relatively stable pattern. Similar to the visitation pattern reported by members in the Australia sample. In terms of visit frequency and pattern, the nature of the decisions to visit the venue by the China sample appear to be largely habitual (see Appendix 4).

Australia sample beer use

The Australia sample comprises of 86.9% current beer users. For this group, mean beer consumption stands at 13.9 glasses (200 ml) for the last seven days. To predict beer consumption frequency and pattern, we use NBD in the same way as to predict respondents' visits to the drinking venue. The results for consumption appear in Figure 6.3.

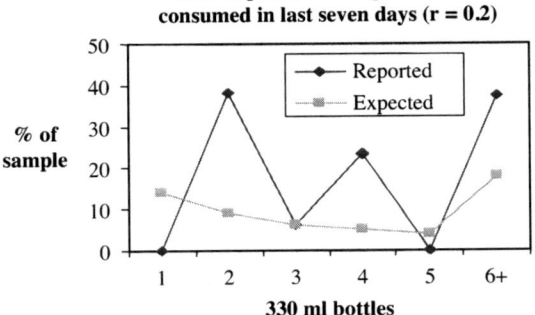

FIGURE 6.4 China sample NBD expected and reported beer consumed in last seven days

Applying a linear regression analysis to the expected and actual visits finds that NBD predicts beer consumption patterns almost perfectly (r = 0.99, p < 0.5), the prediction has 99 percent accuracy. This pattern of use suggests that the Australia sample's beer use is stable and repurchase is potentially highly habitual.

China sample beer use

Of the China sample, 54.7% are current beer drinkers. This group reports a mean consumption of 1.7 glasses (200 ml) of beer in the last seven days. Interestingly, the NBD prediction performs poorly for beer consumption of the China sample (Figure 6.4). NBD cannot predict our China sample members' beer consumption accurately. The result from a regression analysis shows the observed and expected results to be only weakly related (r = 0.20, p < 0.5). This result suggests that the China sample is not stable in using beer, nor do they exhibit habitual patterns in terms of its use. This type of finding is consistent with a product in the early stages of the Product Life-Cycle (East 1997).

The Australia and China sample members' behavior appear to be stable in terms of their visits to the drinking venue. This may reflect the maturity of this format of serving the beer product category – that is, taverns and restaurants are the usual and normal places to serve beer. However, we find a large and statistically different fit for the NBD for the reported drinking of the two samples. The expected use pattern based on the NBD is a very close fit for the Australia sample, but a poor fit for the China sample of current beer drinkers.

Australia and China samples' brand preferences

Table 6.2 reports the Australia and China samples' current beer drinkers' first preference for the beer brands. The Australia sample appears to have a higher preference for the top sales brand – Tooheys New (51.2%) compared to the China sample's preference for the top brand – Tsingtao (45.1%).

TABLE 6.2 Australia and China samples' stated preferred brands

Australia sample respondents' 1st preferred brand

Brands	% share	N
Tooheys New	51.2%	145
Amber Ale	37.5%	106
Swan Draft	11.3%	32
Total	100%	283

China respondents' 1st preferred brand

Brands	% share	N
Tsingtao	45.1%	73
Yanjing	35.8%	58
Snow	19.1%	31
Total	100%	161

We use a 3 × 2 Chi-square test to compare the relative differences between the Australia and China samples' choice of the top three beer brands. This analysis finds the shares of the brands are not significantly different (χ^2 = .57; df = 2, p = 0.6), suggesting that the share of the brands do not differ significantly between the two samples. This adds to our confidence in comparing the samples.

Australia and China current beer drinkers' revealed Brand Loyalty

Each respondent (current drinker or not) was offered a glass of beer after they had completed their survey. This beer was presented as an incentive for their cooperation. All beer-drinking respondents were offered two options for their incentive. These options differed in the price they had to pay for the glass of beer. The price of the beer depended on the respondent's initial choice of their top and second preferred brand. They could stay with their top preferred brand of beer and pay AUD $1.00 for the normally AUD $2.00 (200 ml) glass of beer. Alternatively, they could receive a free glass of their second preferred brand of beer (see question 10 in Appendix 10 English Survey and the last question in Appendix 11 Chinese survey). This option of paying a premium for their top preferred brand or receiving their second preferred beer choice for free was replicated for the China sample. The "stay or switch" results are summarized as Table 6.3.

The results in Table 6.3 show that 38.2% of the Australia sample stayed with their top-preferred brand. This means that 61.8% switched from the top-preferred brand to their second-preferred brand with a discount.

In the China sample, 65.2% stayed with their top-preferred brand, while 34.7% switched from their top-preferred brand to their second-preferred brand with a discount. Comparing the two samples, significantly more members in the China sample

TABLE 6.3 Australia and China samples of current beer drinkers' stay or switch behavior (brand loyalty) when a price incentive was offered

	Australia Sample	China Sample
Choice	**Proportion (n)**	**Proportion (n)**
Stay	38.2% (108)	65.2% (105)
Switch	61.8% (175)	34.7% (56)
Total	**100% (283)**	**100% (161)**

are "brand loyal" – preferring to stay with their top preferred brand when offered a large price discount than for members of the Australia sample (χ^2 = 30.69, df = 1, p = 0.001). Of course, lighter use will necessarily generate higher loyalty by itself (East 1997), this may help explain the higher loyalty in the China sample.

Another possible explanation for higher loyalty is the importance of brand (Lee and Edwards 2013). This is a situation where consumers in less mature markets believe that some brands have superior products – e.g., when the beer market is comparatively less mature in China. In markets where the product category is more mature – like in Australia, increased levels of knowledge increases the product's parity. Increased product parity increases the substitutability between brands – this increases customers' willingness to switch brands because of price.

Factor analysis on Brand Knowledge items

The questionnaire we administered in our field experiment includes 36 statements. These seek to capture information about various aspects of the top and second preferred brands. These statements reflect the Images, Attitudes, Attributes and Benefits of a beer brand and are developed from pre-tests.

We use two orders of questions to determine whether there are any order-bias effects. A post-hoc test shows that there are no significant differences in both sequences of questions on any dependent measures.

Exploratory factor analysis is used to test for the dimensions that make-up the samples' brand knowledge. This test examines the inter-relationships between the data collected for the variables and tries to find common underlying dimensions (Hair et al. 2010). These common dimensions are referred to as "factors".

Using factor analysis, we group respondents' answers about their top preferred brand into factors. This helps us to assess the respondents' knowledge structure about their preferred brand. This should represent the structure that results in Brand Knowledge. We will compare respondents' initial preference for their top preferred brand with their statements about that brand. Further, we will also compare respondents' choice to stay with their preferred brand or switch to the second preferred brand, to their statements about their top preferred brand. When conducting these comparisons, we only use respondents' ratings of their top preferred brand (ratings of brand knowledge). There are two reasons for this. All theories of Brand Knowledge deal with managing the perceptions of one company's brand (our top-preferred brand). We cannot find any that deal with managing a competitors' brand – i.e., the second brand choice. Nonetheless, we attempt to model the respondents' beer brand knowledge from the responses to statements for both top and second preferred brands. The results of these analyses incorporating two brands show that the Brand Knowledge model performs worse than models using the top preference. The use of only the top preferred brand also simplifies data collection and interpretation.

Australia sample factor analysis for the initial brand preferred by buyer

The factor model we specified uses the Varimax rotation method with Kaiser Normalization. Factors identified for the Australian sample are those with eigenvalues above 1.0 and with individual item loadings above 0.6. These are reported in Table 6.4.

Each factor is labeled with an identifier that attempts to capture the meanings that best represent the group of statements clustered as the factor. This task is obviously subjective in terms of the researcher's choice, but may help the reader follow the further use of the factors to determine which are associated with Preference and Loyalty.

From Table 6.4, we can see that the first factor includes five statements, "it has a creative advertising", "it is always available", "it is good value for money", "it is inexpensive compared with competitors", and "it is popular". This factor is labeled "Utilitarian Attributes", and explains 12.4% of total variance in the factorial model.

The second factor identifies five statements with commonalities. These are "it gives me energy and courage", "it reduces my stress", "it gives me enjoyment and satisfaction", "it makes me sociable and lets me make friends easier" and "it makes me happier". We call this factor "Emotional Benefits". This factor explains 11.9% of the total variance.

The third factor includes four statements *when I am consuming or after purchasing . . .* – "I feel trendy", "I feel prestigious", "I feel elegant" and "I feel charming". This factor is labeled "Images", and explains 10.6% of the total variance.

The fourth factor includes two statements, "I like its taste" and "I like this brand". This factor is labeled "Affect", and explains 9.7% of the total variance.

The fifth factor includes three statements, "consuming the beer is good for my health", "it does not get me fat" and "it is interesting and exciting". This factor is labeled "Physical Benefits", and explains 7.5% of the total variance.

A sixth factor includes three statements, "it tastes good", "it is suitable for men" and "it is suitable for celebrations and parties". This factor is labeled "Party Beer", and explains 6% of the total variance.

TABLE 6.4 Australia sample results of factor analysis of beer Brand Knowledge

Factors (% variance explained) Measures	Measure loadings		Extracted factor loading
1. Utilitarian Attributes (12.4% variance explained)			
It has a creative advertising.	.78		
It is always available.	.74		
It is good value for money.	.72		.85
It is inexpensive compared with its competitors.	.69		
It's very popular.	.62		
2. Emotional Benefits (11.9% variance explained)			
It gives me energy and courage.	.76		
It reduces my stress.	.75		
It gives me enjoyment & satisfaction.	.74		.83
It makes me sociable & lets me make friends easier.	.68		
It makes me happier.	.67		
3. Images (10.6% variance explained)			
I feel trendy.		.75	
I feel prestigious.		.74	.80
I feel elegant.		.75	
I feel charming.		.68	
4. Affect (9.7% variance explained)			
I like its taste.		.83	.79
I like this brand.		.73	
5. Physical Benefits (7.5% variance explained)			
It is good for health.		.83	
It does not get me fat.		.83	.84
It is interesting and exciting.		.61	
6. Party Beer (6% variance explained)			
It tastes good.		.78	
It is suitable for men.		.74	.69
It is suitable for celebrations and parties.		.72	

Six factors; 75.6% of total variance explained; Internal scale consistency Cronbach's Alpha = 0.88

(See Appendix 5 factor analysis for the Australia sample)

Overall, these six factors explain 75.6% of the total variance for the factorial model specified with the responses from Australia sample respondents (current drinkers). From this model, we derive normalized factor scores. These scores will be used to test the identification of factors with respondents' choice of their preferred brand.

For the Australia sample factorial model, the Cronbach's Alpha for the inter-item reliability is 0.88. Hair et al. (2010) suggests that this level of internal consistency is suitable for conducting further analyses such as principle components confirmatory factor analysis.

China sample: results of factor analysis of buyers' beer Brand Knowledge

Similar to the analysis for the Australia sample, we use Principle Component factor analysis with the Varimax rotation method and Kaiser Normalization to specify a factorial model for the China sample. This uses their statements about their top preferred brand. In the same way as we did for the Australia analysis, we only report factors with eigenvalues of 1.0 and above and item (statement) loadings of 0.6 or more. These appear in Table 6.5. The responses of the China sample's current beer drinkers helps identify seven factors that portray sample members' knowledge structure for the top preferred brand. Because we label some factors for both Australia and China samples using the same names, we differentiate between the factors for each sample by using capital letters for Australia (e.g., Image Factor) and small letters for China (e.g., image factor).

The first factor is labeled "Images". This factor includes the five items – *when I am consuming or after purchasing* ... "I feel prestigious", "I feel charming", "I feel trendy", "I feel elegant" and "I feel cheerful". This factor contains four of the five statements identified in the Australia sample's factor labeled "Images". The China sample's images factor accounts for 12.3% of the total explained variance. While the images factor is the most important factor for the China sample, the Images factor is ranked as the third most influential factor for Brand Knowledge in the Australia sample.

The second most important factor for the China sample is labeled "affect". This factor explains 11.6% of the total variance in the China Brand Knowledge model. It includes three items; "I like its taste", "it tastes good" and "it makes me feel happier". The China sample's Affect factor is similar to the Australia Affect factor. The difference lies in the China sample perceiving this item as the second most important in their Brand Knowledge construct, while the Australia sample ranks Affect fourth most important. The China Affect factor has one item ("I like its taste") that is similar to the Australia Affect factor.

The third factor in the China Brand Knowledge model is labeled "utilitarian attributes". This explains 10.3% of the total variance. This factor includes four items: "it's good value for money", "it's always available", "it's popular" and "it's inexpensive compared with its competitors". These are four of the five statements that are also included in the Australia factor labeled "Utilitarian Attributes".

The fourth factor in the China Brand Knowledge model is called "experiential attributes". Compared with the Australia sample, this is a largely unique factor to this sample of Chinese beer drinkers. This factor includes two items: "it's refreshing" and "it has nice foam and color". This factor accounts for approximately 9.2% of the total variance.

TABLE 6.5 China sample results of factor analysis of buyers' beer Brand Knowledge components

Factors (% variance explained) Measures	Measure loadings			Extracted factor loading
1. Images (12.3% variance explained)				
I feel prestigious.	.80			.85
I feel charming.	.79			
I feel trendy.	.78			
I feel elegant.	.78			
I feel cheerful.	.72			
2. Affect (11.6% variance explained)				
I like its taste.		.75		.84
It tastes good.		.65		
It makes me happier.		.63		
3. Utilitarian Attribute (10.3% variance explained)				
It's good value for money.		.79		
It's always available.		.74		.85
It's very popular.		.66		
It's inexpensive compared with its competitors.		.64		
4. Experiential Attributes (9.2% variance explained)				
It's refreshing.			.83	.80
It has foam and nice color.			.75	
5. Physical Benefits (9% variance explained)				
It does not get me fat.			.83	.79
It's good for health.			.73	
It's interesting and exciting.			.71	
6. Emotional Benefits (8.5% variance explained)				
It gives me energy and courage.			.75	.77
It reduces my stress.			.75	
It makes me feel cool.			.62	
7. Country Identity (8.2% variance explained)				
It is suitable for men			.77	.80
It is Chinese style beer			.72	
It supports China's economy			.66	
Seven factors; explains 58% of the total variance; Cronbach's Alpha = 0.88				

(See Appendix 6 factor analysis for Chinese sample)

The fifth factor for the China sample contains the same statements as the Australia sample's Brand Knowledge factor labeled "Physical Benefits". This factor includes the statements of: "it does not get me fat", "it is good for health" and "it is interesting and exciting". Similar to the Australia sample's model, the China sample's respondents perceive these attributes to belong to a factor ranked fifth in the factor analysis. However, this factor explains more of the total variance (9%) for the China sample, than the similar factor for the Australia sample (7.5%).

The sixth factor for the China sample's Brand Knowledge construct contains three of the six statements ("it gives me energy and courage", "it reduces my stress" and "it makes me feel cool") that are in the Australia sample's "Emotional Benefits" factor. This factor is labeled "emotional benefits" for the China Brand Knowledge model given its similarity in the statements across the two samples. The statement, "it makes me feel cool" loaded in this factor in the China sample, but not for the Australia sample. This "emotional benefits" factor explains 8.5% variance for the China sample, which is less than what this factor explained for the Australia sample (11.9%).

The seventh China sample factor is called "country identity". It has two of the three statements "it is suitable for men", "it is Chinese style beer" and "it supports China's economy". These statements are conceivably nationalistic. They are different from the Australia sample's factor labeled "Party Beer". This factor explains more of the China sample's Brand Knowledge variance (8.2%) than the Party Beer factor for the Australia sample's Brand Knowledge (6%).

The Cronbach's Alpha for this set of items is 0.88, and above the 0.8 deemed to be the minimum needed for further analyses such as confirmatory research (Joseph F. Hair et al. 2010). This indicates the measures of Brand Knowledge for the Chinese sample has good internal inter-item validity (see reliability tests in Appendix 6). The internal consistency for the China sample's model is close to the Australia sample's results for Cronbach's Alpha. This shows that the items of our Predictive Brand Choice model has consistent internal consistency when used in different countries. This adds a positive note to the external validity of the Predictive Brand Choice model's measures.

Comparing factors across samples

Table 6.6 compares the factors that make up the Australia and China samples members' Brand Knowledge about beer brands. This table also ranks the factors in the models for each country. As we have discussed earlier, the factorial model specified using the data from the Australia sample finds six factors. Responses to the same questions from the China sample has a model showing seven factors. The responses from both the Australia and China samples result in models with the common factors of: Emotional Benefits, Images, Affect, Physical Benefits and Utilitarian Attributes. What differs between the models is the Australia model has the factor Party Beer in its Brand Knowledge construct. The China Brand

TABLE 6.6 Brand Knowledge factors in two samples of beer drinkers

Rank	Sample	
	Australia sample drinkers	*China sample drinkers*
1st	Utilitarian Attributes	brand images
2nd	Emotional Benefits	affect
3rd	Images	utilitarian attributes
4th	Affect	experiential attributes
5th	Physical Benefits	physical benefits
6th	Party Beer	emotional benefits
7th		country identity

Knowledge model has the unique factors of "experiential attributes" and "country identity".

The model specified for each country ranks the latent factors for Brand Knowledge in different orders. Only the fifth factor, "Physical Benefits", is in the same rank. Australian drinkers report more concern about their perception of beer brand's attributes and the emotional benefits they get from drinking their top preferred brand of beer. On the other hand, members of the China sample primarily favor beer brand images and affect toward the brand. The factors in the Australia sample's Brand Knowledge model explains substantially more of the total variance of the responses (75.6% – Table 6.4) than the factors in the China Brand Knowledge model (58% – Table 6.5).

Summary

This chapter has provided an exploratory analysis. This uses descriptive statistics to compare the constituents of the Australia and China samples of current beer drinkers. These are respondents who have drunk at least a 200 ml glass (Australia) or 330 ml bottle (China) of beer in the last seven days. In our interview for this field experiment, we tried to interview all who were present in the venues. However, we chose to include only those with the most recent experience drinking beer in our analyses. Tests of current drinking, age, and the frequency of visits to the drinking venues (university tavern for Australia and university restaurant for China) show that the samples are comparable in these aspects, with the results being very similar. The samples differed in terms of disposable income, with members of the Australia sample having twice the disposable income of respondents in the China sample. Having found this, Australia sample members spent twice the amount of money on beer, drank twice as much, and also drank more frequently than the China sample respondents. These statistics seem to indicate that the samples are comparable. Internal consistency statistics for the scales used (Alpha Cronbach) also show similarities in consistency of scales across the two populations.

This chapter also reported exploratory analyses of the beer Brand Knowledge constructs for each sample. The majority of constructs are found to be very similar, with only very small differences in the make-up of the latent constructs. These Brand Knowledge constructs show high consistency between the two countries were for the factors of Emotional Benefits, Images, Affect, Physical Benefits and Utilitarian Attributes. Three factors stood out as being different. The China sample's model resulted in "country identity" and "experiential attributes" that are unique to the sample. The Australia sample's responses yielded the unique factor of "Party Beer". The Brand Knowledge construct was much stronger for the Australia sample, with the factors that are extracted the analysis being able to explain more of the construct (75.6%) than for the Brand Knowledge construct in China (58%). This supports a proposition of Product Life-Cycle theory, where more mature markets will have more knowledge in the market. In this case, the more mature/declining Australia market for beer has more Brand Knowledge about beer than the China market that is still in the growth stage.

The next step in the analysis will test for the ability of Brand Knowledge to discriminate between the different brands of beer tested in our samples. This discrimination test will indicate whether the Predictive Brand Choice model is able to predict a customer's choice (preference) using their reported Brand Knowledge.

Bibliography

Bennett R. and S. Rundle-Thiele (2005), "The Brand Loyalty Life Cycle: Implications for Marketers", *Journal of Brand Management*, 12 (4), 250.

East, Robert (1997), *Consumer Behaviour – Advances and Applications in Marketing Essex.* England: Prentice Hall Press.

Golder, Peter N. and Gerard J. Tellis (2004), "Growing, Growing, Gone: Cascades, Diffusion, and Turning Points in the Product Life Cycle", *Marketing Science*, 23 (2), 207.

Hair, Joseph F. Jr., Rolph E. Andersen, Ronald L. Tatham and William C. Black (2010), *Multivariate Data Analysis.* Upper Saddle-River, NJ: Pearson Education.

Hair, Joseph F., Jr., William C. Black, Barry J. Babin and Rolph E. Anderson (2010), *Multivariate Data Analysis: Global Edition* (7th ed.). Upper Saddle-River, New Jersey: Pearson Education.

Lee, Alvin and Mark G. Edwards (2013), *Marketing Strategy: A Lifecycle Approach.* Melbourne, Australia: Cambridge University Press.

Pink, Brian (2010), "Australian Yearbook". Canberra: Australian Bureau of Statistics.

Polli, Rolando and Victor Cook (1969), "Validity of the Product Life Cycle", *The Journal of Business*, 42 (4), 385–400.

Statistics China (2010), "China Yearbook". Beijing: National Bureau of Statistics of China.

Thietart, R. A. and R. Vivas (1984), "An Emprical Investigation of Success Strategies for Business along the Product Life Cycle", *Management Science (pre-1986)*, 30 (12), 1405.

7

RESULTS

Predicting brand choice using multiple discriminant analysis

At this point in the analyses, there appears to be support for a construct of Brand Knowledge for both our China and Australia samples. This construct describes the Brand Knowledge related to the top preferred beer brand rated by our samples' respondents. The next step to demonstrate our Predictive Brand Choice (PBC) model is to test whether the factors in each samples' Brand Knowledge construct associates significantly with the respondents' top preferred brand of beer. Statistical tests for association will use multivariate discriminant analysis (MDA) and multiple logistic regression (MLR). These techniques can reveal the relationships between the Brand Knowledge factors for each sample's top preferred beer brand with their actual choice – their top preferred brand of beer. Essentially, this serves to test whether the respondents' Brand Knowledge predicts their choice of brand. If the association is statistically significant, this supports the relationship between Brand Knowledge and purchase preference using an actual choice experiment.

We include other potential variable factors in the analyses. These are the respondents' age; their gender, their disposable income, the number of beer drinks they report to have consumed in the last seven days (glasses of 200 ml beer or 330 ml bottles), and the number of times they report visiting the venue in the last seven days. Following previous research (Yang et al. 2002), we will analyze these factors to see if they add or detract from the power of Brand Knowledge to discriminate between the different brands of beer tested.

Multiple discriminate analysis (MDA)

To see if the sample members' Brand Knowledge about their top preferred brand predicts current beer users' choice of top preferred brand, we use a combination of logistic and MDA to analyze the data. This is a crucial step that our PBC model adds to the understanding and measurement of Brand Choice. The literature we review in chapters three and four of this book clearly highlights that most brand researchers have neglected to include this step in their models. This may be due to difficulties in testing this link, and the low power traditionally found in attempts to link knowledge, preference and actual purchase behavior (Erdem et al. 1999).

We construct the MDA analysis to evaluate group differences. These differences will be based on the top preferred and second preferred groups of brands – it is necessary to group by the top and second preferred brands because individual respondents stated different ranking combinations for Brand Preferences. The MDA is also specified to classify respondents into top brand preference groups using known discriminatory variables. These variables may be the components of the Brand Knowledge constructs for each country, and the effects that arise from respondents' gender, age, disposable income, beer consumption and their visits to the venue.

In order for the linear discriminate functions to produce a minimum probability of misclassification for the top preferred brand, we need to meet certain assumptions about the data. These assumptions are that the data must have multivariate normality. The data must also demonstrate homoscedasticity, where the covariance matrices must be equal for the independent variables that are spread across different groups of dependent variables. Finally, the data must meet the assumption that the relationship between the independent and dependent variables are linear (Hair et al. 2010). The data from both the Australia and China samples meet all required assumptions (see Appendix 7 for the rationale and analyses supporting these assumptions).

Australia sample MDA for first brand preference

The multiple discriminant analysis model identifies two functions. The first discriminant function explains 86.9% of the differences between groups, whereas the second discriminate function explains 13.1% of the differences. Both functions are statistically significant (Group 1: Wilk's λ = s 0.46, $\chi2$ = 192.33, df = 24, p < 0.001; Group 2: Wilks λ = 0.88, $\chi2$ = 31.82, df = 11, p < 0.001). These results in Table 7.1 show the first discriminant function to provide the best separation of groups. The second function, orthogonal to the first, separates groups on the basis of associations that are not used in the first function.

In order to identify variables within the functions that may be useful in discriminating between preference groups, we place an emphasis on group differences in the analysis. Here, we use the significance and magnitude of the standardized canonical discriminate function coefficients from the analysis output to assess the relative importance of predictor variables. When the valence signs (+/−) are ignored, the weights show the relative effect of the variable in the MDA function. Variables with larger weights are believed to have higher discriminating power. For the MDA structure matrix in Table 7.1, the eigenvalue for Function 1 is 0.91 and Function 2 is 0.14. Canonical correlations for Functions 1 and 2 are 0.69 and 0.35 respectively.

The MDA Structure Matrix reported in Table 7.1 orders the Australia sample's standardized canonical discriminate function variables by their absolute size of

TABLE 7.1 Australia MDA structure matrix

	Function	
	1	*2*
Utilitarian Attributes	−.75*	
Images	.24*	
Physical Benefits	.16*	
Visit	.14*	
Party Beer	−.08*	
Gender		.34*
Affect		.23*
Glasses Drank		−.19*
Emotional Benefits		−.16*
Age		−.14*
Disposable Income		.07*

Note: *Largest absolute correlation between each variable and the discriminant function, non-significant loadings are not reported.

TABLE 7.2 MDA classification of Australia sample's first preferred brands

Actual choices			*Predicted Group Membership*		
	n	*Brand*	*Tooheys New n (%)*	*Amber Ale n (%)*	*Swan Draft n (%)*
n total = 257	129	**Tooheys New**	118 (91.5%)	9 (7%)	2 (1.5%)
	96	**Amber Ale**	24 (25%)	**70 (72.9%)**	2 (2.1%)
	32	**Swan Draft**	18 (56.3%)	7 (21.9%)	**7 (21.9%)**

correlation with each function. For Function 1, the most important Brand Knowledge variables are "Attributes", "Images" and "Physical Benefits". The number of visits to the Tavern over the last seven days "Visits" ranks slightly above "Party Beer". For Function 2, the most important variable is "Gender", followed by "Affect" and "Glasses Drank".

The MDA model we have specified is further applied to the Australia sample's responses to test for the PBC model's ability to discriminate on the top preferred brand of beer. The MDA produced the classification reported in Table 7.2. This table reports the actual and predicted group membership for each discriminant group and the brand as a measure of accuracy.

Referring to guidelines on how to interpret the accuracy of MDA classifications/ predictions (Hair et al. 2010), correctly judging a model's classification accuracy is crucial. However, the determination of accuracy for MDA models is not straightforward. The rule of thumb suggested by Hair et al. (2010) suggests the model should be at least 25% better at classification than the probability of a chance occurrence – that is, the prediction should be at least 25% better than if it is left to chance alone.

The field experiment we are using to demonstrate the PBC model uses three brands in each country. This makes the prior probability of classification into a group by chance to be approximately 33.3% (100% divided by three brands = chance of classification). Hair et al. (2010) argues for the classification accuracy to be higher than 33.3%. Because we know the actual brand share allocation from respondents' replies during the experiment, we have data for a more rigorous comparison. Hair et al. (2010) recommends using this actual share plus 25%; that is to specify a threshold of 125% above the actual share percentage to determine significance.

There is a second significance testing criteria that is more stringent. This is based on the actual market share of the top preferred brand. In our case, this second criteria requires a 62.8% identification accuracy [50.2% × 125% = 62.8%] in order to be sure that our prediction holds. Table 7.3 displays the actual choice, predicted choice and the level of improvement against the more stringent second criteria.

Table 7.3 shows that our MDA model correctly classifies 75.9% of the respondents for their top preferred brand across all the three beer brands tested. The MDA model is able to correctly identify respondents' overall top brand preferred significantly above the levels expected for chance occurrence. According to the results reported in Table 7.3, the MDA model correctly categorizes 91.5% of the respondents that indicated preference for Tooheys New as their top brand. This is well above the required level of 62.8% to be considered a significant improvement over chance. This means that using the PBC model, we can predict respondents' top brand preference very well using their Brand Knowledge. For the Australia sample, respondents' demographics and their reported use perform 82.3% above what would be expected when the shares of the brands are known. The classification for Amber Ale (72.9%) and Swan Draft (21.9%), are also significant improvements; although we theoretically only estimate the top preferred brand.

Given the significant improvement of the PBC model to predict the link between Brand Knowledge and the respondents' top brand choice (Brand Equity), it seems

TABLE 7.3 Australia sample classification against significance criteria

	Tooheys New	Amber Ale	Swan Draft	Overall
Actual	50.2%	37.4%	12.5%	40.7%[1]
MDA	91.5%	72.9%	21.9%	75.9%
Improvement[2]	82.3%*	94.9%*	75.2%*	38.5%*

Note: [1] $(129/257)^2 + (96/257)^2 + (32/257)^2 = 54.8$

[2] *significant if 125% above chance

appropriate to determine which factors are associated with the performance of the MDA component of the PBC model.

When MDA manages to specify two or more discriminate functions, the test provides a summary measure of the contribution of a variable across all the significant functions as an output. This result is useful to help assess the overall discriminatory power (correctly identifying top and second preferred brand) of a factor as compared to other factors. A relative measure that includes the contribution of the functions to the overall solution is calculated and reported in Table 7.4

Referring to Table 7.4, Function 1 has a contribution at 86.9%, and Function 2 has 13.1%. The "Utilitarian Attributes" factor reports loading coefficients of −0.88 (Function 1) and 0.67 (Function 2). Using these results, we can calculate the "potency value" of the "Utilitarian Attributes" factor. This can be calculated as:

$$0.869 \times (0.88) \, 2 + 0.131 \times (0.67) \, 2 = 0.74.$$

By calculating the potency values of all factors, we can determine the rank of each factor by their discriminatory ability. These calculations find the top preferred brand's "Utilitarian Attributes" factor to be the best discriminator between the preferred brands for the Australia sample. The next factor, "Affect", has substantially less discriminating power on brand choice (0.24). From the third factor onwards, the factors reported in Table 7.4 have very weak influence on brand choice and are very similar in their low levels of discriminating power. This suggests that there may be only one factor, "Affect", that the Australia sample members use to help them determine which brand of beer is their top preferred brand.

TABLE 7.4 Rank of factors for standardized canonical discriminate function

Factors	Function 1	Function 2	Overall ranks
	86.9%	13.1%	
Utilitarian Attributes	−0.88	0.67	0.74
Affect	0.49	0.45	0.24
Glasses of Beer	−0.28	−0.08	0.07
Visits	0.26	−0.07	0.06
Images	0.20	0.03	0.04
Gender	0.04	0.37	0.02
Physical Benefits	0.11	0.25	0.02
Party Beer	0.14	−0.03	0.02
Emotional Benefits	0.05	−0.28	0.01
Disposable Income	0.05	0.17	0.01
Age	0.21	−0.14	0.003

China sample MDA for first brand preference

Preliminary tests of the data provided by the China sample shows the data to meet Box's Test requirements. This indicates that the data complies with the required assumption of equality of co-variance matrices needed to perform a MDA. We have chosen to use a different approach to ascertaining the data requirements with the China sample data to demonstrate the flexibility and different methods to deal with basic statistical requirements. This extends the range and flexibility of our PBC model. Meeting Box's M statistical requirements from Box's test means the groups in the China sample can be classified. This also means that we are able to proceed with a test of the relationships between the factors and Brand Preference (see Appendix 7).

By following the rules for significant and accurate classification that guide MDA modeling (Hair et al. 2010), the classification should be at least one quarter greater than that achieved by chance (+25%) – we discussed this earlier with the Australia sample MDA model. Table 7.5 shows the actual and predicted choices and the improvement against criteria for the MDA results using the data provided by the China sample. For example, the classification accuracy for Tsingtao should be higher than 57% (45.6 × 125% = 57%) to be regarded as a significant improvement in explanation and identification. In this case, the results in Table 7.5 show that MDA cannot predict the China sample members' top preference (Tsingtao) because the MDA classification is 48.6%, this falls below the critical threshold of 57%. However, the MDA model provides a significant improvement over "chance" (share × 125%) for the overall classification across the three brands (52.5%), and significantly better than chance for Yanjing (51.8%) and Snow (63.3%) – see also Table 7.6. This is particularly surprising in that the model is based on the sample's reported perceptions of the first preferred brand, and the first brand (Tsingtao) constitutes 45.6% of the respondents.

Table 7.7 shows the variables' overall contribution to the functions for the China sample. As with the analyses for the Australia sample, the product of the two functions indicates the magnitude of the model's influence.

Eigenvalues of the discriminate functions indicate discriminatory power, but only the first discriminate function is statistically significant ($\lambda = 0.76$, $p = 0.02$) for our China sample. The first discriminate function in Table 7.7 explains 67.6%

TABLE 7.5 MDA classification of China sample's first preferred brands

Actual choices			Predicted Group Membership		
	n	*Brand*	*Yanjing n (%)*	*Tsingtao n (%)*	*Snow n (%)*
n total = 158	56	**Yanjing**	**29 (51.8%)**	15 (26.8%)	12 (21.4%)
	72	**Tsingtao**	18 (25%)	**35 (48.6%)**	19 (26.4%)
	30	**Snow**	8 (26.7%)	3 (10%)	**19 (63.3%)**

of the differences between brand preference groups, whereas the second (p = 0.24) discriminate function is not significantly associated with the identification.

The best discriminators for the sample of current beer drinkers in the China sample are based on the Function 1 factors. These are the respondents' "disposable income", the brand's perceived "physical benefits", their "gender", "emotional benefits", "affect" toward the brand and "300 ml glasses of beer" consumed in the last seven days.

As previously discussed, our PBC model uses standardized canonical discriminate function coefficients from MDA to assess the relative importance of predictors. These are predictors that are significantly associated with the customers' top

TABLE 7.6 China sample's classification against significance criteria

	Tsingtao	Yanjing	Snow	Overall %
Actual Choice	45.6%	35.4%	19%	37%[1]
MDA Predicted Choice	48.6%	51.8%	63.3%	52.5%[3]
MDA Predicted Choice minus Actual Choice	3%	16.4%	44.3%	15.5%
Improvement[2]	6.6%	46.3%	233.2%	41.9%

Note: n=158 = 56 + 72 + 30 = (Yanjing + Tsingtao + Snow), see Table 7.5
[1]$(56/158)^2 + (72/158)^2 + (30/158)^2 = 36.92\%$ = adjusted share criteria
[2]must be 25% or above choice to be significant. Calculated as:
(MDA predicted choice – Actual Choice)/Actual choice
[3]first brand correctly classified from Table 7.5

TABLE 7.7 Standardized canonical discriminate function coefficients

Factors by Rank of Effect	Function 1	Function 2 Not significant
	67.6%	32.4%
1. disposable income	−0.69	0.07
2. physical benefits	0.68	0.08
3. gender	0.20	0.22
4. emotional benefits	−0.19	0.39
5. affect	0.12	−0.31
6. glasses of beer drank in last 7 days	0.10	0.89
7. age	−0.08	0.39
8. utilitarian and experiential attributes	0.08	−0.53
9. visits	0.08	−0.75
10. country identity	−0.05	0.22
11. images	−0.003	−0.40
12. quality	0.002	0.40

preferred brand. The higher the percentage returned by the standardized canonical discriminate coefficient, the more important the predictor. Table 7.7 shows the structure matrix for the variables in the model. These variables are ranked by the absolute correlation between each variable and any discriminate function. As the second function is not a significant discriminator, the rankings from function one are sufficient for interpreting the results.

The results in Table 7.7 show the highest correlations of factors to the top preferred brand for the China sample are "disposable income", perceptions of the brand's "physical benefits", the top brand's "images", the respondents' "gender", and the respondents' perceptions of the top brand's "quality".

The second and non-significant function shows the highest correlations with "reported glasses of beer drank in the last seven days', their perceptions of the brand's "attributes", their "age", their reported "visits", the brand's "emotional benefits", their "affect" toward the brand, and the brands' perceived "country identity". However, these are not significant discriminators.

Comparing brand classifications of the Australia and China samples

The MDA component used to analyze our PBC model can correctly classify across the three brands we tested. This classification uses data from our China and Australia samples to build separate discriminatory models. We find different levels for accuracy of classification. PBC can classify about 76% of the Australia sample of current beer users by their first brand choice. This accuracy is much higher than that managed for the sample of respondents in China – the China sample manages a classification accuracy of 52.5%. This finding suggests that the beer Brand Knowledge components may be more developed of for the Australia sample of current beer users. This result also shows that Brand Knowledge plays a more important role in determining choice of brand for the Australia sample members as compared to the China sample members who are current beer drinkers.

The rank of factors for the two samples reported in Table 7.8 reveal that the university students making up the Australia sample of current beer drinkers are more

TABLE 7.8 Significant factors associated with brand preferences

Order	Australia	China
1st	Attributes	income
2nd	Affect	physical benefits
3rd	Images	gender
4th	Gender	emotional benefits
5th	Physical benefits	affect
6th		glasses of beer drank in the last seven days

concerned with their perceptions of the brand's "Attributes", "Affect" toward the brand, and perceived brand "Images".

The perceptions of the brand's "physical benefits" and their "gender" are relatively stronger effects in the China sample respondents' first Brand Preference. The factor that has the highest discrimination power for Brand Preference/Choice in the China sample is "disposable income". The Chinese respondents' "gender" is a weak third factor.

Summary

This chapter demonstrates the use of MDA to provide discrimination between top preferred and lesser preferred brands. This extends the analytical spectrum of the Brand Knowledge and Brand Equity spectrum to prediction. The MDA model can use the respondents' Brand Knowledge to predict their choice of brand very well, especially for the Australia sample. Although our PBC model using MDA can predict the Australia sample's preference well, it is less accurate at predicting brand choice for the China sample – especially for the top preferred brand. This may be due to differences in the stage of maturity between the Australia and China beer market. A more mature beer market like that found in Australia would reasonably have a higher level of Brand Knowledge (and overall category knowledge) compared to a growing market like China.

While MDA is very accurate and very suitable to analyze the discriminatory component of our PBC model, there may be situations when metric data is unobtainable – for example, when surveying children. In the next chapter, we use an alternative analysis that has less stringent requirements for data. We use the same data from the Australia and China samples and demonstrate analyzing the discriminatory function of PBC by utilizing multinomial logistic regression analysis.

Bibliography

Erdem, Tulin, Joffre Swait, Susan Broniarczyk, Dipankar Chakravarti, Jean-Noel Kapferer, Michael Keane, John Roberts, Jan-Benedict E. M. Steenkamp and Florian Zettelmeyer (1999), "Brand Equity, Consumer Learning and Choice", *Marketing Letters*, 10 (3), 301–19.

Hair, Joseph F., Jr., William C. Black, Barry J. Babin and Rolph E. Anderson (2010), *Multivariate Data Analysis: Global Edition* (7th ed.). Upper Saddle-River, New Jersey: Pearson Education.

Yang, Sha, Greg Allenby, M. and Geraldine Fennell (2002), "Modeling Variation in Brand Preference: The Roles of Objective Environment and Motivating Conditions", *Marketing Science*, 21 (1), 14–32.

8

RESULTS

Predicting brand choice using multinomial logistic regression analysis and binary logistic regression analysis

To improve the usability of the Predictive Brand Choice (PBC) model, we also demonstrate modeling the data by using multinomial logistic regression (MLR) and binary logistic regression (BLR). MLR is a test that can discern effects in the respondents' top preferred brand of beer. The MLR test provides greater scope for analysis as it is less restrictive in its requirements for data normality, and is able to accommodate a mix of continuous and categorical variables (Hair et al. 2010). While it is more robust in its ability to handle non-parametric data, it is also less conservative when testing of hypothesis.

MLR analyses identifying the Australia sample's brand preference

Here, we demonstrate MLR in testing for the reliability of the findings for the top preferred brand in each of our samples (Australia and China). We also use MLR results to compare the respondents' decision to stay with the top preferred brand or switch to their second preferred brand. One of the ways this buyer choice analysis of loyalty can be undertaken is by using MLR. As such, this test presents an improvement over testing by using multiple discriminant analysis (MDA) that was presented in the previous chapter. Comparing the results of MLR against MDA will also offer an added degree of statistical insight that may be useful when judging the hypotheses.

Testing using the MLR analysis finds similar relationships to those found by the MDA analysis. The MLR classification Table 8.1 reports the overall percentage of accurate classification to be 77.4%, and this is 4% higher than the MDA classification of 73.5% for the Australia sample that was reported in the previous chapter. The MLR classification of 27% in Table 8.1 exceeds the critical value of 25% better

TABLE 8.1 Australia sample's MLR classification results

Observed	Predicted			
	Tooheys New (n)	Amber Ale (n)	Swan Draft (n)	Percent Correct
Tooheys New	116	10	3	**89.9%**
Amber Ale	18	76	2	**79.2%**
Swan Draft	18	7	7	**21.9%**
Overall percentage	59.1%	36.2%	4.7%	**77.4%**

TABLE 8.2 Australia sample's MLR classification against significance criteria

	Tooheys New	Amber Ale	Swan Draft	Overall
Actual	50.2	37.4	12.5	**54.8%**
MLR	89.9	79.2	21.9	**77.4%**
Improvement over actual	79.1%	111.7%	75.2%	**41.2%**

than if classification is by chance alone. This means the MLR classification model is reliable and the prediction is clear.

We specify a MLR model using data from the Australia sample of current drinkers. From Table 8.1, for the individual brands, this model can identify 89.9% (n = 116) of the respondents who prefer Tooheys New as their top brand, and 79.2% (n = 76) of the respondents who say Amber Ale is their top choice. These classification results are close to those obtained with the MDA, where 91.5% of respondents were correctly identified as preferring Tooheys New, and 72.9% Amber Ale. Both the MDA and MLR models correctly identify 21.9% of Swan Draft preferences.

Consistent with the findings for MDA, the MLR results suggest that Brand Knowledge data from the Australian sample of current beer drinkers can be used to accurately identify sample members' top preference among the three most popular brands of beer in the University of Western Australia tavern. These results lend support for the Brand Knowledge – Brand Equity model that is being tested.

Table 8.2 reports the MLR model's improvement over the actual prediction. We can see from the table that the MLR identification exceeds the significance threshold requirement of 25% more than the actual observed percentage by a wide margin. Tooheys New identification is 79.1%, Amber Ale 111.7% and Swan Draft 75.2%. This statistics show that the model is robust and can identify the sample members who chose each brand as their top choice of beer to drink. Overall, the improvement over chance for the three brands tested is 41.2%, and this is well above the required significance criteria of 25% above chance.

MLR analyses identifying factors in the China sample's brand preference

We use the same method and analysis as that with our Australia sample for data collected from our China sample. The MLR model specified with the China sample data explains preference at a statistically significant level ($\chi2$ = 44.3, df = 24, p = 0.007), with a Pseudo R-square from 0.25 (Cox and Snell) to 0.28 (Nagel-Kerke). The Pseudo R-square is lower than the same statistic in the Australia sample MLR model (Cox and Snell = 0.53, Nagel-Kerke = 0.62). The classification matrix for the MLR model with the China sample data is shown in Table 8.3.

The MLR results in Table 8.3 correctly identify 70.8% of current drinkers who say Tsingtao is their top preferred brand, 55.4% respondents naming Yanjing as their top choice and 23.3% the working sample of current drinkers who like Snow beer as their top brand. In comparing the MLR identification rate to the actual reported top preferences for brands, only the classification for the Snow brand is less than the required 25% threshold. This may be partially due to the small numbers of respondents naming Snow as their top preferred brand – predictions are more accurate when there are sufficient numbers of responses to the question. Classification for the two brands with higher share performs very well. Yanjing (35.4%) and Tsingtao (53.8%) both exceed the required 25% significance threshold with good margins.

When we compare the MDA (Chapter 7) and MLR (Table 8.4) findings for the China sample data, using MLR as a prediction test appear to provide a better model for identifying the respondents' top preferred brand. These are models that

TABLE 8.3 China sample's MLR classification results

Observed	Predicted			
	Yanjing (n)	Tsingtao (n)	Snow (n)	Percent Correct
Yanjing	31	20	5	**55.4%**
Tsingtao	16	51	5	**70.8%**
Snow	9	14	7	**23.3%**
Overall percentage	35.4%	53.8%	10.8%	**56.3%**

TABLE 8.4 China sample's MLR identification, actual shares by brand

	Tsingtao	Yanjing	Snow	Overall
Actual	45.6	35.4	19	**36.9%**
MLR	70.8	55.4	23.3	**56.3%**
Improvement over actual	35.6%	56.5%	22.6%	**52.6%**

incorporate the respondents' reports of their brand knowledge, their demographic background and their past consumption. The MLR can predict at 70.8% for Tsingtao and 55.4% for Yanjing preferences. Preference for Snow can be predicted at 23.3%. The overall amount of correct brand preference classification using Brand Knowledge, demographic and use data is 56.3%.

Modeling the China sample data using MLR (56.3%) results in a 13% better prediction than that achieved with MDA (41.1%). These results suggest a better classification rate of both samples' respondents' top preferred brand with MLR than with MDA.

Binary logistic regression test

To further demonstrate the PBC model, we use BLR to test the data collected from the Australia and China samples. Similar to the tests we have performed with MDA and MLR, we will use respondent's reported brand knowledge of their top preferred brand, respondents' demographics and reported beer use in the MLR models. These variables will predict the dependent variable whether the respondents decide to stay with their top preferred brand while paying a premium price, or to switch to their second preferred brand without paying the price premium. Essentially, this mimics the situation that is regularly encountered at the point of sale, where one brand will be on "discount" hoping to entice buyers away from their favorite brand. This will test whether a buyer's brand knowledge about their top brand can predict who will switch and who will stay loyal to their nominated top brand. Given the binary dependent response of stay or switch, the BLR test seems to be the most appropriate test for this decision (Hair et al. 2010). In essence, this tests the "brand loyalty" component for our PBC model.

BLR of the Australia sample's loyalty to the first preferred brand

We specify a BLR model using the data from the Australia sample of current beer drinkers. BLR provides a model that shows the Homer and Lameshow measure of overall fit. The Homer and Lameshow test answers the question, "How well does my model fit the data?" – It is basically a goodness of fit test. Homer and Lameshow will test for differences between the observed and prediction models. In the model for the Australia sample, the results indicate no statistically significant differences between the observed and predicted classifications ($\chi2 = 7.83$, df $= 8$, p $= 0.45$). In this case, there is no significant difference between the data we have collected from the Australia sample and our specified predictive model. This shows that our BLR model can be judged as adequate and dependable when predicting using this dataset. The rationale and output from the tests can be found in Appendix 9. Table 8.5 shows the accuracy of classifying whether the Australia sample respondents stayed with their top preferred brand, or switched to the less expensive second preferred brand.

Table 8.5 shows the observed and predicted statistics of respondents from the Australia sample staying with their top preferred brand and second preferred brand. The predicted model uses the factors from the respondents' reports about their brand knowledge of their top preferred brand. The factors of the brand's perceived "Country Identity", "Physical Benefits" and "Attributes" are all significant (p < 0.05) factors that help the predictive model accurately discriminate and predict the choice a sample member will make.

For the Australia sample, the BLR model provides a significant and strong classification and prediction for "switch" (Table 8.6), showing a significant improvement in this area for predicting which respondents will switch to their second preferred brand. For this, the BLR model can predict with an improvement of 87.9% over the actual observed 61.8%; this is an improvement of 42%. However, the model only provides increased accuracy for switching (87.9%), not for staying (34.7%) with the

TABLE 8.5 Australia sample's BLR classification of loyalty

		Predicted		
		Stay with Top Preferred Brand	*Switch to Second Preferred Brand*	*Percentage Correct*
Observed	**Stay with top preferred brand**	34	64	**34.7%**
	Switch to second preferred brand	19	138	**87.9%**
				Overall **67.5%**

Cox and Snell R^2 = 0.86
Nagelkerke R^2 = 0.12
Hosmer and Lameshow test χ^2 = 7.83, df = 8, p = 0.45

TABLE 8.6 Australia sample's BLR classification vs. actual choice

	Stay with Top Preferred Brand	*Switch to Second Preferred Brand*	*Overall*
Actual	38.2%	61.8%	**52.7%**
BLR	34.7%	87.9%	**67.5%**
Improvement over actual	−9.2%	42%	**28.1%**

Items significant in BLR model
Attribute B = −0.58, p = 0.004
Benefits B = 0.36, p = 0.04
Country identity b = 0.55, p = 0.08

top preferred brand. The model performs significantly worse (−9.2%) than chance for classifying those that stay loyal to the brand. This is an important finding, that our measurement of Brand Knowledge can be used to predict which customers are likely to purchase their second preferred brand because of a price discount.

BLR of China sample's stay or switch decision

The result of the China sample's "stay" or "switch" decision is shown in Table 8.7. The overall correct classification rate for the sample is 67.1%. Although this rate is very similar to the 67.5% obtained with the Australia sample, accuracy is quite different for the areas tested.

When the classification accuracy of the BLR model is compared against the actual decisions of the respondents in the China sample, the overall accuracy does not reach the +125% of actual threshold level (see Table 8.8). The model falls just short (+22%) of the criteria (+25%) and may be called only marginally, but not significantly better.

TABLE 8.7 BLR China sample's stay or switch classification

| | | Predicted | | |
		Stay with Top Preferred Brand	Switch to Second Preferred Brand	Percentage Correct
Observed	**Stay with top preferred brand**	93	11	**89.4%**
	Switch to second preferred brand	41	13	**24.1%**
				Overall **67.1%**

Cox and Snell R^2 = 0.52
Nagelkerke R^2 = 0.07
Hosmer and Lameshow test χ^2 = 1.46, df = 2, p=0.48

TABLE 8.8 China sample's BLR identification vs. actual shares by brand

	Stay with Top Preferred Brand	Switch to Second Preferred Brand	Overall
Actual	65.4%	34.6%	**55%**
BLR	89.4%	24.1%	**67.1%**
Improvement over actual	36.7%	−30.3%	**22%**

Significant items in BLR model
Income B = −0.002, p = 0.001

The BLR model using the data from the China sample finds "disposable income" to be a significant predictor of which respondent will stay with their top preferred brand or switch to their second preferred brand (p = 0.001). The result in Table 8.8 shows the model can very accurately classify and predict which respondents will stay with their top preferred brand (89.4%). However, the model cannot accurately predict who will switch (24.1%). This is the reverse of the finding with our Australia sample.

BLR model of loyalty for Australia vs. China samples

It is important to have a measurement component in the branding process that can predict whether a customer will stay with the brand or switch. Our contribution to the measurement of brands and branding activities, the PBC model, is able to use a customer's brand knowledge of their top preferred brand, simple demographic data, and product usage data to predict which customers will stay with their top preferred brand and pay a premium price and which customers will switch brands when the second preferred brand is cheaper.

In our demonstration of the PBC model, the sample of current drinkers forming the Australia sample provided data that allowed us to develop a model that predicts who will switch to the second preferred brand. PBC's prediction accuracy for this is 77.4% overall. This prediction of switching is based on the respondents' perceptions of their top preferred brands' Attributes and their beliefs of the brands' Benefits. Brand Attributes have a negative relationship with their choice – causing them to prefer not to switch. The respondents' beliefs about the brands' Benefits associate positively with switching behavior – making them switch to their second preferred brand.

In our model using the data from current beer drinkers in our China sample, the respondents' reported "disposable income" is the only significant factor to predict which respondents' will stay with their top preferred brand. This factor exhibits a negative relationship with switching behavior. In other words, the more disposable income they reported, the lower the tendency for them to switch to a second preferred brand. This is logical as respondents may be less price sensitive if they have a higher level of income. Our PBC model can correctly predict 89.4% of the respondents in this sample who will stay with their top preferred brand. However, the relationship between choice and income is extremely weak (the index is 0.002).

Our PBC model can accurately classify the Australia sample beer drinkers into those who switch (42% above chance), but not those who stay (9.2% below "share"). In contrast, the China sample beer drinkers can be more accurately predicted if a respondent stays with their top preferred brand (36.7% above "share"), but not those who switch to their second preferred brand (−30.3% below "share"). Nonetheless, only the model for the Australia sample shows a significant improvement in predicting those respondents that both stay and switch.

TABLE 8.9 Classification comparisons preferences and loyalty

Sample	Overall % MLR (1st preference)	Overall % BLR (loyalty/equity)
Australia sample	77.4%	67.5%
China sample	56.3%	67.1%[1]

[1] not significantly better than "share"

Table 8.9 shows the classification ratio for prediction by different analysis methods for judging the consistency of the results. The Australia sample beer drinkers' top preference and second preference can be correctly classified at 77.4% with MLR, and their "stay with the top preferred brand or switch" to the second preference can be predicted for 67.5% of the respondents.

For the sample of beer drinkers interviewed in China, their top preference and second preference can be correctly classified at 56.3% with MLR, and their "stay or switch" can be correctly predicted at 67.1%. The China sample's "stay or switch" BLR model does not predict significantly better than MLR in terms of classification by brand "share".

Formal testing of the hypotheses

Based on the literature, we proposed four hypotheses to test our PBC model. This chapter reports the analyses associated with different components of the PBC model. These results enable responses to each hypothesis.

H1: Respondents' favorable images about a brand will be a significant effect in their brand knowledge, their brand preference and their loyalty to their preferred brand.

We included statements in both the Australia and China samples' questionnaire that asked respondents for their knowledge of their top preferred brand of beer. This questionnaire was completed by respondents in a field experiment in a drinking venue.

The responses we managed to collect can be modeled to form a factor that we labeled "Images". Table 8.10 shows the items that make up the respondents' top preferred beer's brand "Image" ("when I drink this brand") from each sample.

As a part of our PBC model, we apply MDA and MLR analyses to test H1. These analyses provide results showing the respondents' perceptions of brand images to affect their top preference of brands for both samples. This result supports part of H1. However, the brand images of the top preferred brand fails to produce significant effects in the respondents' decision to stay with their top preference or switch their loyalty to their second preferred brand in both samples. This results in rejecting the part of H1 that relates to the association between brand images with brand loyalty.

TABLE 8.10 Components of each sample's beer brand images

In response to a question, "When I drink this brand of beer. . ."

Australia sample	China sample
I feel trendy.	I feel prestigious.
I feel prestigious.	I feel charming.
I feel elegant.	I feel trendy.
I feel charming.	I feel elegant.
	I feel cheerful.

TABLE 8.11 Components of each sample's factor of Affect

In response to a question, "When I drink this brand of beer. . ."

Australia sample	China sample
I like its taste.	I like its taste.
I like this brand.	It tastes good.
	It makes me happier.

H2: Respondents' favorable affect toward a brand will be a significant effect in their brand knowledge, their brand preference and their loyalty to the brand.

The factor we label "Affect" towards the brand comprises of similar items in both the Australia and China samples. Table 8.11 shows the items that make up this factor for each sample.

For both samples, "Affect" toward the preferred brand is a significant effect in their choice of the top preferred brand. This result is reported by both the MDA and MLR models and analyses. These results support part of H2 for both samples. However, affect toward the top preferred brand is not an effect in the BLR analyses of switching for both samples. Therefore, we reject H2 for the respondents' loyalty to their most preferred brand. Affect is not a predictor for respondents' choosing to stay with their top preferred brand or to switch to their second preferred brand.

H3: Respondents' favorable perceptions of a brand's attributes will be a significant effect in their brand knowledge, their brand preference and their loyalty to the preferred brand.

Our results from undertaking the analytical process for the PBC model shows that Brand Knowledge as a factor of brand attributes is consistent across the two samples (see Table 8.12). The Australia sample's factor of "Utilitarian Attributes" is very similar to the Chinese factor we call "utilitarian attributes". Additionally, the factor "experiential attributes" is reported by the China sample's current beer drinkers.

TABLE 8.12 Statements in the factor of attributes related to first brand preference

Australia sample	*China sample*
Utilitarian Attributes	**utilitarian attributes**
It has creative advertising.	It's good value for money.
It is always available.	It's always affordable.
It is good value for money.	It's very popular.
It is inexpensive compared to its	It's inexpensive compared with its
competitors.	competitors.
	experiential attributes
	It is refreshing.It has foam and nice color.

The Australia sample's factor, "Utilitarian Attributes", is reported to be the most influential factor that determines the respondents' top brand preference. However, both of the two factors we label "utilitarian attributes" and "experiential attributes" do not significantly predict top brand preference for the China sample. These results only partially support (Australia sample only) H3.

Only the current beer drinkers from our Australia sample are affected by their top preferred beer brand's "Utilitarian Attributes" when deciding whether to remain loyal to their top preferred brand. None of the factors labeled "utilitarian attributes" nor "experiential attributes" affect the switch or stay decision for respondents in our China sample. These results only partially support (again, Australian sample only) H3.

H4: Respondents' favorable perceptions of a brand's benefits will be a significant effect in their brand knowledge, their brand preference and their loyalty to the preferred brand.

Following our method in our Predict Brand Choice (PBC) model, the "Benefits" factor results in two sets of Brand Knowledge items. We call these "Physical Benefits" and "Emotional Benefits". Table 8.13 shows the statements for these two factors in our Brand Knowledge construct. The results also show the relative ranking of each factor in the Brand Knowledge construct for each sample.

Both the Brand Knowledge factors we call "emotional benefits" and the "physical benefits" are significant for identifying the top brand preference of the current beer drinkers in our China sample – these are significant in both MDA and MLR results (see Table 8.13). The "physical benefits" factor has a stronger effect than the "emotional benefits" for the China sample's beer drinkers. For the Australia sample, only the corresponding "Physical Benefits" factor significantly discriminates between the choice to stay or switch. This means that H4 is only partially supported.

Hypothesis 4 also proposed that the Brand Knowledge factor we label "Brand Benefits" would affect the respondents' decision to stay with or switch (brand loyalty/ equity measure) from their top preferred brand. In our PBC process, the BLR analysis

TABLE 8.13 Rank and statements in Benefits related to first brand preference

Australia sample	China sample
2nd Emotional Benefits	**6th emotional benefits**
It gives me energy and courage.	It gives me energy and courage.
It reduces my stress.	It reduces my stress.
It makes me enjoy and be satisfied.	It makes me feel cool.
It makes me sociable and lets me make friends easier.	
5th Physical Benefits	**5th physical benefits**
It does not get me fat.	It does not get me fat.
It is good for health.	It is good for health.
It is interesting and exciting.	It is interesting and exciting.

component found the Brand Knowledge factor of "Physical Benefits" (see Table 8.13 to see statements) to significantly affect the respondents' decision to stay or switch. However, no Brand Knowledge factor, including either form of "benefits" (Physical or Emotional), affected the Chinese sample's decision to stay loyal or to switch brands. As such, H4 is only partially supported. The effects of favorable perceived benefits in loyalty occurs only with the Australia sample of current beer drinkers.

The analyses presented in the PBC modeling process includes two sets of non-Brand Knowledge factors. We see these as correlates that need to be accounted for in analyses. The respondents' demographics are represented by age, gender and self-reported disposable income. The respondents' reported consumption (200 ml glasses in Australia and 330 ml bottles in China that we converted to 200 ml to enable comparison) of beer, and their visits to the venue (University of Western Australia tavern or China Agricultural University restaurant) over the last seven days serve as factors of use frequency.

Using BLR analyses, a number of these factors are found to be effects in the respondents' top brand preference for both samples. For the Australia sample, the respondents' "Gender" is a significant effect in their top brand preference. The respondents' "disposable income", "gender" and "bottles of beer consumed" in the last seven days are significant effects in our China sample's top brand preference.

The BLR analyses finds only the respondents' "disposable income" as an effect in the China sample's decision to stay or switch. However, that model does not provide a significant increase in accurate identification (22% vs. 25% necessary) to be considered significant.

Summary

This chapter provided the process necessary to determine whether the PBC model can accurately predict which respondents will stay loyal to their top preferred brand

and pay a premium for this loyalty, and which respondents will switch to their second preferred brand. We used demographic factors and factors that make up the respondents' Brand Knowledge construct about their top preferred brand of beer to perform these predictions. The analyses used MLR and BLR. Both these tests are very suitable to determine membership classification. By having classifications that reach and surpass the significance threshold (+125%), we can be confident that our predictions will hold.

Both MLR and BLR models for data from our Australia and China samples return very similar results. The results overall are positive. Our PBC model and modeling process can find and classify respondents to different groups with confidence. That means that PBC can predict who will stay loyal, and who will switch brands. This is a significant step forward in brand measurement and prediction.

Bibliography

Hair, Joseph F. Jr., Rolph E. Andersen, Ronald L. Tatham and William C. Black (2010), *Multivariate Data Analysis.* Upper Saddle-River, NJ: Pearson Education.

9

DISCUSSION OF RESULTS AND SUMMARY

Predictive Brand Choice model specification, testing and refinement

We developed the Predictive Brand Choice (PBC) model and documented the process in this book to help improve the process for measuring brand performance. This book provides details of the rationale underlying the PBC model. PBC uses data about customers' brand knowledge, demographics and product use to uncover their brand knowledge constructs for their most preferred brand in the category. Using this data, PBC provides a process to predict whether the customer will stay loyal to the brand, or switch to a cheaper competing brand. This competing brand is their second most preferred brand. This ability to predict, to model a result that provides a reliable discrimination between brands is a step forward in modeling customer brand choice. The great majority of previous models do not provide a way to use a customer's brand knowledge to discriminate between the customers preference for different brands in their buying repertoire. The remaining studies that we reviewed when developing our PBC model provided some discrimination for intentions to buy. So far, PBC appears to be the only model that can reliably use brand knowledge, demographics and product use frequencies to predict whether a customer will remain loyal to his or her favorite brand, or whether that consumer will switch to his or her second preferred brand when this less-preferred brand offers a discount. This prediction is the missing link that has long been a handicap in predicting the effect of brand knowledge on brand choice during purchase.

The PBC model offers other improvements over previous methods. We have presented PBC as a model, a process and a method. This improves the clarity of how to model the link between Brand Knowledge and Brand Equity. To do this, PBC uses factorial analysis to determine the existence of constructs that correspond to the Brand Knowledge theorized by Keller (1993) and Aaker (Aaker and Keller

1990). This provides specificity for the PBC model. To build the Brand Knowledge construct for PBC, we followed Keller's method of building questions and constructs from the ground up. This used a series of pre-tests to identify items associated with the brand knowledge for beer brands and purifying these with different samples of respondents through a series of tests.

We also include work from the NBD – Negative Binomial Distribution – models that help forecast and predict patterns of repurchase (Uncles et al. 1994). These models can predict for comparability of purchase patterns in different markets.

In order to increase the external validity of our Predictive Brand Choice (PBC) model, we test PBC with similar samples in the same product category, but in two different countries – Australia and China. Not only are there well-documented differences in culture, language and society between the markets of these countries, but the market for beer (our test product) also differs between the two countries. While the market is declining in Australia, beer consumption is growing in China. By choosing the same product, but in markets where the brand knowledge about beer and the reasons for drinking beer are very different, we can test for our model's ability to predict brand choice under different conditions. We expected predictions to be very accurate for the mature market (Australia) because of the higher level of brand knowledge about the product category (mature and declining market). PBC was expected to be less accurate at predicting in the China market where knowledge about the beer brands and category are not yet settled.

To improve and fine-tune the PBC modeling process, we model the data collected from the samples using multiple discriminant analysis (MDA) to see if PBC can correctly discriminate between respondents. These respondents had stated as their top preferred, second preferred and third preferred brands, brands of beer that were available for sale in the test venues. These venues were a university tavern in Australia and a university restaurant in China. Respondents in these venues selected different brand-combinations as their most, second and third preferred beers. Using these data, and data about their brand knowledge of their most preferred brand, we tried to predict their top, second and third most preferred brands by placing respondents into groups according to their named top preferred brand. PBC can accurately model this and discriminates with high degrees of accuracy for both the Australia and China samples.

To provide predictive power, that is to use brand knowledge, demographics and usage data to predict choice of brand, and to predict switching from the most preferred brand to second preferred brand, we used multinomial logistic regression (MLR) and binary logistic regression (BLR) analysis. We make post-hoc comparisons between these predictive methods and to fine-tune the PBC process.

The process for collecting data from customers/respondents uses only data collected at the point of purchase. This simplifies the data requirements to use the PBC model. Data can be collected at the point of sale using a relatively short survey. Unlike other predictive methods, no previous purchase (time series) data are required. We also only require a short survey that collects respondents' brand knowledge – this is only for their top preferred brand. This is a great improvement over previous methods with onerous data demands. The following paragraphs provide a detailed summary of our process.

Summary of findings from the PBC model development and testing process

The PBC model introduced in this book was developed with data that come from two samples of young (18- to 24-year-old) beer drinkers. These beer drinkers had consumed at least a 200 ml glass (Australia) or a 330 ml bottle of beer (China) in the last seven days. We recruited these participants for our field experiment for PBC from the University of Western Australia (Perth, Australia) and China Agricultural University (Beijing, China). We interviewed the Australia sample in the university tavern and the China sample in the university restaurant. These are places that students frequent to purchase and consume beer. Both venues serve meals.

As a part of their participation in the field experiment, respondents nominated their top, second and third preferred beer brands from the brands that were available for sale in the respective venues. They also answered a survey that sought to capture the existence, and possible effects of consumer beer brand knowledge in their beer preference and brand loyalty. Although we picked respondents using a predetermined random selection pattern, we only analyzed data from current drinkers – those who reported they had consumed at least a glass (Australia) or a bottle of beer (China) in the last seven days.

Using the data from current beer drinkers from our Australia and China samples, we found the PBC model could identify a construct that can be called Brand Knowledge for each sample. This used the samples' responses to questions about their perceptions of their top preferred beer brand. The statements ordered on quite similar factors in both samples, but the order of the factors was different (see Table 6.10).

Using the PBC modeling process, we found each sample's Brand Knowledge factors to have effects on their top preferred brand choice. The PBC process provided models that were a significant improvement in correctly identifying respondents' top preferred brand. There were some similar factors in the two samples' models. These similarities were factors we called "Affect" toward the brand, perceived "Physical Benefits", respondents' "Gender". These factors were shown to differ in their relative strength to affect the samples' preference and loyalty towards the brands of beer that were tested.

Finally, only two factors of the first preferred brand's knowledge were significant effects in explaining brand loyalty. These were factors we named "Physical Benefits" and "Utilitarian Attributes". These effects were only found in the Australian sample of beer drinkers.

Limitations

This study was always positioned as an exploratory study, particularly adding a second sample that introduced the potential confounds of culture and stage of the Product Life-Cycle. These confounds were added to test the robustness of the PBC model in different markets, although it was for the same product category. The category of beer has a long history of investigation by researchers but it is not clear whether similar products in other categories (e.g., cola) would be expected to have similar findings to those we have reported in this book. A program of research like that mounted by researchers in Signaling Theory would need to be conducted to see how consumers would respond to other products when modeled with the PBC model. The extent to which consumer beer choice is similar to other products would also require some further study. Perhaps the more subjectively based products would be most similar.

The issue of causality is an important consideration and the cross-sectional design prohibited the determination of the direction of the link between brand knowledge and brand equity in our study. Aaker (1991) argued that preference and use can reinforce and change what Keller would call the knowledge of a brand. Therefore, the direction of causality could be in both ways, or non-recursive as some previous research has suggested.

Comparison to previous research

The findings of our PBC model provided an empirical test of the effects of the "cognitive psychologists" views of brand knowledge, and its links with brand preference and brand loyalty behavior. These are two of several theoretical outcomes of Consumer-Based Brand-Equity (CBBE) (Aaker 1991). Essentially, we have managed to demonstrate a strong empirical link between the psychological and behavioral dimensions in the buyer choice process. We believe our link is stable, and the results are strong. We can also provide high levels of accuracy in prediction.

An Information Economics model of Brand Equity based on Signaling Theory has been replicated (e.g., Wang et al. 2008). This may provide a useful rough comparison to the findings we have derived from the PBC model. There are significant differences in the methods used by each modeling approach, so any comparisons must be viewed with caution. In particular, very large differences occur in the product categories, measures and models used. The Signaling Theory CBBE model was largely tested on products like financial services (credit cards, loans etc.). These categories have more objective criteria, and these criteria are assumed to be used by respondents when evaluating different brands.

Perhaps the easiest way to compare between the Signaling Theory CBBE model and PBC would be by comparing the models' ability to identify respondent preferences. This would be the measures of the models' accuracy of classifying respondents. While both models were able to identify respondent preferences among brands, our PBC model reported in this book provided a much higher hit rate (77% vs. 55–65%) for brand preference when tested using data from our Australia sample. It could also be argued that the ability to identify the respondents' top preferred beer brands in this research was more difficult than for previous work (Wang et al. 2007) because the brand shares were more difficult to identify. Choosing the top three brands would be more difficult than choosing brands with top and bottom shares in a category. Choosing the top three brands is also a more realistic test of the way customers make choices. Customers tend to habitually purchase within a brand field, this repertoire of several (three to five) brands tends to represent very close substitutes (e.g., top three brands in a category). Previous research that had respondents rate the top versus the bottom brand in a category seems unrealistic.

The types of perceptions tested in the two approaches were also quite different. The Signaling Theory approach arguably uses more objective or utilitarian perceptions in comparison to the very perceptual and subjective nature of brand knowledge tested by the PBC model. Obviously, much more research needs to be done to replicate these PBC findings on other samples, for example, by using a program similar to Erdem and Swait (1998; Erdem et al. 2006). Nonetheless, PBC has the ability of using present brand knowledge to model and correctly identify respondents' top preferred brand. The PBC model's results using data from our China sample of current beer drinkers achieve about the same "hit rate" (56.3%) as Wang et al. (2008) achieved on their Australian sample. Our PBC prediction for our Australia sample far surpasses Wang et al.'s hit rate. This shows quite strong performance where the application of PBC with the weakest results matches the best results achieved by other researchers.

No previous research had tested the brand equity output with actual behavior. The Predictive Brand Choice model that measures and links Brand Knowledge to Brand Equity was able to provide a 67.5% "hit rate" of the Australia respondents stay versus switch choice – the hit rate is the percent correct identification. This hit rate may be understood as being a prediction of which customers will stay with their top preferred brand and which will switch to their lesser preferred brands. The Chinese sample had a 67.1% correct classification, but fell a bit short (22% vs. 25% necessary) for a significant improvement over informed "chance".

Conclusion

The psychological based approach to CBBE ranges from models that reflected a multi-attribute model similar to the Theory of Planned Behavior (Park and Srinivasan, 1994), to Lambert's (2008) model that looked at three- and four-year-olds' brand knowledge for fast-food restaurants. There is a surprising diversity of measures and models compared to the Information Economics literature with Signaling Theory.

The most similar approach to the PBC model described in this book is the Lambert (2008) study; even though the PBC tested products (fast-food vs. beer) and samples of respondents (three- and four-year-olds vs. 18- to 24-year-olds) were quite different. Both Lambert's (2008) model and PBC have similar constructs and model of Brand Knowledge linking to Brand Equity.

While Lambert (2008) found some evidence of brand awareness being influential in Brand Equity (preference and loyalty factors), awareness was so unanimous that she could not use this factor to discriminate between her respondents' brand choices. While brand image and affect toward the brand were significant effects in beer brand knowledge, the lack of competing brands' imagery and affect were strong effects in young children's preference and loyalty for a meal at a fast food restaurant. Clearly, the effects of the product studied and the sample used are significant factors and should be addressed in future research.

The previous two studies that looked at beer (Krishnan 1996; Rajh et al. 2003) would seem to provide an opportunity to look at competing psychological based CBBE models for the same product. There were big differences between these two, and certainly different from the PBC model we presented in this book.

The lack of an actual choice is common in the previous literature using the psychological approach to model Brand Knowledge. The closest to actual behavior may be the discrete choice used by researchers in Signaling Theory (e.g. Erdem et al. 2006). However, beer drinkers actually received and consumed the brands tested in the PBC interview process (in the loyalty experiment). PBC's ability to test actual behavior and obtain very good discrimination between the brands being considered; especially in the Australian sample, provides a contribution for marketers.

It is also useful to find that the best discrimination was obtained with respondents' top preferred brand. This would expedite the data collection process and reduce respondent fatigue. In commercial practice, this would significantly reduce costs. Perhaps consumers tend to think of their top preferred brand but none or few of the other brands.

The level of accuracy achieved with the PBC model is similar to the best results from Theory of Planned Behavior (TPB) tests (East 1997). This would suggest that the very extensive TPB method with many more measures may not be as accurate when applied to outcomes like preference and loyalty, and products with very subjective perceptions of the product. Obviously, more investigation on these comparisons may be a useful area for further research.

Comparisons of the responses of our two samples (Australia vs. China) must be speculative until further research. However, the general model of Brand Knowledge to Brand Equity appeared to be similar in the two samples. One would expect the importance of Brand Knowledge components to differ between most samples, but the same factors tended to be present in both samples' Brand Knowledge. While it would be expected that the effects of culture may be large, an objective factor like "disposable income" is not an unsurprising element in the Chinese sample's Brand Equity. This may be at least partially due to the developing nature of the Chinese economy and wealth of the student population sampled.

One would also expect some product usage effects in the factors that were linked to Brand Equity in each sample. The Australia sample is consuming more volume (adjusting for a 200 ml glass vs. a 330 ml bottle), more alcohol and more often. This may be partially due to the Product Life Cycle of beer in each sample, or the drinking culture of Australia. Perhaps even these two factors are mutually affected by the Product Life Cycle. How much does use versus culture explain differences? This must be largely conjecture until further research can more adequately compare the findings of this study.

In summary, this research provides more empirical support for the Lambert et al. (2009) model of Brand Knowledge. This model posits that Brand Knowledge leads to Brand Equity. Brand Knowledge may be also affected by Brand Equity as others (Aaker 1991) have argued. The very subjective nature of the factors of Brand Knowledge in both this and the Lambert et al. (2009) model were effectively accounted for in generating very accurate discrimination and possible future prediction. This will hopefully be useful for those researchers that need just a few accurate measures that are rapidly completed.

Bibliography

Aaker, David A. (1991), *Managing Brand Equity: Capitalizing on the Value of a Brand Name.* New York: Free Press.

Aaker, David A. and Kevin Lane Keller (1990), "Consumer Evaluations of Brand Extensions", *Journal of Marketing*, 54 (1), 27–41.

East, Robert (1997), Consumer Behaviour – Advances and Applications in Marketing Essex, England: Prentice Hall Press.

Erdem, Tulin and Joffre Swait (1998), "Brand Equity as a Signaling Phenomenon", *Journal of Consumer Psychology*, 7 (2), 131–57.

Erdem, Tulin, Joffre Swait and Ana Valenzuela (2006), "Brands as Signals: A Cross-Country Validation Study", *Journal of Marketing*, 70 (1), 34.

Keller, Kevin Lane (1993), "Conceptualizing, Measuring, and Managing Customer-Based Brand Equity", *Journal of Marketing*, 57 (1), 1–22.

Krishnan, Shanker H. (1996), "Characteristics of Memory Associations: A Consumer-Based Brand Equity Perspective", *International Journal of Research in Marketing*, 13 (4), 389.

Lambert, Claire (2008), "Young Children's Fast Food Brand Knowledge, Preference and Equity", The University of Western Australia.

Lambert, Claire, Dick Mizerski and Doina Olaru (2009), "Young Children's Fast Food Knowledge and Preference", in Society for Marketing Advances 2009 Conference. New Orleans.

Park, Chan Su and V. Srinivasan (1994), "A Survey-Based Method for Measuring and Understanding Brand", *Journal of Marketing Research*, 31 (2), 271–89.

Rajh, Edo, Tihomir Vranesevic and Davor Tolic (2003), "Croatian Food Industry-Brand Equity in Selected Product Categories", *British Food Journal*, 105 (4/5), 263.

Uncles, M. D., K. A. Hammond, A. S. C. Ehrenberg and R. E. Davis (1994), "A Replication Study of Two Brand-Loyalty Measures", *European Journal of Operational Research*, 76 (2), 375–84.

Wang, Haizhong, Yujie Wei and Chunling Yu (2008), "Global Brand Equity Model: Combining Customer-Based With Product-Market Outcome Approaches", *Journal of Product & Brand Management*, 17 (5), 305–16.

Wang, Paul, Constantinos Menictas and Jordan Louviere (2007), "Comparing Structural Equation Models with Discrete Choice Experiments for Modelling Brand Equity and Predicting Brand Choices", *Australian Marketing Journal*, 15 (2), 12–25.

10

WORKSHOP

Predictive Brand Choice (PBC) work process

This chapter serves as an extension to the previous chapters to provide a workshop for the processes linked to the Predictive Brand Choice (PBC) model. The different steps laid out in this chapter help readers who are interested in undertaking the process work through our steps and logic.

Creating and measuring brand equity

This chapter defines and demonstrates a way to create Brand Knowledge and to link it empirically to Brand Preference. Brand Preference is the decision made by a customer to choose one brand over another brand. This preference for purchase is the cornerstone for building Brand Equity. In introducing the PBC brand measurement process, we will also touch upon the brand building process – this will help researchers understand brands better, leading to building better measurement models. In doing this, we will describe an empirical process in PBC for identifying, defining and measuring Brand Knowledge. Brand Knowledge is then used to predict Brand Preference.

The PBC process described here appears to be among the first to empirically demonstrate that Brand Preference can be predicted using Brand Knowledge. Until now, the literature appears to provide fuzzy associative models that link the two constructs. This may be due to this cognate area lacking a dominant theory to measure Brand Equity. This has led to the adoption of many different, and sometimes dubious and unsupported, methods aimed at creating Brand Preference.

This chapter is designed with worksheets to help readers work through the Brand Knowledge creation process. We also present methods to measure Brand Knowledge and to predict its effects on Brand Preference. This format gives readers the chance to "workshop" this method using data that they may possess or that are available from the Authors. A good way to begin understanding this analysis methodology is to revisit the different components of branding that are linked to Brand Equity (BE).

The way Brand Knowledge is created

Brand Equity metrics are measurements that seek to quantify the value of a brand. These evaluate its dimensionality. A brand's dimensions form nodes of Brand Knowledge in consumers' minds that help them ascribe meaning to a brand. Together, Brand Knowledge (BK) and Brand Meaning can be used to predict Brand Preference, and ultimately to predict Brand Choice during purchase. This continuum of brand effects (Knowledge–Meaning–Preference–Choice) is crucial to building successful and profitable brands; the most successful brand in a market is the one that is purchased (chosen) the most often by consumers (Aaker and Biel 1993; Keller 2001; Uncles et al. 2003).

A brand is an attitudinal construct (Uncles et al. 2003). It lives in people's minds and exists as a perception of value (Aaker 1991). This value is represented by what the brand stands for (a promise), and the way a consumer derives a benefit from this promise. An attitude towards a brand results from the brand owner's efforts to communicate its meaning and value through formal marketing communication channels (MARCOMS). Attitude towards a brand may equally be influenced informally through socialization towards the brand by significant others (e.g., in a family or school setting), exposure to the brand through mediums like word-of-mouth (e.g., discussion or recommendations), by associating with the brand's users (e.g., getting a ride on a BMW motorcycle), and through incidental exposure (e.g., coming across a brand when surfing the internet).

Socialization and exposure to a brand

A brand is attitudinal and perceptual in nature. These properties make it difficult to accurately quantify a brand's value and meaning. Difficulty in measurement stems from the way an audience learns about a brand, doing so by interacting with brand information through the senses – sight, touch, smell, sounds and taste (Berger et al. 2007). These encounters with a brand serve to create nodes in a person's memory that stores the brand experience (Keller 1993). Over time, familiar sensory stimuli like an advertising jingle, particular shade of a color or a brand logo serve to "jog" or "prompt" a person's memory, eliciting recall of the brand and what it stands for. The measurement of the level and the meaning of this knowledge provides the bases for brand management and for building Brand Equity. We will present a hypothetical example to foster understanding of this brand-building process. This example draws on our understanding of the way brand knowledge is formed (Keller 1993), and how this knowledge translates into brand equity through preference for a brand at the time of purchase.

Brand-building process for a beer

Initial exposure

Little Al is exposed to the Tsingtao beer brand as a child by observing his father drinking Tsingtao beer at the dinner table. This exposure to the Tsingtao brand is registered as a node in the Little Al's memory that is associated with *Drink*.

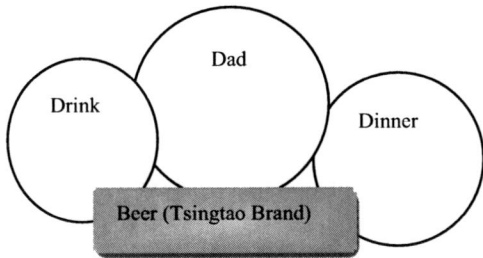

FIGURE 10.1 Formation of memory nodes through mere exposure

At this stage, the brand name may not be explicitly registered in the child's memory node because of his limited power of comprehension; the child perceives the beer as being a *Drink*. This memory is connected to two other nodes, *Dad* and *Dinner* (see Figure 10.1). In this case, Dad takes a salient position in the child's memory because of Dad's relative influence on Al's life. Little Al may perceive Tsingtao as being a green bottle at the dinner table. Over time, this linkage tends to strengthen because of repeated exposure to Dad drinking from this green bottle during dinner.

Making sense of a brand through MARCOMS

Over time the child is exposed to more diverse messages from the Tsingtao brand. Some of these are in the form of Tsingtao's advertising and promotional efforts (e.g. bottle opener premium). Little Al will be more likely to take notice of these MARCOMS (marketing communications) because he is familiar with the brand's logo or the shape-color of the Tsingtao bottle. This familiarity has developed through mere exposure (Zajonc and Markus 1982) to the beer brand drunk by Dad.

After many repeated exposures Tsingtao's MARCOMS, Little Al picks up different snippets of information about Tsingtao and begins to link these snippets together. These connections begin to form an "image" in the child's mind; Little Al is beginning to form Brand Image.

This ability to learn about a brand means that brand image is dynamic. This means that altering the information or the relationships between information about a brand can change a brand's image and along with it, a person's attitude towards a brand. This ability to build and change brand image is the foundation for brand building.

Returning to our example, let's say that exposure to Tsingtao's MARCOMS has led to the child associating Tsingtao with China (see Figure 10.2 – map). In the child's mind, the memory node containing China is also associated with Dad, who is also from China. This association is specific to Little Al. This suggests that a brand's image will be slightly different for each audience member. These slight individual differences account for the "fuzziness" around the edges of constructs when measuring Brand Image, Brand Knowledge and Brand Meaning.

By this time, Little Al has developed enough associations to call the brand *Tsingtao* – it is no longer the familiar green bottle at the dinner table. The child also begins to associate Tsingtao with the word beer because his exposure to a Tsingtao logo that contains the word beer (Figure 10.2 – red, green and yellow neon sign). In this case, the child has modified the construct of *Drink* to *Beer*. This shows that as the child becomes more knowledgeable about a brand, they are able to define it in more specific ways.

The Tsingtao logo also depicts a dragon, another element that that the child associates with China. This cross referencing of memory nodes creates an association in the child's mind that serves to strengthen their knowledge about the Tsingtao brand.

At home, Dad has a Tsingtao bottle opener. This brand premium has the Tsingtao logo and the word Beer. The child associates this with Dad as he uses it to open his beer. This premium may help give the abstract idea of Tsingtao and beer a real life link, providing a concrete physical representation for Little Al. This helps because the child has not tasted Tsingtao beer. To the child, this may help to signify that the brand is "real".

As Figure 10.2 depicts, the child has added to their knowledge about the brand by forging new links between existing knowledge-nodes for the Tsingtao brand and nodes. These links were created through socialization and mere exposure that were developed through exposure to the brand's marketing communications –

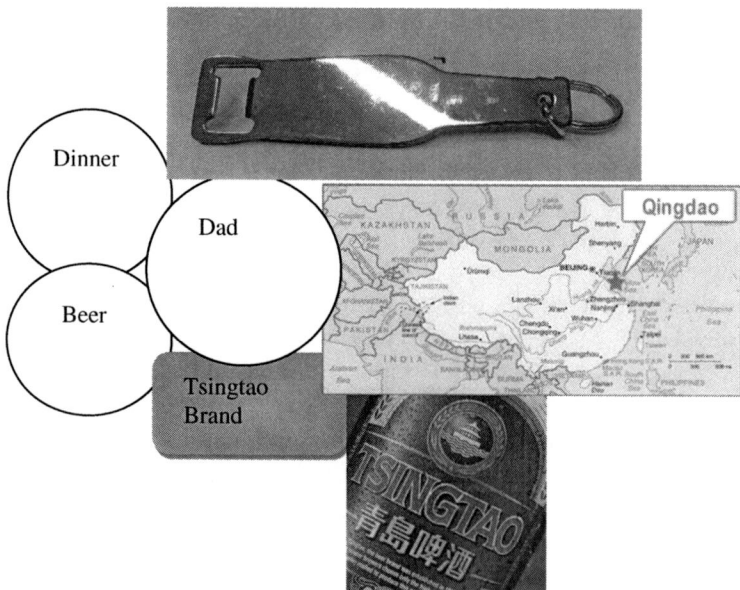

FIGURE 10.2 Dynamic learning about brand through MARCOMS

Source of graphics: Photographs by Jinchao Yang

*All product and company names are trademarks™ or registered® trademarks of their respective holders.

Use of them does not imply any affiliation with or endorsement by them.

MARCOMS. The child has added to and reorganized their understanding of their knowledge dimensions associated with the Tsingtao brand.

Formation of brand image

As the child grows and reaches adolescence, they will acquire more knowledge about Tsingtao. Chances are, more recently acquired knowledge will become more salient than previous knowledge, modify existing knowledge and strengthen the knowledge. The stronger memory imprint of more recent knowledge is an effect of the primacy and recency phenomenon, this is where people tend to remember more recent experiences, especially for knowledge areas that are still developing (Ebbinghaus 1913). Primacy and recency is a serial position effect in memory, where more recently encountered information is likely to be remembered more accurately. Therefore, this information would carry more weight in forming perception and understanding.

As Little Al reaches adolescence, he begins to comprehend more about the effects of beer. This comprehension results from complex interactions between the nodes of memory representing the Tsingtao brand, and associations with *use* contexts for the brand. By adolescence, the child has probably witnessed beer being used during celebratory dinners like weddings and birthdays. Beer is used to *Toast* people's health. This is likely to create the perception that beer is a healthy drink. This process describes the formation of a brand image – in this case a positive image of the Tsingtao brand that is associated with *Celebration* and *Health* (see Figure 10.3).

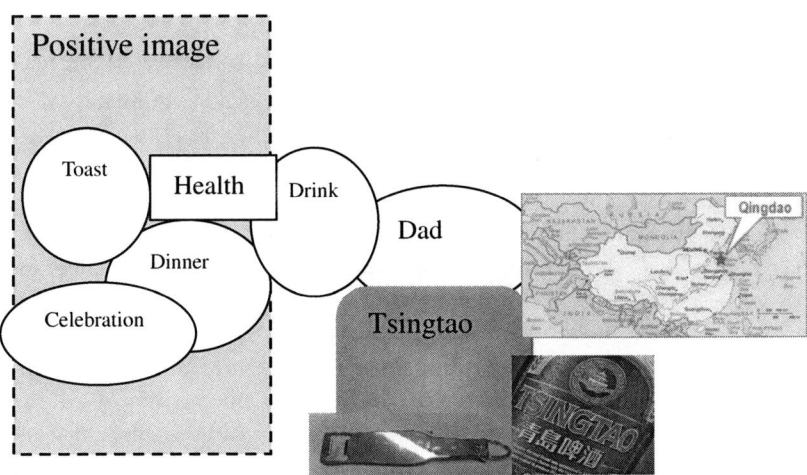

FIGURE 10.3 Formation of a positive image about beer

⋆All product and company names are trademarks™ or registered® trademarks of their respective holders.

Use of them does not imply any affiliation with or endorsement by them.

Formation of brand preference

Through exposure to MARCOMS, socialization and by mere exposure to the brand, Adolescent Al will have picked up that there are different brands of beer. These are organized as "chunks" in his memory. The way consumers organize and represent brand information has been an enduring topic in marketing research. However, the ability of consumers to complete "top-box" recall tests supports the notion of chunking. Top-box recall tests are where consumers respond by naming brands for a product category (Mayer and Anderson 1991). For example, when asked to name three brands of beer – the adolescent may answer:

(1) Tsingtao
(2) Snow Beer
(3) Yanjing

It is widely believed that the first named brand, the top-box brand, is the brand that is the most memorable to the person. In this case, Tsingtao is Adolescent Al's top ranked brand for the beer category. In more academic terms, the first named brand tends to be regarded as having the highest level of brand recall (top of mind recall) and is regarded as being having the highest level of salience in memory (Keller 1991).

Consumers' ability to provide top-box recall scores is thought to result from the way the human brain stores and files information (Alba and Chattopadhyay 1986). The brain tends to group "chunks" of information under categories – e.g., beer brands. The ranking of different brands in a category tends to develop over time and appears to have some positive correlation with the "share of voice" and recency of MARCOMS; more recently advertised brands and those with more advertising tend to perform better in top-box recall tests (Ng and Houston 2009).

When forming brand image, Adolescent Al can form either positive or negative images of groups of brands. The directionality of perceived brand image will affect his preference, for example, for certain brands of beer. There is also likely to be a third category of brands that Adolescent Al is aware of but is neutral about – these brands are likely to be brands that have little salience to Adolescent Al.

In Figure 10.4, we have depicted the salient brands as preferred versus not preferred brands. In our example, Adolescent Al is patriotic and prefers locally produced beers. In forming this preference, the adolescent has drawn upon other more deeply rooted belief schemas (e.g., patriotism) that he may associate with the constructs of *Dad* and *China* from earlier encounters with the Tsingtao beer brand. This suggests that brand preference or dislike of a brand may be contingent on more general psychological schemas like personality and the things that people hold salient (Alba and Chattopadhyay 1986; Ng and Houston 2009). This theory suggests that brand preference may be affected by elements other than MARCOMS and socialization. There appears to be some truth about the ability of deeper psychological schemas to affect brand preference – many brands find success by using MARCOMS that are salient with their target markets. These messages are necessarily contextually and temporally appropriate for specific consumer groups – this

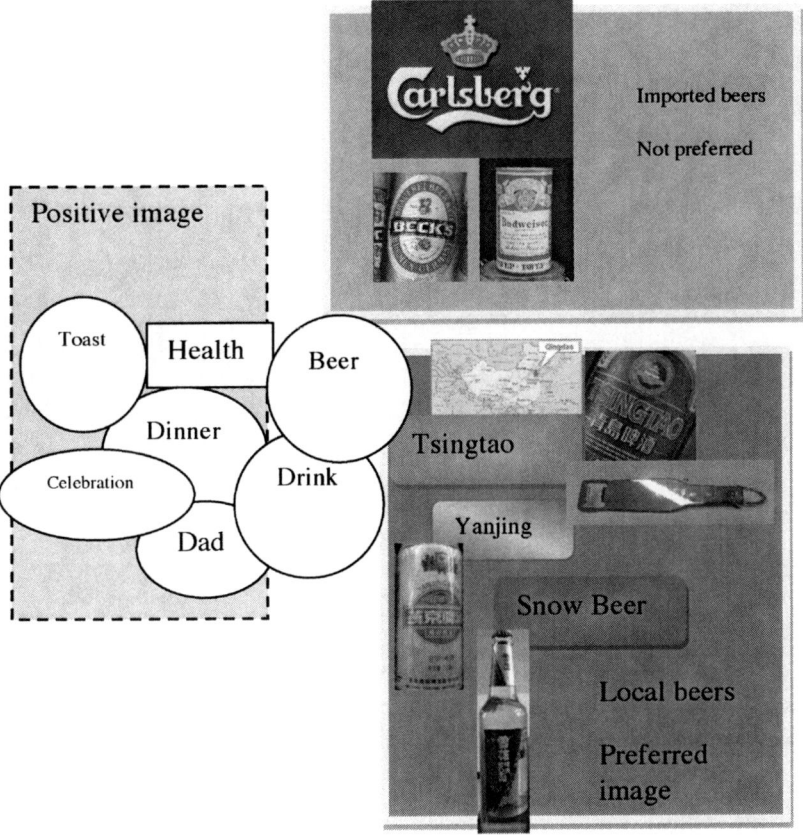

FIGURE 10.4 Formation of a preference for brands

Images by Jinchao Yang

★All product and company names are trademarks™ or registered® trademarks of their respective holders.

Use of them does not imply any affiliation with or endorsement by them.

means that these messages must appeal to the deeper collective psychological schemas that are common to these groups (e.g., some people like excitement, others value health etc.).

Most preferred brand in brand field

As Adolescent Al becomes Teenager Al, the opportunity to try beer presents itself. If Teenager Al does not buy the beer at the initial trial, he will likely drink whatever brands are available; for example, when offered by friends. The opportunity to purchase beer may arise after the initial trial. This opportunity to purchase "jogs" the teenager's memory about brand imagery and preference. If their preferred brand is available and accessible (i.e., not too expensive), there is high probability that Teenager Al will buy his preferred brand. This is when brand preference results in brand

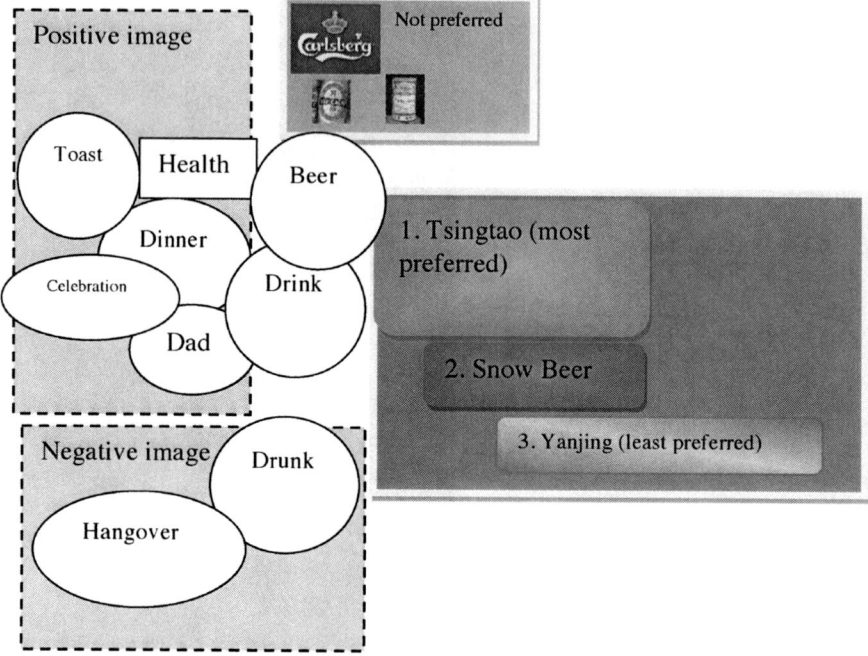

FIGURE 10.5 Formation of most preferred brand and brand field

★All product and company names are trademarks™ or registered® trademarks of their respective holders.

Use of them does not imply any affiliation with or endorsement by them.

choice (see Figure 10.5). The brand that is chosen most often is the brand that has the highest level of "Brand Equity" with the buyer/user.

Reinforcement of brand choice

With trial, the teenager may arrive at a conclusion that the beer met their expectations (i.e., the brand fulfilled its promise). A brand that delivers on its promise to the consumer will likely be bought again. Continued purchase tends to positively reinforce the brand's position and image for Teenager Al. After a period of use, he may indicate that Tsingtao is his "favorite" brand. Favorite brands tend to be preferred brands. This means that the brand has a better chance to be purchased more often, and in larger quantities. When this preference for a brand leads to choosing the brand more often during purchase occasions, "brand loyalty" occurs. In marketing and brand building, regular purchase behavior and strong brand preference is strong evidence of Brand Equity.

Purchase patterns where brands are regularly bought and are bought regardless of market changes (e.g., changes to price or promotions or other competitive actions) appear to parallel behavioral buying patterns. This type of purchase pattern may be thought of as being habitual buying (Ehrenberg 1988). In habitual buying situations, a buyer tends to buy from a narrow field of a few brands (brand field). They will predominantly buy the brands in this field, but tend to have a clear preference for buying one of the brands. This situation is depicted in Figure 10.5 where Tsingtao is the most preferred (favorite) and most bought brand, Snow Beer is second, and the Yanjing brand is the third preferred brand of beer in Teenager Al's brand field.

Trial of a brand may also result in negative reinforcement for the consumer. This happens when the brand does not live up to its promise, or when the trial results in negative consequences (e.g., getting drunk, sick and having a hangover). In this case, trial creates negative associations with the beer product class. If the negative associations are strong enough, the consumer may not try the product any more. This leads to a negative effect on brand equity.

The next section of this workshop chapter formalizes the constructs that we have discussed and provides a method of testing brand knowledge and equity. We begin by looking at a way for building Brand Knowledge and lead into turning Brand Knowledge into Brand Equity.

Building BK and BE

From the example for Al and Tsingtao branded beer, it appears that brands are a type of "shorthand". Brands act as a "placeholder" that makes it easier for people to understand product markets. A brand acts like a search-word on an electronic database. Access to this word "activates" memory nodes that are formed by the brand's advertising messages the consumer is aware of and the consumer's experiences with brand. These memory/knowledge nodes act like files that the brain can read and use to understand abstract schemas. Depending on which nodes are activated, the brain links the nodes to arrive at a meaning for the brand. Therefore, it is important to convey and represent your brand in a manner that creates the desired meaning in customers' minds. The following are steps for building a construct that can be called Brand Knowledge:

1. Define your brand's positioning – best to use singular position

Brands can be positioned, repositioned or de-positioned. Brand positioning is a process instigated by the firm that owns the brand. It seeks to create an identity or image for the brand in the minds of the brand's target audience. Repositioning seeks to change the brand's identity relative to competitor brands. De-positioning is a process that seeks to change the identity of competing brands relative to the firm's own brand.

While we have used the terms product and brand interchangeably, products and brands have different positioning processes.

Process for creating a brand position

This process for creating a brand position is founded on the notion of strategic differentiation. It is a process that seeks to avoid mediocrity, to communicate the distinctiveness of your brand from the competition. One way for achieving this is by:

Articulating your brand's own positioning – write in one sentence of less than 10 words, what your brand stands for to the customer. Use only one position. Generally, brands use these positions:

Symbolic – enhance user's image, ego identification, belongingness, meaningful in a social sense, affect – the brand promises that using it will lead to fulfillment of self or social needs.

Utilitarian – solve problem, provide desired benefit – the brand promises that its products will provide a desired function to solve customer's problem.

Experiential – sensory or cognitive simulation – the brand promises to stimulate the senses or provide a function that will create good or bad feelings (e.g., the Disney brand).

Identifying your firm's most direct competition – This deals with strategic group analysis. Essentially, if a competing brand can be substituted for your brand, it is considered to be in head-on competition with your brand. List these direct competitors and group them according to the sub-markets serviced by your brand.

List the basis of differentiation for each direct competitor – This step lists the strategic positioning of each competitor brand. Sometimes, there may be groups of competitors that occupy a specific differentiation position – e.g., three competitors with "cheap" positioning, six with "best service" positioning, four with "everyday low price" positioning etc. If this is the case, then it is best to group these competitors strategically.

Compare to competition to identify viable differentiation position – find a defendable position in each sub-market that fits your firm's capabilities. Remember, your brand position is linked to deliverables. If you cannot deliver what you promise in your brand position, then your branding has failed – e.g., cannot deliver cheaper goods if brand positioning is cheapest in the market.

Develop positioning statement – this entails developing a consistent brand positioning statement based on your intended differentiated position. This statement will influence all the key messages your firm releases in relation to the brand. This position will ultimately affect the types of value propositions that your firm associates with products that carry the brand.

Strategic group analysis may be modified to identify groups of brands by their promise. Figure 10.6 is an example of a hypothetical analysis of the Chinese Beer Market.

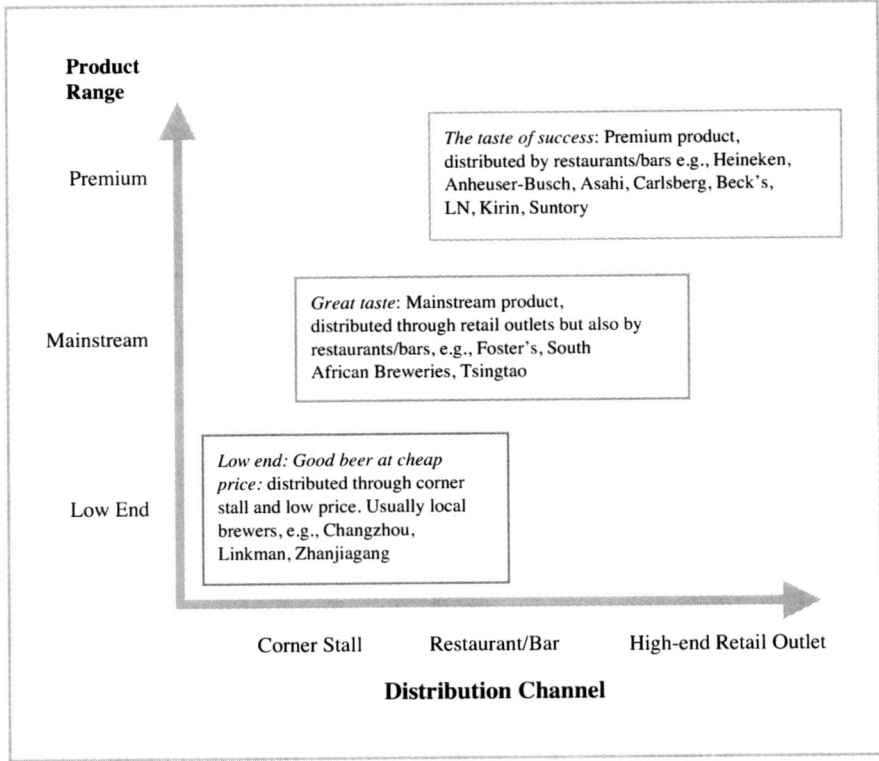

Product Range

Premium

The taste of success: Premium product, distributed by restaurants/bars e.g., Heineken, Anheuser-Busch, Asahi, Carlsberg, Beck's, LN, Kirin, Suntory

Mainstream

Great taste: Mainstream product, distributed through retail outlets but also by restaurants/bars, e.g., Foster's, South African Breweries, Tsingtao

Low End

Low end: Good beer at cheap price: distributed through corner stall and low price. Usually local brewers, e.g., Changzhou, Linkman, Zhanjiagang

Corner Stall   Restaurant/Bar   High-end Retail Outlet

Distribution Channel

FIGURE 10.6 Strategic group analysis of beer brands in China

We have provided a worksheet related to the points discussed. This worksheet helps you make notes to position your brand.

Worksheet 10.1 Brand positioning		
I	Brand's position in 10 words or less – choose 1 positioning + 1 promise	
II	Most direct competitors are: (list names of each competing brand that can substitute for your brand)	
III	Group most direct competitors by their positioning promise:	Group 1 Group 2 Group 3 Group n
IV V	How does my position compare with these competitor groups? How do I change my brand positioning statement?	Current brand position statement (see I): Repositioned statement:

Process for creating a product position

While we depict three hypothetical positioning segments in Figure 10.6 and in worksheet 10.1, it is likely that most markets will have more than three distinct brand positions. In practice, it is useful to identify distinct and strongly defined market segments for your product market. Note that the segments are likely to differ for each market (e.g., Australia versus China) where you operate.

Returning to the context of our worksheet, if our company is Tsingtao, then we will further break the mainstream segment into subsets of beers (product lines) – a way to categorize these subsets is according to the beers' brand positioning statements. By breaking individual market segments down to product lines, we are performing the product positioning process. A product line is a "variation" of the product – usually also called a stock-keeping unit (SKU); for example – 560 ml bottles, 330 ml cans of Tsingtao branded beer are two separate product lines. Note that when grouping products, most product lines are designed for specific markets. Figure 10.5 shows the segmentation for the China beer market. This market has premium, mainstream and low end segments. It follows that each of these markets are serviced by specific types of distribution outlets (see Figure 10.6). For example, premium beer is sold in high-end retail outlets, restaurant and bars. Low end beer is typically sold in corner stalls, some restaurants and bars. Whereas mainstream beers tend to be carried by all types of outlets. This shows that a brand's positioning is closely associated with where its products are sold – this means that a way for determining positioning in a market sub-segment is through the type of distribution channel that is used. Typically, the type of distribution outlet will also dictate the price that can be charged for a product.

The process to define product positioning in a sub-market is:

> *Define the market where the product carrying the brand will compete* – it helps to define the sub-market by articulating the profile of the target buyer. For example, the buyer buys this beer to impress friends and guests at high end restaurants. Alternatively, the buyer buys this beer from the corner store near their home to consume at home.
>
> *Articulate the attributes that define that sub-market* – these are the motivators for buyers within a sub-market. For example, Chinese alcohol buyers who buy beer for business entertainment tend to choose the most expensive beer available, and will buy large quantities. This is driven by the notion of being a good host, and the notion of having "face". It helps to have some market research that can describe reasons for purchase.
>
> *Determine top-box recall for each branded product in the sub-market* – work out the product's share-of-mind for consumers in the sub-market. Does the brand's share-of-mind correspond with advertising and promotional expenditures? This gives insight into the brand's equity.

What is the relative position of each product in the sub-market – a useful tool to determine relative brand positioning is multiple discriminant analysis. Each sub-market will have a preferred combination of product attributes – this is called the *Ideal Vector* of attributes. This is a line that rises at a 45-degree angle left to right in the perceptual map of brand positions. This perceptual map can be generated by most software that is capable of multiple discriminant analysis. Theoretically, the brand that best fits the Ideal Vector will be the most successful over the long-run. Therefore, examine the position of your product against the Ideal Vector.

Figure 10.7 is a perceptual map generated with Multiple Discriminant Analysis (MDA) that shows beer brands from our hypothetical market in China. This perceptual map is drawn for the mainstream market. Because mainstream beers compete in

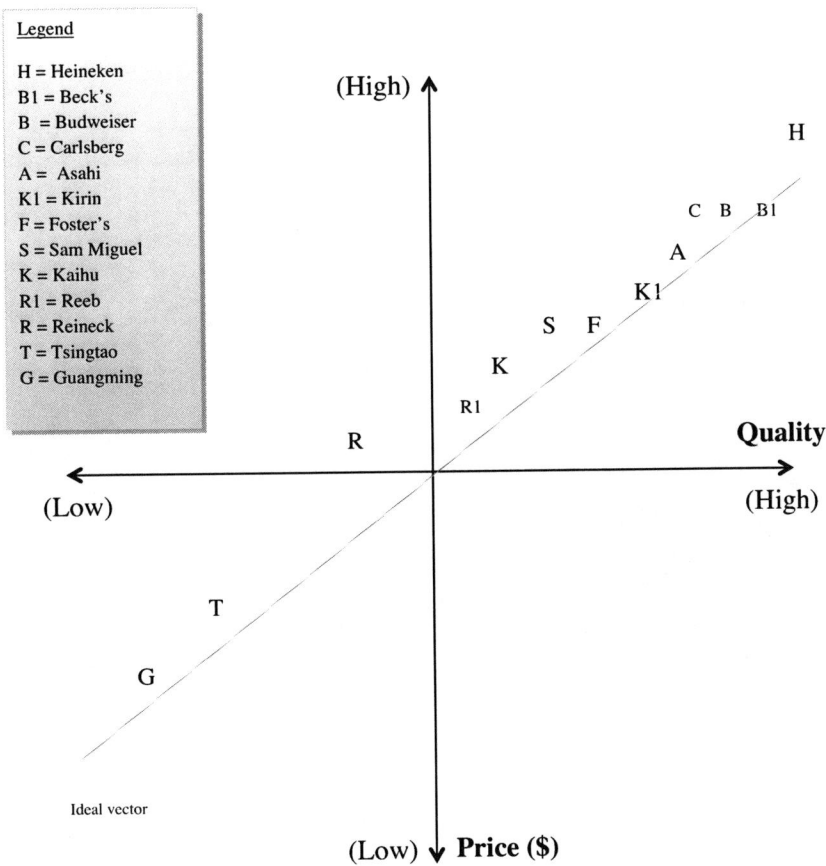

FIGURE 10.7 Positioning – perceptual map (price vs. quality)

some of the same markets (i.e., is distributed in through the same outlets) as premium and low-end beers, some premium and low-end brands appear in the map.

According to this perceptual map, consumers in China evaluate brands according to price and quality factors. The brands appear to cluster around a rather orderly positive slope. This slope is the Ideal Vector for this sub-market. It can be seen that successful brands tend to follow the vector quite closely. In Figure 10.7, the vector appears to be quite linear, representing a trade-off between price and quality (positively correlated). Beer brands in this market must be positioned to fit closely to the sloped line in order to succeed. If the brand's product is far away from the Ideal Vector, then that product is perceived by buyers to be either too expensive or too cheap for the quality obtained.

In order to work-out the type of competition faced by your brand in a sub-market, you may wish to define competition in the following manner (example of beer market) – Figure 10.8:

- *Generic competition:* other forms of indulgences that compete for the consumer's budget for beer.
- *Form competition:* beverages that can substitute for beer (e.g., carbonated drinks, juice etc.)
- *Product competition:* all brands of beer (premium, mainstream and low end)
- *Brand form competition:* the specific competition in your product's sub-market.

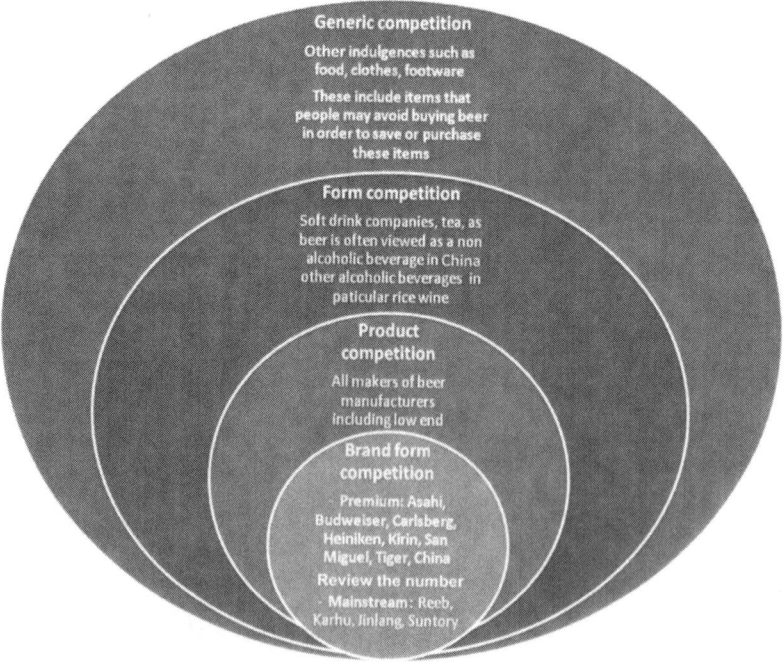

FIGURE 10.8 Different types of competition

Next is a worksheet for working through the product positioning process:

Worksheet 10.2 Product positioning process		
I	What are the characteristics of the market where the product carrying the brand competes? Market size, profitability, market boundaries, profile of target buyer, market head-room, intensity of competition.	
II	What are the buying motivations for the main buyer group in the market? If more than one, rank or weight.	
III	From market research, what is top box recall for brands in sub-market?	Brand 1 Brand 2 Brand 3 Your brand?
IV	Chart relative position of each brand in the sub-market. How well does your brand fit the Ideal Vector?	

2. Positioning statements – how to convey to market

The next step to build Brand Knowledge is to create a brand positioning statement that will be used to guide the firm's activities. The information we need is:

Worksheet 10.3 Positioning statements
I What business are we in? _____
II Who does my brand serve? _____
III What does my target market need/want when buying my brand? (2 things only) _____
IV Who are my competitors who give customers the identical things in III? (List closest competing brands) _____
V Why is my brand different from these competitors? (10 words) _____
VI What are the unique benefits that my brand's buyers derive from buying my brand and not the competitors' brands? _____
VII Is this unique selling proposition really unique? If not, redevelop and when happy, publish.

> • Statement must be clear and defensible – clear, concise, consistent and must have continuity.
> • Company must be able to deliver on promise in statement.
> • Should address III, V and VI.

3. Build awareness and brand recognition before the transaction

This next step of the brand building process is concerned with developing awareness of your brand in your target market. This seeks to create brand familiarity in your target audience. Ideally, the buyer will be familiar with your brand before they get to the checkout. Brand Recognition and Brand Familiarity is positively associated with the chance your product will be purchased (Campbell and Keller 2003; Pham et al. 2009), the more familiar your brand is, the more it is recognized, the more likely it will be bought.

Initially, word about your brand and its market position can be spread using MARCOMS. Advertising creates awareness. Editorials and other content intensive mediums can be used to facilitate a deeper understanding of your brand. If your brand is targeting the younger internet-web-able generation, then having the organizational ability to perform Search Engine Optimization (SOE), create and popularize apps and to monitor discussions on social media is crucial to getting noticed. We will not go into detail about media and mediums here. Interested readers should consult the many good sources of information about MARCOMS and IMC – integrated marketing communication.

One of the cheapest ways to create brand awareness is to use promotion – give something useful away for free. This item should have your brand's logo and should be connected with what your brand or product stands for. For example, a good tie-in would be a bottle opener as a free-gift with purchase of Tsingtao beer. A bad tie in would be a pen that has the Tsingtao logo.

4. Measure your efforts at building Brand Knowledge

We present a way to measure the effect of Brand Knowledge in Brand Equity that was developed by Lambert (2008) and tested on three- to four-year-old children's Brand Knowledge and Brand Equity of fast-food. Yang (2010) modified Lambert's model and used it to compare young people's beer Brand Knowledge and Brand Equity in China and Australia. This model posits Brand Knowledge as an antecedent of Brand Equity. The model is fully reflective and has five dimensions. Figure 10.9 depicts Lambert's BK-BE Model.

Yang (2010) uses the same structure for linking between Brand Knowledge and Brand Equity but test four slightly different dimensions. These are Brand Image, Brand Attitude, Brand Attributes and Brand Benefits (see Figure 10.10). These reflect the endogenous construct Brand Knowledge. Brand Knowledge leads to Brand Equity. In turn, Brand Equity is composed of Brand Preference and Brand Loyalty.

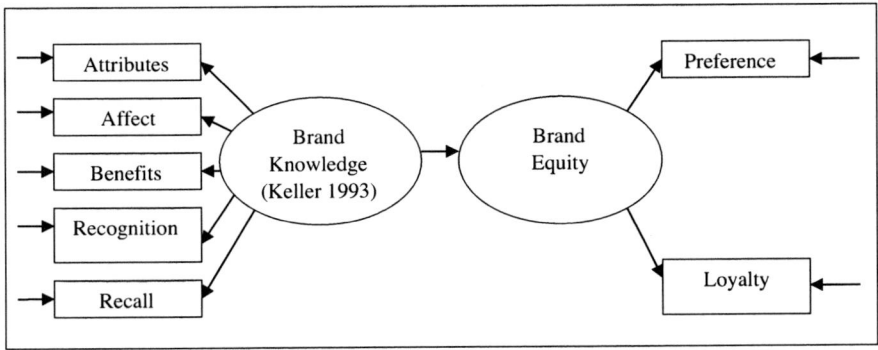

FIGURE 10.9 Adapted from Lambert BK–BE Model (2008)

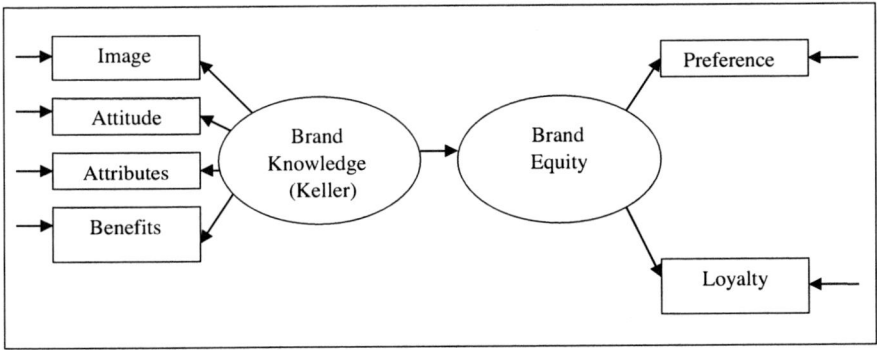

FIGURE 10.10 Adapted from Yang's BK–BE Model (2010)

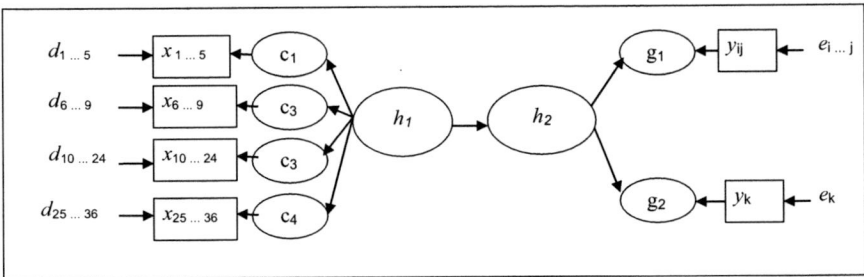

FIGURE 10.11 Formalized model for Yang's BK–BE model

We will use Yang's model as the example to workshop the process for measuring BK–BE. Therefore, it helps to more formally specify Yang's BK–BE Model.

Figure 10.11 depicts the formalized Yang BK–BE model. The associated explanations for the model are in Figure 10.12. The endogenous variables for Yang's model (Brand Knowledge) comprise four dimensions labeled ξ_1 to ξ_4.

Evaluative dimension		Measurement attribute
Endogenous construct	h_1	Brand knowledge
Exogenous construct	h_2	Brand equity
Errors	d	Endogenous measurement attribute ($x_{i\,to\,j}$) measurement error
	e	Exogenous measurement attribute ($g_{i\,to\,j}$) measurement error
c_1 Image	x_1	I feel prestigious.
	x_2	I feel cheerful.
	x_3	I feel elegant.
	x_4	I feel charming.
	x_5	I feel trendy.
c_2 Attitude	x_6	I like this brand.
	x_7	I like its taste.
	x_8	I am interested in this brand.
	x_9	This brand attracts me.
c_3 Attributes	x_{10}	It tastes good.
	x_{11}	It has good quality.
	x_{12}	It has foam and nice color.
	x_{13}	It's refreshing.
	x_{14}	It's suitable for celebration and party.
	x_{15}	It's suitable for men.
	x_{16}	It's (Chinese/Australian/any country of origin) beer.
	x_{17}	It supports the (country of origin) economy.
	x_{18}	It's very popular.
	x_{19}	It's always available.
	x_{20}	It's good value for money.
	x_{21}	It's inexpensive compared with competitors.
	x_{22}	It represents the (country of origin) identity.
	x_{23}	It has creative advertising.
	x_{24}	It can cool you down in hot weather.
c_4 Benefits	x_{25}	It makes me happier.
	x_{26}	It makes me feel cool.
	x_{27}	It reduces my stress.
	x_{28}	I enjoy and am satisfied with it.
	x_{29}	It gives me energy and courage.
	x_{30}	It improves my status.
	x_{31}	It makes me sociable and makes it easier for me to make friends.
	x_{32}	I get attention when I drink this beer.
	x_{33}	I use it to welcome guests warmly.
	x_{34}	It is good for health.
	x_{35}	It does not get me fat.
	x_{36}	It's an interesting and exciting beer.
g_{ij} Preference	$y_{1j,\,k\ldots ith}$	1st preferred brand, 2nd preferred brand and so on – for 1st beer
	$y_{2j,\,k\ldots ith}$	1st preferred brand, 2nd preferred brand and so on – for 2nd beer
g_k Loyalty	y_1	Did subject accept 2nd most preferred beer after price premium.

FIGURE 10.12 Evaluative dimensions for Yang's BK-BE model

Experiment and stimuli

Previous research into Brand Knowledge – Brand Equity has often used survey-based self-reports that sought to capture respondents' intended behaviors. As mentioned in Chapter 2, this research has often tested two or more categories. However, three of four cross-cultural studies used only one category, as did all the retail, sports, experimental, subscription markets and the Lambert study from which some theory and method is used. Given the complexity of studying the link between Brand Knowledge and Brand Equity and the unique use of an actual behavioral test of loyalty, it is more suitable to study the effects of Brand Knowledge in Brand Equity in one product category.

Sampling

Testing for the existence and effects of beer brand knowledge will use a sample of beer users. For much of the world, the heaviest users of beer are usually students enrolled in university (Toner-Schrader and Mizerski 1997). This group is also developing their brand knowledge about beer brands.

Field experiment data collection

Step 1 – determine whether beer consumers/buyers have a mental construct that we can model into a factorial construct that approximates Brand Knowledge.

Step 2 – if it is found that we can model a concept called Brand Knowledge from responses, then there will be tests for the association of the elements of Brand Knowledge (e.g., imagery, affect) with the respondents' equity toward their preferred beer.

Step 3 – Finally, their loyalty will be tested. Loyalty to the brand preferred will be tested by whether they will choose to stay with their preferred choice when tempted by a price-off of a second preferred brand of beer.

Predictor variables for stay or switch – uses both the respondent's initial brand preference, and their decision to stay or switch (loyalty). These are indicators of a brand's equity (Aaker 2003).

Incentives – actual beer is used as an incentive for the beer drinker's co-operation.

Pretests – this obtains individuals' rating of how they perceived brands in terms of the factors believed to make up the construct of brand knowledge (e.g., images, benefits). These factors would first be elicited from samples of buyers of beer that were similar to the sample used in the final survey and choice experiment using a series of pre-tests.

Interview – uses a choice experiment. We use the method to elicit brand knowledge, preference and loyalty developed by Lambert (2008) and reported used in Lambert et al. (2009).

The individuals in the sample are asked to rate the top three brands in the venue in terms of their preference for a beer. After they provide their first and second preference, they provide responses to questions about beer brand knowledge of their top two preferred brands of beer. They rate the top preferred brand first using the measures in Figure 10.11.

At the end of the survey, the respondents are told they can either have a 200 ml glass of their second preferred brand free, or pay a small fee (50% of the regular price for both samples) and get a 200 ml glass of their first preference. The respondents are told the beer was a "thank you" for their cooperation. This latter measure tests their loyalty in a situation where they would need to pay a premium to stay with their initially preferred brand (Netemeyer et al. 2004). This willingness to pay a premium is an important aspect of brand equity (Aaker 1991; Lambert 2008).

Data

After the survey is transcribed into an electronic database, the data should be cleaned and inspected for normality and for any non-random missing values. There are procedures in Hair et al. (2010) that are useful for accomplishing these tasks. Once the data reasonably satisfies data entry error checks, it can be used to model the link between Brand Knowledge and Brand Equity. This modeling process begins by understanding the data by undertaking these steps:

1. Descriptive profiling of respondents
2. Enumeration of subjects' drinking and venue patronage pattern using:

    a. descriptive statistics
    b. by fitting the predicted and actual drinking and venue patronage statistics by using a NBD (Negative Binomial Distribution) software

3. Enumeration of subjects' actual and predicted brand preference
4. Testing the dimensionality of the model

This modeling process adheres to the principles raised in the Occam's Razor Paradigm; our modeling simultaneously strives for parsimony and adequate levels of explanatory power.

1. Descriptive profiling of respondents

Description of a sample is useful towards helping to establish the validity of the sample. In many cases, a company may wish to measure the profiles of customers from two different markets (e.g., local and overseas customers). This measurement may yield perceptual differences towards a brand between customer groups. Figure 10.13 lists the descriptive statistics that are useful in this profiling process.

Item	Descriptive	Significance if more than one group
Age	Percentage	t–test
Gender	Percentage	t–test
Income	Median and modal	t–test
Amount of beer consumed (define a consuming unit, e.g., 200 ml glass).	Consuming units	t–test
Visits to drinking venue	Number of times visited	t–test

FIGURE 10.13 List of descriptive statistics used to profile sample

Note: To simplify analysis, an ANOVA may be used instead of multiple t-tests. However, the Anova cannot be interpreted for meaning unless we have specified a model to test drinking and demographics.

Worksheet 10.4 (next) is useful for documenting the results of a descriptive profile analysis:

Worksheet 10.4 Descriptive statistics used to profile sample		
Item	**Group 1**	**Group 2**
Age	(%)	(%)
Gender	(%)	(%)
Income	Median: Modal:	
Amount of beer consumed in last seven days (_____consuming unit).	units	units
Frequency of visits to drinking venue	times	times

Note: Indicate significant differences in cells using *

2. Enumeration of subjects' drinking and venue patronage pattern using NBD

To derive a fit between reported and expected patronage and the amount of beer drunk, it is useful to fit a Negative Binomial curve. The reported and expected statistics can be easily obtained using East's (1997) NBD software. This software provides a "fit" value that is very similar to the R-square statistic used in Multiple Regression.

By using purchase frequency and brand penetration, the NBD can model a consumer's decision about which brand to buy (e.g., Tsingtao or Yanjing Beer), the frequency that they buy the brand, the amount bought during each purchase occasion (e.g., do they buy one bottle of beer or a carton?), and the place of purchase. These four sub-processes of purchase are considered to be the only universal "law" of marketing that accurately describe the observed behavior of consumers with stationary choice patterns (regular users) in a stationary and stable market (*cf.* discussion and review of the Goodhardt et al. 1984 in Royal Statistical Society Journal by Bartholomew, D. J., Kemp, A. W., Sharot, T., Bloom, D., Jephcott, J. G., Cox, D. R., Bass, F., Buck, S. F., Ciggle, P. J., Jeuland, A., Phillips, F., Shoemaker, R. W., Wrigley, N., Dunn, R., and Zufryden, F. S.).

In many Western countries like Australia, the beer market is considered to be stationary. These markets are mature, stable and tightly controlled by industry players and by policy makers. The beer market's characteristics also meet the assumptions needed to use NBD modeling; alcohol purchase and use in the population is a well-defined industry that is distinguished by a specific use and benefit, it is a stable market in terms of the number of drinkers, the average frequency of repurchase of alcohol products is more than once a year, and repeat purchase rates fit the Poisson statistical distribution (East 1997).

Formally specifying NBD (East 1997):

$$p_r = (1 - m)/(m + k)^{-k}$$
Where:
k parameter is estimated from purchase frequency and penetration $(1 + x)^n$ are binomial
p_r is a negative binomial because the exponent is negative
m is mean population purchase rate
Using some algebraic transposition, calculating the NBD requires the solution to: $$1 - b = (1 + m/k)^{-k}$$ This gives us the parameter of k. The requirement for this are statistics on: 1. purchase frequency 2. penetration of product in the population

NBD can be used to ascertain the stage of the market life cycle. In mature and stationary markets, the fit values should be extremely good. Using the East (1997) software, expected and reported beer consumption can be compared. Worksheet 10.5 can be used to write down the NBD fit values:

Worksheet 10.5 NBD fit values			
	Expected	**Reported**	**Fit**
Group 1	Time 1 = 2 = 3 = 4 = 5 = 6 = 7 = n . . .	Time 1 = 2 = 3 = 4 = 5 = 6 = 7 = n . . .	

| Group 2 | Time
1 =
2 =
3 =
4 =
5 =
6 =
7 =
n . . . | Time
1 =
2 =
3 =
4 =
5 =
6 =
7 =
n . . . | |

This data can also be graphed using an electronic spreadsheet with graphing functions (e.g., MS Excel). Graphing provides readers with a visual representation of how well the reported data and the expected data match. Modelers may wish to provide these graphs:

- Group 1 reported vs. expected patronage in last seven days
- Group 1 reported vs. expected amount drunk in last seven days
- Group 2 reported vs. expected patronage in last seven days
- Group 2 reported vs. expected amount drunk in last seven days

3. Enumeration of subjects' actual and predicted brand preference

The analysis of brand preference entails describing the relative share of each brand. Worksheet 10.6 can be used to document relative brand share for groups of consumers in different markets:

Worksheet 10.6 Stated brand preferences		
Brands	**% share**	**n**

Group 1
    y_1j_1
    y_1j_2
    y_1j_3		

Group 2
    y_2j_1
    y_2j_2
    y_2j_3		

Following this, the relative differences between those who chose to stay with their favorite brand and those who chose to switch to their second most preferred brand is estimated. Chi-square tests can be used to compare the relative differences between the top choices of beer brands between Groups 1 and 2. If 3 brands, then it the Chi-square test uses a 3×2 matrix, if four brands a 4×2

matrix, if 3 groups with two brands a 2 × 3 matrix and so on. This matrix will indicate the amount of brand loyalty to a brand. Brand loyalty equals brand equity in the market as it measures the number of times a customer will choose your brand over the competitors' brands. Worksheet 10.7 can be used to document chi-square differences.

Worksheet 10.7 Comparison of those who remained loyal to brand and those who chose to switch brands		
	Group 1 **% (n)**	**Group 2** **% (n)**
Stay		
Switch		
Total		
Difference between Stay & Switch × 2 significance		

4. Testing for dimensionality of model

The dimensionality of our Brand Knowledge model (endogenous construct h1) must be tested. This is because the dimensions of Brand Knowledge are expected to vary depending on the market, its life cycle stage and market characteristics. In a market like China where beer is a relatively new product, consumer knowledge of beer may not have "settled". This may affect the way beer brands are understood.

To explore the dimensionality of Brand Knowledge, the data collected for the exogenous variables $\chi 1$ to 36 from Figure 10.12 are analyzed using exploratory Factor Analysis. This is a multivariate technique that can be used to identify endogenous relationships from exogenous variables. In this case, the endogenous relationships form the Brand Knowledge (h1) and Brand Equity (h2) constructs, the exogenous variables are represented by the x (BK) and g (BE) measurement variables and their associated e (BK) and d (BE) errors. The use of Factor Analysis assumes that the data meets these assumptions:

- Data normality
- Adequate numbers of significant correlations among the variables
- Low values in Partial Correlations (Anti-image Correlation Matrix, Measure of Sampling Adequacy, Bartlett Test of Sphericity)
- Some underlying structure exists in the variables

Terminology for factor analysis

These are three tests that are essential for undertaking Exploratory Factor Analysis. The Anti-image Correlation Matrix can be obtained as a part of the post-hoc results of Factor analysis. This Matrix provides analysis of the partial-correlations among the variables that are entered into the factorial model. The Anti-image Correlation Matrix provides an inverse test of partial-correlations. This is a statistical technique where the correlation between two variables is calculated by taking into account the moderating effects of all other variables present. Hair et al. (1998) suggests that partial-correlations values should be small, otherwise, there are no "true" underlying factors in the data. Therefore, it is important to count the number of significant values in the Anti-image Correlation Matrix. Fewer than half of the correlations should be significant.

Bartlett's Test of Sphericity is a statistical test that is employed to identify the presence of between-variable correlations. Correlations between variables are important in factor analysis as these correlations help determine the factors (dimensions) of the factor solution. Bartlett's Test of Sphericity provides a significance test for the presence of at least some significant correlations among the variables. Therefore, a significant Bartlett's Test is desirable.

The Measure of Sampling adequacy (MSA) is used to quantify the degree of intercorrelations among the variables and assists in assessing the appropriateness of applying factor analysis. MSA values in excess of 0.5 are deemed adequate (with values above 0.8 considered excellent).

Deriving BK factor matrix

The endogenous factorial structure of Brand Knowledge can be identified using exploratory factor analysis. This analysis is normally done by modeling with a Varimax rotation and Kaiser Normalization. The Varimax rotational method is the most conservative method. Rotating the data will improve its "fit" to the model in a manner that results in more clearly defined factors. Kaiser Normalization is a statistical criterion that identifies the number of factors to be extracted by the factor modeling process; this criterion drops factors that have eigenvalues of less than 1. In many statistical packages such as SPSS, the implementation of the Kaiser criterion occurs as a result output called the Scree Plot. This is a graphical representation of the number of factors with eigenvalues more than 1 that are extracted by and retained in a factorial model.

Identifying and naming factors

The results generated in Factor Analysis should be organized for clarity. These results are normally organized as a list of factors, with each factor comprising of a mix of exogenous x variables. The output may look like this:

Factors (% variance explained) Measures	Measure loadings		Extracted factor loading
1. Images (12.3% variance explained)			
I feel prestigious.	.80		
I feel charming.	.79		
I feel trendy.	.78		.85
I feel elegant.	.78		
I feel cheerful.	.72		
2. Affect (11.6% variance explained)			
I like its taste.	.75		
It tastes good.	.65		.84
It makes me happier.	.63		
3. Utilitarian attribute (10.3% variance explained)			
It's good value for money.	.79		
It's always available.	.74		
It's very popular.	.66		.85
It's inexpensive compared with its competitors.	.64		
4. Experiential attributes (9.2% variance explained)			
It's refreshing.	.83		.80
It has foam and nice color.	.75		
5. Physical Benefits (9% variance explained)			
It does not get me fat.		.83	
It's good for health.		.73	.79
It's interesting and exciting.		.71	
6. Emotional benefits (8.5% variance explained)			
It gives me energy and courage.		.75	
It reduces my stress.		.75	.77
It makes me feel cool.		.62	
7. Country identity (8.2% variance explained)			
It is suitable for men.			.77
It is Chinese style beer.			.72 .80
It supports China's economy.			.66
Seven factors; explains 58% of the total variance; Cronbach's Alpha = 0.88			

FIGURE 10.14 Depiction of factorial loadings

Multiple loadings – During the analysis process, some x variables are expected to load on more than one factorial dimension. In presenting the results of exploratory, loadings of less than 0.6 are generally disregarded. The modeler is really interested in loadings that are in excess of 0.8. Factor loadings are a standardized score and range between 0 and 1, with 1 being a "perfect" loading. If the model is based on sound a-priori constructs and is specified correctly, then the loadings should be quite "clean" – this means that there will be very few variables that load across different factors.

Parsimony – Not all exogenous x variables are expected to load. This is a good thing as factor models are supposed to reduce the data, striving for parsimony in the factorial solution. This method attempts to provide the maximum amount of explanation by using the simplest model (Occam's Razor concept).

Naming factors – Each of the factors should be given a name that reflects the combination of the χ exogenous measures that have loaded on the factor. For example, the x variables for prestige, charming, elegant, trendy and cheerful loaded on a single factor. These were judged by the analyst to represent the construct of Brand Image. This process is repeated for each identified and retained factor in the analysis.

Extracted factor loadings – It is also common practice to derive extracted factor loadings. These extracted loadings can be found in the output of most factor analysis packages. Higher loadings (i.e., closer to 1.0) signify stronger factors.

How many factors? – As a rule of thumb, it is best to have between three and five factors. Each factor should optimally be comprised of five exogenous variables. However, many researchers will be satisfied if a small number of factors have only three exogenous variables – provided that the extracted factor loading is sufficiently high (0.7 and more). It is important not to include single variable factors in any factorial model.

Internal consistency – Cronbach's Alpha is a measure of internal consistency for the exogenous x measures. This is a test to see if the questions in a construct appear to measure the same phenomenon or the same component of a phenomenon. In other words, it tests for the reliability of the questions. Cronbach's Alpha can be derived using a separate test. Measures of internal consistency are normally reported for the factorial models as a whole.

Variance explained – The final statistic that is important is the "variance explained" statistic. This can be obtained from the factor analysis output. This statistic gives an indication of the "explanation power" that is similar to a R-square statistic in Multiple Linear Regression; it indicates the contribution of the questions that have loaded in the factorial model towards explaining the Brand Knowledge construct in our sample.

Figure 10.14 suggests that beer Brand Knowledge has seven dimensions. These are listed in their order of importance and have been labeled:

1. Image
2. Affect
3. Utilitarian Attributes
4. Experiential Attributes
5. Physical Benefits
6. Emotional Benefits
7. Country Identity

If there are multiple market segments (e.g., different countries, rural vs. urban, business vs. private consumer), then the factor analysis can be repeated for each segment and differences in perceptions of Brand Knowledge can be compared. Worksheet 10.8 (next) can be used to depict the results of your factor analysis:

Worksheet 10.8 Factor structure for Brand Knowledge								
Factors (% variance explained) Measures	**Measure loadings**							**Extracted factor loading**
Factor number	*1*	*2*	*3*	*4*	*5*	*6*	*7*	
Factor 1 (name):								
How many factors? total variance = % Cronbach's Alpha =								

5. Predicting brand preference

The ability to accurately predict brand preference is central to brand knowledge management. In turn, sensible management of a brand's image will contribute towards a firm's equity. What is unclear, and not discussed in the literature, is the way Brand Knowledge leads to Brand Preference and subsequently to Brand Choice (purchase). It is only through purchase that a brand enjoys increased equity. This section provides details of a procedure for using Brand Knowledge to predict Brand Choice. This methodology represents a way to empirically link Brand Knowledge and Brand Equity.

The MDA is used to predict Brand Choice. This is achieved by using the Brand Knowledge dimensions that are extracted from the factor analysis and using these dimensions to predict whether a customer will switch brands. This is achieved by calculating the relative share of brand preference among beer drinkers in a sample and by constructing a potency index to identify the salience of each Brand Knowledge dimension at predicting choice.

Using the Brand Knowledge factorial dimensions from Figure 10.14, beer Brand Knowledge is comprised of Image, Affect, Utilitarian Attributes, Experiential Attributes, Physical Benefits, Emotional Benefits and Country Identity. During the experiment, subjects were also asked to provide information about their:

- Disposable income
- Gender
- Age
- Number of bottles of beer consumed in the last seven days
- Number of visits to drinking outlet (restaurant) in the last seven days

These demographic and beer use/venue visit data will also be used to predict brand choice.

Assumptions to use MDA

The MDA uses a linear process to derive discriminating functions between different "dimensions" in the data. These functions seek to minimize the probability of misclassifying the first preferred brand that respondents' have stated. MDA tests can be found in most popular statistical software packages. To use MDA, the data must:

1. have multivariate normality
2. be homoscedastic (covariance matrices of independent variables across the groups of dependent variables are equal – use Box's M test)
3. be able to depict a linear relationship between independent and dependent variables

Classification of actual vs. preferred brands

Step 1 – classify first preferred brands

The subjects' most preferred brands can be identified by using simple counts. The three most popular brands are used as the basis for discrimination. From the MDA

	Tsingtao	Yanjing	Snow	Overall %
Actual choice	45.6%	35.4%	19%	37%[1]
MDA predicted choice	48.6%	51.8%	63.3%	52.5%[3]
MDA predicted choice minus Actual choice	3%	16.4%	44.3%	15.5%
Improvement[2]	6.6%	46.3%	233.2%	41.9%

FIGURE 10.15 Sample classification against significance criteria

Note: n = 158 = 56 + 72 + 30 = (Yanjing + Tsingtao + Snow), see Table 7.5

[1] $(56/158)2 + (72/158)2 + (30/158)2 = 36.92\%$ = adjusted share criteria
[2] must be 25% or above choice to be significant. Calculated as:
$$\frac{(\text{MDA predicted choice} - \text{Actual choice})}{\text{Actual choice}}$$
[3] first brand correctly classified from Figure 10.14

TABLE 10.1 MDA classification of first preferred brands

	Actual choices		Predicted Group Membership		
	n	Brand	Yanjing n (%)	Tsingtao n (%)	Snow n (%)
n total = 158	56	**Yanjing**	**29 (51.8%)**	15 (26.8%)	12 (21.4%)
	72	**Tsingtao**	18 (25%)	**35 (48.6%)**	19 (26.4%)
	30	**Snow**	8 (26.7%)	3 (10%)	**19 (63.3%)**

output, a table about the actual choices vs. predicted group membership can be constructed (e.g., Figure 10.15).

From Figure 10.15, we can see that 158 respondents ranked their favorite brands. The most popular brand was Tsingtao (n = 72), followed by Yanjing (n = 56) and Snow Beer (n = 30) – these are depicted in the area of the table that is shaded darker.

To interpret predicted group membership, we read the intersecting cells for the same brands (e.g., Tsingtao vs. Tsingtao) – in Figure 10.15 these are the values in bold. Predicted group membership are the cells in a lighter shade. In Figure 10.15, the ranking for brand preference remains consistent – the MDA model predicts Tsingtao as the most preferred beer (n = 35), Yanjing as the second most preferred beer (n = 29), Snow Beer remains third (n = 19).

Step 2 – constructing classification vs. significance criteria table

To work out if the MDA predictions are significantly better than that achieved by chance alone, a classification vs. significance criteria table must be constructed. To construct this table, two statistics have to be calculated – chance for classification and the significant classification criterion. The way to calculate these are:

1. Chance for classification
The number of brands signifies chance – i.e., two brands = 50/50% chance, four brands = 25/25/25/25% chance
The MDA in Figure 10.15 classifies three brands of beer.
Therefore chance for classification is 100% ÷ 3 = 33.33%.
In this case, the chance for classification is 0.33.

2. Significant classification criterion
To be "sure" that the MDA classification is above that achieved by chance alone, classification has to be 25% greater than chance. For example, to be classified as "significant", the classification for Tsingtao beer should be:

48.6% × 125% = 60.75%.

The classification statistic 48.6% is obtained from Table 7.5.

The actual choice criterion (expressed as a percentage) is:
Brand Share ÷ Total Number of Subjects in the Sample being analyzed.
For example, for Tsingtao, it is 72 ÷ 158 = 45.6%

These two calculated statistics are used to construct Figure 10.15 to determine the significance criterion.

As can be seen from the last line in Figure 10.15 (Improvement), Tsingtao brand (6.6%) is not predicted significantly better than chance. However, Yanjing (46.3%) and Snow (233%) branded beers are classified significantly better than chance.

Worksheet 10.9 can be used for documenting the classification vs. significance criteria for your data:

Worksheet 10.9 Classification vs. significance criteria			
	Brand 1	**Brand 2**	**Brand 3**	**Overall %**
Actual choice	%	%	%	%[1]
MDA predicted choice	%	%	%	%[3]
MDA predicted choice minus Actual choice	%	%	%	%
Improvement [2]	%	%	%	%

Note: n = _____ = _____ + _____ + _____ = (Brand 1 + Brand 2 + Brand 3)

[1] (_____ ÷ _____)² + (_____ ÷ _____)² + (_____ ÷ _____)² = _____% = adjusted share criteria

[2] must be 25% or above choice to be significant. Calculated as:

(MDA predicted choice – Actual choice)

Actual choice

[3] first brand correctly classified

Factors by Rank of Effect	Function 1	Function 2
		Not significant
	67.6%	32.4%
1. Disposable income	−0.69	0.07
2. Physical benefits	0.68	0.08
3. Gender	0.20	0.22
4. Emotional benefits	−0.19	0.39
5. Affect	0.12	−0.31
6. Bottles of beer drank in last seven days	0.10	0.89
7. Age	−0.08	0.39
8. Attributes	0.08	−0.53
9. Visits to the restaurant	0.08	−0.75
10. Country identity	−0.05	0.22
11. Images	−0.003	−0.40

FIGURE 10.16 Standardized canonical discriminate function coefficients

Step 3 – Derive Standardized Canonical Discriminate Function Coefficients

Standardized Canonical Discriminate Function Coefficients can be obtained from the output of MDA analysis. This is standard output for post-hoc analysis provided by the MDA modules. Returning to our worked example, the Standardized Canonical Discriminate Function Coefficients appear in Figure 10.16.

Figure 10.16 shows two discriminate functions, Function 1 significantly discriminates between dimensions of brand knowledge. When sorted by rank effect (as is portrayed in Figure 10.16), the ranked dimensions indicate the relative strength of each at influencing predicted brand choice. This provides managers with an indication of the relative effect of each of the exogenous x or g variables.

The product of the summed function coefficients (top row) derives the size of each function's influence in the model. In this case, meaningful interpretation indicated that strong predictors of brand choice are:

- Disposable income
- Physical benefits (does not get me fat, good for health, is exciting and interesting)
- Gender
- Emotional benefits (gives energy and courage, reduces stress, and makes me feel cool)
- Affect (like its taste, taste good, and makes me feel happier)
- The amount of beer drunk in the past seven days

This indicates that managers should focus more on these elements when attempting to build brand knowledge. These elements appear to be able to predict brand preference. For brands operating in different markets and segments, these steps for modeling using MDA should be repeated. The results are expected to be different for each market.

Worksheet 10.10 can be used for ranking Standardized Canonical Discriminate Function Coefficients from your data.

Worksheet 10.10 Ranking standardized canonical discriminate function coefficients		
Factors by Rank of Effect	**Function 1**	**Function 2**
	__%	__%
1.		
2.		
3.		
4.		
5.		
6.		
7.		
8.		
9.		
10.		
11.		

Summary

This chapter has introduced a method for identifying the dimensions that form Brand Knowledge. Brand Knowledge is expected to differ by market segment, which is reflected in its dimensionality identified using Factor Analysis. These Brand Knowledge dimensions can be used to predict Brand Choice. The MDA provides a way for classifying a brand's buyers relative to competing brands. This classification ranks brands by preference. More importantly, the derived post-hoc results from MDA provide an indication of each dimension's relative effect of Brand Knowledge dimensions on Brand Choice. This information is useful for managing Brand Knowledge and a brand's image. Ultimately Brand Knowledge leads to Brand Preference and to Brand Choice. In turn, increased Brand Choice is a causal precursor for increased Brand Equity.

Bibliography

Aaker, D. A. (2003), "The Power of the Branded Differentiator", *MIT Sloan Management Review*, 45 (1), 83–7.

Aaker, David A. (1991), *Managing Brand Equity: Capitalizing on the Value of a Brand Name*. New York: Free Press.

Aaker, David A. and Alexander L. Biel (1993), *Brand Equity & Advertising: Advertising's Role in Building Strong Brands*. Hillsdale, NJ: Lawrence Erlbaum Associates.

Alba, Joseph W. and Amitava Chattopadhyay (1986), "Salience Effects in Brand Recall", *Journal of Marketing Research*, 23 (4), 363–9.

Berger, Jonah, Michaela Draganska and Itamar Simonson (2007), "The Influence of Product Variety on Brand Perception and Choice", *Marketing Science*, 26 (4), 460–72.

Campbell, Margaret C. and Kevin Lane Keller (2003), "Brand Familiarity and Advertising Repetition Effects", *Journal of Consumer Research*, 30 (2), 292–305.

East, Robert (1997), *Consumer Behaviour – Advances and Applications in Marketing Essex*. England: Prentice Hall Press.

Ebbinghaus, Hermann (1913), *On Memory: A Contribution to Experimental Psychology*. New York: Teachers College.

Ehrenberg, E. (1988), *Repeat Buying: Theory and Application* (2nd ed.), London: Charles and Griffin & CO.

Goodhardt, G. J., A. S. C. Ehrenberg and C. Chatfield (1984), "The Dirichlet: A Comprehensive Model of Buying Behaviour," *Journal of the Royal Statistical Society. Series A (General)*, 147 (5), 621–55.

Hair, J. F. Jr., R. E. Anderson, R. L. Tatham and W. C. Black (1998), *Multivariate Data Analysis* (5th ed.). New Jersey: Prentice Hall.

Hair, Joseph F. Jr., Rolph E. Andersen, Ronald L. Tatham and William C. Black (2010), *Multivariate Data Analysis*. Upper Saddle-River, NJ: Pearson Education.

Keller, K. L. (2001), "Building Customer-Based Brand-Equity", *Marketing Management*, 10 (2), 14.

Keller, Kevin Lane (1991), "Memory and Evaluation Effects in Competitive Advertising Environments", *Journal of Consumer Research*, 17 (4), 463.

——— (1993), "Conceptualizing, Measuring, and Managing Customer-Based Brand Equity", *Journal of Marketing*, 57 (1), 1–22.

Lambert, Claire (2008), "Young Children's Fast Food Brand Knowledge, Preference and Equity", The University of Western Australia.

Lambert, Claire, Dick Mizerski and Doina Olaru (2009), "Young Children's Fast Food Knowledge and Preference", in Society for Marketing Advances 2009 Conference. New Orleans.

Mayer, Richard E. and Richard B. Anderson (1991), "Animations Need Narrations: An Experimental Test of a Dual-Coding Hypothesis", *Journal of Educational Psychology*, 83 (4), 484–90.

Netemeyer, Richard G., Balaji Krishnan, Chris Pullig, Guangping Wang, Mehmet Yagci, Dwane Dean, Joe Ricks and Writh Ferdinand (2004), "Developing and Validating Measures of Facets of Customer-Based Brand Equity", *Journal of Business Research*, 57 (2), 209–24.

Ng, Sharon and Michael J. Houston (2009), "Field Dependency and Brand Cognitive Structures", *Journal of Marketing Research*, 46 (2), 279–92.

Pham, Thang, Katherine Mizerski, Saalem Sadeque and Richard Mizerski (2009), "The Effect of Product Familiarity in Perceptions and Preferences of Private Label and National Brands", in ANZMAC. Melbourne: Australia New-Zealand Marketing Educators Association.

Toner-Schrader, Julie and Richard Mizerski (1997), "An Investigation of the Relationship Between Need for Affect and Responses to Alcohol Public Service Announcements", *Journal of Nonprofit & Public Sector Marketing*, 5 (3), 41.

Uncles, Mark D., Grahame R. Dowling and Kathy Hammond (2003), "Customer Loyalty and Customer Loyalty Programs", *The Journal of Consumer Marketing*, 20 (4/5), 294.

Yang, Jinchao (2010), "Beer Brand Knowledge and Its Effects in Brand Preference and Brand Loyalty: A Comparative Study of Australian and Chinese Young Heavy Users", The University of Western Australia.

Zajonc, Robert B. and Hazel Markus (1982), "Affective and Cognitive Factors in Preferences", *Journal of Consumer Research,* 9 (2), 123–32.

APPENDIX 1

FORMULA USED TO CALCULATE DISPOSABLE INCOME

Disposable income calculation formula

Formula used to determine the relative cost of beer consumption as a percent of their disposable income = amounts of beer consumed (by 200 ml glass) × frequency of visits × price per glass/self-reported disposable income × 100%

APPENDIX 2

DEMOGRAPHIC FACTORS INDEPENDENT SAMPLE TEST TABLE

Independent Samples Test

		Levene's Test for Equality of Variances		t-test for Equality of Means					95% Confidence Interval of the Difference	
		F	Sig.	t	df	Sig. (2-tailed)	Mean Difference	Std. Error Difference	Lower	Upper
age	Equal variances assumed	9.532	.002	−7.869	446	.000	−1.163	.148	−1.454	−.873
	Equal variances not assumed			−8.297	388.760	.000	−1.163	.140	−1.439	−.888
gender	Equal variances assumed	10.607	.001	1.554	446	.121	.071	.046	−.019	.161
	Equal variances not assumed			1.581	352.361	.115	.071	.045	−.017	.159
income	Equal variances assumed	10.270	.001	2.778	427	.006	335.500	120.768	98.126	572.873
	Equal variances not assumed			3.506	305.096	.001	335.500	95.689	147.205	523.794
amounts	Equal variances assumed	87.264	.000	6.440	446	.000	8.422	1.308	5.852	10.992
	Equal variances not assumed			8.150	366.852	.000	8.422	1.033	6.390	10.454
visit times	Equal variances assumed	18.877	.000	4.090	446	.000	.633	.155	.329	.937
	Equal variances not assumed			4.327	392.074	.000	.633	.146	.345	.921

APPENDIX 3

TABLE OF AUSTRALIAN BEER USERS VISITING TIMES PREDICTION RESULT (UWA)

Table of Australian beer users visiting times prediction result (UWA)

Repeat buying over two equal (stationary) periods

Type of Buyer	Proportion of Population (b)	Proportion of Buyers	Average per Buyer (w)
Repeat buyers (buy in both periods)	0.7395	0.8510	2.3266
Lapsed buyers (first period only)	0.1295	0.1490	2.1481
'New' buyers (second period only)	0.1295	0.1490	2.1481
Non-buyers (buy in neither period)	0.0015	n/a	n/a

NBD predicted consuming amounts outputs for UWA beer users

	1 day	1 wk	4 wks	12 wks	24 wks	48 wks	365 days
Penetration (b)	0.58	0.87	0.95	0.98	0.99	0.99	0.99
Purchase frequency (w)	2.97	13.90	50.92	148.49	294.23	585.10	635.28
Repeat purchase %	77.39	94.39	97.95	99.06	99.43	99.65	99.67
Pur freq of rpt buyers	3.37	14.62	51.95	149.88	295.92	587.16	637.38
Pur freq of new buyers	1.59	1.78	1.81	1.82	1.82	1.82	1.82
Proportion buying 0:	0.42	0.13	0.05	0.02	0.01	0.01	0.01
buying once:	0.21	0.09	0.04	0.02	0.01	0.01	0.01
twice:	0.13	0.07	0.03	0.01	0.01	0.01	0.01
three times:	0.08	0.06	0.03	0.01	0.01	0.00	0.00
four times:	0.05	0.05	0.02	0.01	0.01	0.00	0.00
five times:	0.04	0.05	0.02	0.01	0.01	0.00	0.00
six plus:	0.08	0.56	0.81	0.91	0.94	0.97	0.97

APPENDIX 4

TABLE OF CHINA BEER USERS VISITING TIMES PREDICTION RESULT (CAU)

Table of Chinese beer users visiting times prediction result (CAU)

Repeat buying over two equal (stationary) periods

Type of buyer	Proportion of population (b)	Proportion of buyers	Average per buyer (w)
Repeat buyers (buy in both periods)	0.3340	0.6105	1.6404
Lapsed buyers (first period only)	0.2130	0.3895	1.7934
'New' buyers (second period only)	0.2130	0.3895	1.7934
Non-buyers (buy in neither period)	0.2400	n/a	n/a

NBD predicted consuming amounts outputs for CAU beer users

	1 day	1 week	4 weeks	12 wks	24 wks	48 wks	365 days
Penetration (b)	0.24	0.55	0.71	0.80	0.85	0.88	0.88
Purchase frequency (w)	1.76	5.50	16.87	44.93	85.39	164.33	177.81
Repeat purchase %	55.98	83.38	91.49	94.76	96.08	97.03	97.13
Pur freq of rpt buyers	2.07	6.28	18.29	47.33	88.81	169.30	183.02
Pur freq of new buyers	1.35	1.56	1.61	1.62	1.62	1.62	1.62
Proportion buying 0:	0.76	0.45	0.29	0.20	0.15	0.12	0.12
buying once:	0.15	0.14	0.10	0.07	0.05	0.04	0.04
twice:	0.05	0.09	0.06	0.05	0.04	0.03	0.03
three times:	0.02	0.06	0.05	0.04	0.03	0.02	0.02
four times:	0.01	0.05	0.04	0.03	0.02	0.02	0.02
five times:	0.01	0.04	0.03	0.03	0.02	0.02	0.02
six plus:	0.01	0.18	0.43	0.60	0.68	0.75	0.76

APPENDIX 5

FACTOR ANALYSIS FOR AUSTRALIA SAMPLE BEER USERS

Australian sample factor analysis process (FA)

From the rotated component matrix, there are nine factors which can explain 63.33% total variance. Nine factors have been extracted, after removing four items including "nice color", "refreshing", "getting attention"; "welcome guests", were removed from the analysis as being not significant for the latent consistent. Several new extractions were performed: eliminating gradually the less contributing items. There are eight factors left.

Eight factors have been extracted; removing "cheerful", "cool down", "good quality", there are still eight factors; finally, after removing " improve my status" item, and the factor analysis suggests six factors which can totally explain 75.6% variance.

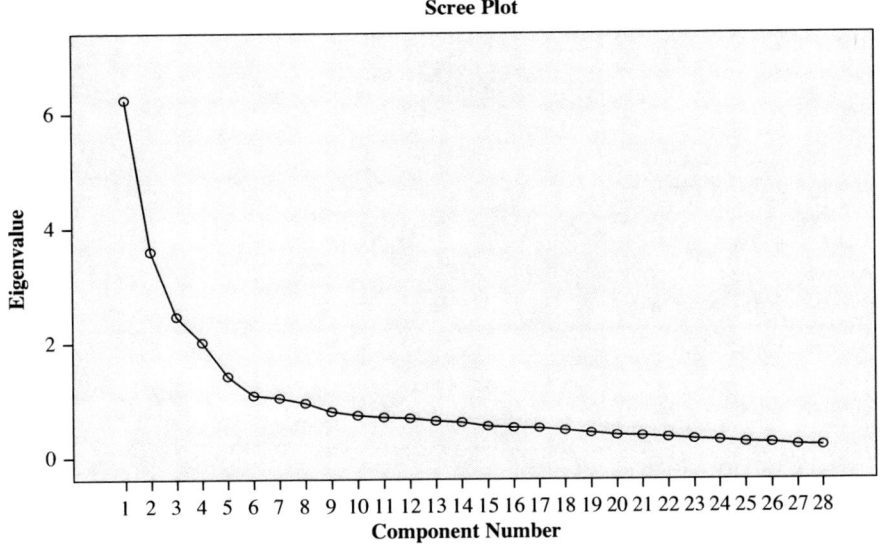

Scree Plot

FIGURE A-1 Australia sample 286 users' scree plot

From SPSS outputs, some main figures are as follows:

Six factors extracted from 28 items

Australia sample 286 users' scree plot shows there are 28 items left with six factors.

KMO and Bartlett's test result

Kaiser–Meyer–Olkin measuring of sampling adequacy is .807 bigger than .60, Chi-Square 3184, degree of freedom df 378 and significance .000. This KMO result suggests factor analysis is appropriate.

Australia Sample Rotated Component Matrix[a]

	Component					
	1	2	3	4	5	6
prestigious			.74			
elegant			.75		.31	
charming			.68			.30
trendy			.75			
like brand				.73		
like taste				.83		.35
tastes good					.78	
celebration and party	.32				.74	
for men					.74	
Australian style	.70					
popular beer	.62					
available	**.74**					
good value for money	.72					
inexpensive	.69					
happier		.67				.42
reduce stress		.75				.36
creative advertising	**.78**					
enjoyable and satisfaction		.74				
give energy & courage		.76				
sociable		.68				
good for health						.83
not getting fat						.83
interesting and exciting						.61

Extraction Method: Principal Component Analysis
Rotation Method: Varimax with Kaiser Normalization
[a]Rotation converged in 10 iterations.

Total variance is explained as 63.75%.

Australia sample factor analysis reliability test

Case Processing Summary

		N	%
Cases	Valid	160	98.8
	Excluded[a]	2	1.2
	Total	162	100.0

[a]Listwise deletion based on all variables in the procedure.

Reliability Statistics

Cronbach's Alpha	N of Items
.875	26

Alpha is higher than 0.80, it refers the test is reliable.

APPENDIX 6

FACTOR ANALYSIS OF CHINA SAMPLE BEER USERS

China sample factor analysis process detail (FA)

Put 36 items to run factor analysis, there are nine factors which can explain 67.11% variance.

After removing "like brand", "interested in brand", "attracts me", "celebration and party", and" improve my status" five items, eight factors which can explain 66.78% total variance.

Further elimination of item "increase China's identity", eight factors with 69.24% variance explained are extracted.

Finally after removing "welcome guests", "cool down", "getting attention from others" and "sociable" the final solution includes seven factors with 69.13% variance explained with 25 items left.

SPSS outputs, figures are as follows:

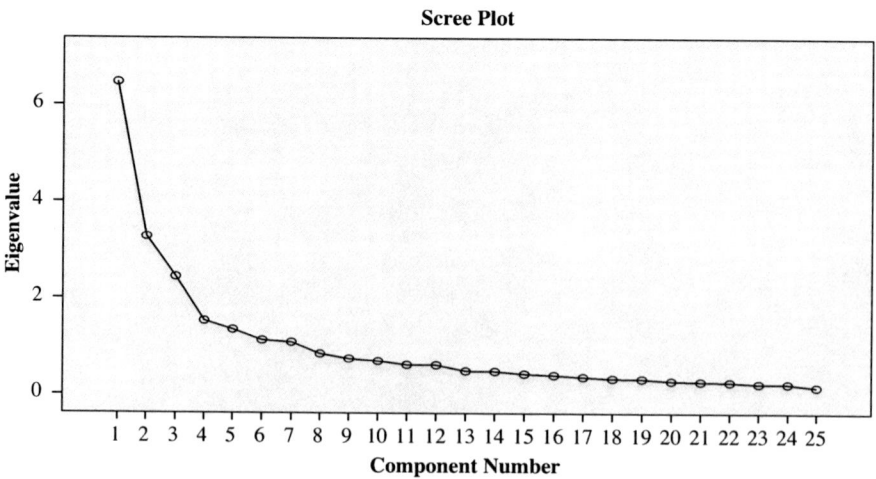

FIGURE 0-1: China sample 162 users' scree plot

Seven factors extracted from 25 items

China sample 162 users' scree plot shows there are 25 items left with seven factors.

China sample samples KMO and Bartlett's test result

Kaiser–Meyer–Olkin measuring of sampling adequacy is .811 bigger than .60, Chi-Square 1906, degree of freedom df 325 and significance .000, it's required for the factor analysis.

Table of China sample 162 users rotated component matrix

Rotated Component Matrix[a]

	Component						
	1	2	3	4	5	6	7
prestigious	.80						
charming	.79						
trendy	.78						
elegant	.78						
like taste		.75					
cheerful		.739					
tastes good		.65		.48			
happier		.63				.38	
good value for money			.79				
available			.74				
popular beer			.66				.36
inexpensive			.64				
refreshing				.83			
nice color		.34		.75			
not getting fat					.83		
good for health					.73		
interesting and exciting					.71		
give energy						.75	
reduce stress						.75	
feel cool	.38					.62	
for men							.77
Chinese style			.31				.72
support economy			.31				.66

Extraction Method: Principal Component Analysis.
Rotation Method: Varimax with Kaiser Normalization.
[a]Rotation converged in 11 iterations.

China sample factor analysis reliability test results

Case Processing Summary

		N	%
Cases	Valid	160	98.8
	Excluded[a]	2	1.2
	Total	162	100.0

[a]Listwise deletion based on all variables in the procedure.

Reliability Statistics

Cronbach's Alpha	N of Items
.875	26

Alpha is higher than 0.80, it refers the test is reliable.

APPENDIX 7

MDA ANALYSIS

Australia sample MDA analysis: goodness-of-fit and pseudo R-square test

Case Processing Summary

		N	Marginal Percentage
First preferred brand	Tooheys new	129	50.2%
	Amber ale	96	37.4%
	Swan draft	32	12.5%
gender	male	172	66.9%
	female	85	33.1%
Valid		257	100.0%
Missing		29	
Total		286	
Subpopulation		256[a]	

[a]The dependent variable has only one value observed in 256 (100.0%) subpopulations.

Descriptive statistics show that 50.2% users prefer Tooheys new, 37.4% Amber ale, and 12.5% Swan draft.

Goodness–of–Fit

	Chi-Square	df	Sig.
Pearson	1219.464	486	.000
Deviance	307.929	486	1.000

Pseudo R-Square

Cox and Snell	.527
Nagelkerke	.615
McFadden	.384

Chi-square results confirm that the logistic regression model is valid and the variables contribute to the discriminations ($x^2 = 192302$. $p = 0.000$), that is further confirmed by pseudo r^2 with values above 0.38Y.

China sample MDA: classification test table

Classification

Observed	Predicted			
	Yanjing	*Tsingtao*	*Snow*	*Percent Correct*
Yanjing	31	20	5	55.4%
Tsingtao	16	51	5	70.8%
Snow	9	14	7	23.3%
Overall Percentage	35.4%	53.8%	10.8%	56.3%

From the classification table the classification can be predicted at 70.8% for Tsingtao and 55.4% for Yanging. Preference for Snow can be predicted at 23.3%. The overall percentage classification is 56.3%.

Table of case summary for China sample

Case Processing Summary

	Brands	N	Marginal	Percentage	25% higher
first preferred brand	Yanjing	56	0.35443	0.369332	0.461665
	Tsingtao	72	0.455696		
	Snow	30	0.189873		
	Total	158			

Brand preference for three beer brands can be classified at overall percentage 56.3%, which is about 13% higher than the MDA classification at 41.1% and 10% higher than the multinominal logistic regression analysis needed at 46.17%. These results suggest the higher classification rate by multinomial logistic regression than the results by MDA.

Comparing the factors that associated with brand preference suggested by logistic analysis and MDA, they are mostly same except the age. The relative contribution differs between the two techniques. The logistic analysis result decreases from health, income, amounts, visiting times to attributes but the order by MDA is drinking amounts, visiting times, health, income, attributes and age.

APPENDIX 8

MLR ANALYSIS

Australia sample MLR: likelihood ration tests table

Likelihood Ratio Tests

Effect	Model Fitting Criteria	Likelihood Ratio Tests		
	−2 Log Likelihood of Reduced Model	Chi-Square	df	Sig.
Intercept	307.929[a]	.000	0	.
Q4	314.630	6.701	2	.035
Q7	310.473	2.544	2	.280
Q8	313.837	5.907	2	.052
Q9	313.824	5.895	2	.052
attribute	385.569	77.640	2	.000
benefits	309.683	1.754	2	.416
image	311.998	4.069	2	.131
attitude	331.430	23.501	2	.000
health	309.910	1.980	2	.371
party	309.136	1.207	2	.547
country identity	330.193	22.263	2	.000
Q5	311.460	3.531	2	.171

The chi-square statistic is the difference in −2 log-likelihoods between the final model and a reduced model. The reduced model is formed by omitting an effect from the final model. The null hypothesis is that all parameters of that effect are 0.

[a]This reduced model is equivalent to the final model because omitting the effect does not increase the degrees of freedom.

Australia sample MLR: parameter estimates table

Parameter Estimates

First preferred brand[a]		B	Std. Error	Wald	df	Sig.	Exp(B)	95% Confidence Interval for Exp(B)	
								Lower Bound	Upper Bound
Tooheys new	Intercept	7.466	3.258	5.250	1	.022			
	Q4	−.275	.163	2.860	1	.091	.759	.552	1.045
	Q7	.000	.000	1.681	1	.195	1.000	1.000	1.001
	Q8	.000	.014	.001	1	.980	1.000	.973	1.028
	Q9	−.118	.149	.630	1	.427	.889	.664	1.189
	attribute	1.710	.385	19.726	1	.000	5.529	2.600	11.758
	benefits	−.409	.315	1.683	1	.194	.664	.358	1.232
	image	−.200	.314	.406	1	.524	.819	.442	1.516
	attitude	.281	.337	.699	1	.403	1.325	.685	2.563
	health	.189	.283	.447	1	.504	1.209	.694	2.106
	party	−.319	.378	.710	1	.399	.727	.346	1.526
	country identity	−1.148	.402	8.167	1	.004	.317	.144	.697
	[Q5=1]	−.877	.564	2.423	1	.120	.416	.138	1.255
	[Q5=2]	0[b]			0				

(Continued)

(Continued)

First preferred brand[a]		B	Std. Error	Wald	df	Sig.	Exp(B)	95% Confidence Interval for Exp(B)	
								Lower Bound	Upper Bound
Amber ale	Intercept	.257	3.540	.005	1	.942	1.061	.751	1.499
	Q4	.059	.176	.113	1	.736	1.001	1.000	1.001
	Q7	.001	.000	2.251	1	.134	.969	.937	1.002
	Q8	−.032	.017	3.490	1	.062	1.181	.870	1.603
	Q9	.167	.156	1.143	1	.285	.466	.218	.999
	attribute	−.763	.389	3.847	1	.050	.725	.354	1.484
	benefits	−.322	.366	.775	1	.379	1.421	.711	2.840
	image	.351	.353	.988	1	.320	4.639	2.111	10.197
	attitude	1.535	.402	14.585	1	.000	1.524	.833	2.790
	health	.422	.308	1.870	1	.171	.978	.437	2.193
	party	−.022	.412	.003	1	.958	.173	.074	.404
	country identity	−1.756	.433	16.441	1	.000	.332	.095	1.162
	[Q5=1]	−1.102	.639	2.976	1	.084			
	[Q5=2]	0[b]			0				

[a]The reference category is: Swan draft.

[b]This parameter is set to zero because it is redundant.

Note:

Q4 = age
Q5(1) = male
Q5(2) = female
Q7 = income
Q8 = amounts
Q9 = visiting times

Australia sample MLR: Classification test results

SPSS output for classification result:

Classification

Observed	Predicted			
	Tooheys new	*Amber ale*	*Swan draft*	*Percent Correct*
Tooheys new	116	10	3	89.9%
Amber ale	18	76	2	79.2%
Swan draft	18	7	7	21.9%
Overall Percentage	59.1%	36.2%	4.7%	77.4%

Considering the classification by chance confirm 54.8% the classification results for brand preference among the top three beer brands in UWA is higher than 68.5% (25% above classification by chance) suggesting that logistic model is explaining the first preference for beer brand.

Table of case summary

Case Processing Summary

	N	*Marginal*	*Percentage*	*25% higher*
Tooheys new	129	0.501946		
Amber ale	96	0.373541		
Swan draft	32	0.124514		
Total	257		0.406986	0.508732

From the classification tables, the overall percentage is 77.4%, which is 4% higher than the discriminate classification 73.5%, and 27% higher than the classification by chance. These results suggest that the Australia university student beer users can make clear preference among top three beer brands and the factors attitudes, attributes, country identity strongly contribute to the preference. The results are more robust than those from the discriminate analysis.

China sample MLR: goodness-of-fit and pseudo R-square test

The results of the multinomial logistic regression for China sample beer users are given below.

Case Processing Summary

		N	Marginal Percentage
first preferred brand	Yanjing	56	35.4%
	Tsingtao	72	45.6%
	Snow	30	19.0%
gender	Male	116	73.4%
	Female	42	26.6%
Valid		158	100.0%
Missing		4	
Total		162	
Subpopulation		158[a]	

[a]The dependent variable has only one value observed in 158 (100.0%) subpopulations.

From 162 current beer users, 45.6% prefer Tsingtao and 35.4% prefer Yanjing. The remaining prefer Snow brand. There are 73.4% male users and 26.6% female users in the sample.

Model Fitting Information

Model	Model Fitting Criteria			Likelihood Ratio Tests		
	AIC	BIC	−2 Log Likelihood	Chi-Square	df	Sig.
Intercept Only	333.029	339.154	329.029			
Final	336.648	416.276	284.648	44.381	24	.007

Goodness-of-Fit

	Chi-Square	df	Sig.
Pearson	302.996	290	.288
Deviance	284.648	290	.578

Pseudo R-Square

Cox and Snell	.245
Nagelkerke	.280
McFadden	.135

Goodness-of-fit results are not as good as for Australian sample, however the model explains differences in preferences ($x2 = 44.38$, p = 0.07).

China sample MLR: likelihood ratio tests table

Likelihood Ratio Tests

Effect	Model Fitting Criteria			Likelihood Ratio Tests		
	AIC of Reduced Model	BIC of Reduced Model	−2 Log Likelihood of Reduced Model	Chi-Square	df	Sig.
Intercept	336.648	416.276	284.648[a]	.000	0	
Q4	334.936	408.438	286.936	2.288	2	.319
Q7	344.619	418.121	296.619	11.971	2	.003
Q8	338.661	412.163	290.661	6.013	2	.049
Q9 image	337.326	410.828	289.326	4.678	2	.096
attitude	334.829	408.331	286.829	2.181	2	.336
attributes	333.700	407.202	285.700	1.051	2	.591
quality	336.002	409.504	288.002	3.354	2	.187
health	334.513	408.016	286.513	1.865	2	.394
benefits	343.425	416.927	295.425	10.777	2	.005
country identity	334.946	408.448	286.946	2.297	2	.317
Q5	333.059	406.562	285.059	.411	2	.814
	334.154	407.656	286.154	1.506	2	.471

The chi-square statistic is the difference in -2 log-likelihoods between the final model and a reduced model. The reduced model is formed by omitting an effect from the final model. The null hypothesis is that all parameters of that effect are 0.

[a]This reduced model is equivalent to the final model because omitting the effect does not increase the degrees of freedom.

China sample MLR: parameter estimates table

Parameter Estimates

first preferred brand[a]		B	Std. Error	Wald	df	Sig.	Exp(B)	95% Confidence Interval for Exp(B)	
								Lower Bound	Upper Bound
Yanjing	Intercept	5.939	4.506	1.738	1	.187			
	Q4	-.270	.212	1.625	1	.202	.764	.504	1.156
	Q7	.001	.001	.390	1	.532	1.001	.999	1.003
	Q8	-.166	.071	5.410	1	.020	.847	.737	.974
	Q9 image	.440	.260	2.855	1	.091	1.553	.932	2.586
	attitude	.495	.344	2.070	1	.150	1.641	.836	3.222
	attributes	.268	.361	.551	1	.458	1.307	.645	2.650
	quality	.535	.323	2.752	1	.097	1.708	.907	3.214
	health	-.515	.393	1.714	1	.190	.597	.276	1.292
	benefits	-.396	.370	1.149	1	.284	.673	.326	1.388
	country identity	-.356	.351	1.029	1	.310	.700	.352	1.394
	[Q5=1]	-.184	.377	.237	1	.626	.832	.397	1.743
	[Q5=2]	.531	.561	.897	1	.344	1.701	.566	5.110
		0[b]			0				

(Continued)

(Continued)

first preferred brand[a]	B	Std. Error	Wald	df	Sig.	Exp(B)	95% Confidence Interval for Exp(B)	
							Lower Bound	Upper Bound
Tsingtao Intercept	1.307	4.362	.090	1	.764			
Q4	-.071	.203	.121	1	.728	.932	.626	1.387
Q7	.003	.001	6.828	1	.009	1.003	1.001	1.004
Q8	-.089	.063	1.950	1	.163	.915	.808	1.036
Q9 image	.091	.278	.107	1	.744	1.095	.635	1.889
attitude	.249	.318	.611	1	.434	1.282	.688	2.391
attributes	-.009	.351	.001	1	.981	.991	.498	1.974
quality	.182	.313	.336	1	.562	1.199	.649	2.214
health	-.264	.380	.482	1	.487	.768	.365	1.617
benefits	-1.008	.367	7.549	1	.006	.365	.178	.749
country identity	.038	.342	.012	1	.912	1.039	.532	2.029
[Q5=1]	-.008	.369	.001	1	.982	.992	.481	2.044
[Q5=2]	.686	.567	1.466	1	.226	1.987	.654	6.036
	0[b]			0				

[a]The reference category is: Snow.

[b]This parameter is set to zero because it is redundant.

Note:

Q4 = age

Q5(1) = male

Q5(2) = female

Q7 = income

Q8 = amounts

Q9 = visiting times

APPENDIX 9

BLR ANALYSIS

Australia sample BLR: Hosmer and Lemeshow tests

Dependent Variable Encoding

Original Value	Internal Value
first preferred brand	0
second preferred brand	1

Dependent variable (1, 2) has been changed into logistic analysis's (0, 1). It means stay on the first preferred brand is 0 and switch to the second preferred brand is 1.

Variables in the Equation

		B	S.E.	Wald	df	Sig.	Exp(B)
Step 0	Constant	.471	.129	13.401	1	.000	1.602

Wald = 13.401, P value <.001, it has significant logistic regression relationship. This shows the next analysis is reasonable and the dependent variable and independent variables does have the logistic regression relationships.

Omnibus Tests of Model Coefficients

		Chi-square	df	Sig.
Step 1	Step	22.852	12	.029
	Block	22.852	12	.029
	Model	22.852	12	.029

Model Summary

Step	−2 Log likelihood	Cox and Snell R Square	Nagelkerke R Square
1	316.877[a]	.086	.116

[a]Estimation terminated at iteration number 4 because parameter estimates changed by less than .001.

Hosmer and Lemeshow Test

Step	Chi-square	df	Sig.
1	7.831	8	.450

The three tables above show the brand equity model summary for UWA beer users. The chi-square for change in the-2LL value from the base model indicated the chi-square value was statistically significant at the .029 level. The Hosmer and Lemeshow measure of overall fit indicated there was no statically significant difference between the observed and predicted classifications (p = .45 > .05). Both tests provide the support for the acceptance of the seven dependent variables model as significant analysis (see Appendix 15, Hosmer and Lemeshow tests).

Australia sample BLR: classification test

Classification Table[a]

Observed		Predicted		
		choice		Percentage Correct
		first preferred brand	second preferred brand	
Step 1 choice	first preferred brand	34	64	34.7
	second preferred brand	19	138	87.9
Overall Percentage				67.5

[a]The cut value is .500.

Table of the case summary table for Australia sample

Case summary table

Choices	N	Classification %	25% higher
First choice (stay)	98	0.384314	
Second choice (switch)	157	0.615686	
Total	255	0.526767	0.658458

The hit ratio table shows the first preference brand (choice 0, stay 1), was predicted correctly in 34.7% of cases, but switch to the second preference brand choice (classification) was correctly predicted in 87.9% of the cases, overall 67.5% correct. The conclusion may be that for Australian beer users the switching behavior can be correctly predicted but stay with the brand needs further developed.

Australia sample BLR: variables in the equation

Variables in the Equation

	B	S.E.	Wald	df	Sig.	Exp(B)	95.0% C.I. for EXP(B)	
							Lower	Upper
Step 1ª attribute	−.576	.202	8.122	1	.004	.562	.378	.835
benefits	.361	.177	4.130	1	.042	1.434	1.013	2.031
image	.127	.185	.469	1	.493	1.135	.790	1.632
attitude	−.221	.190	1.355	1	.244	.802	.553	1.163
health	−.160	.172	.863	1	.353	.852	.608	1.195
party	−.103	.210	.242	1	.623	.902	.598	1.361
country identity	.545	.205	7.041	1	.008	1.724	1.153	2.577
Q4	−.122	.094	1.687	1	.194	.885	.737	1.064
Q5	−.205	.310	.435	1	.509	.815	.444	1.497
Q7	.000	.000	2.111	1	.146	1.000	.999	1.000
Q8	.007	.010	.451	1	.502	1.007	.988	1.026
Q9	−.089	.085	1.099	1	.295	.914	.774	1.081
Constant	3.465	1.916	3.270	1	.071	31.972		

ªVariable(s) entered on Step 1: attribute, benefits, image, attitude, health, party, country identity, Q4, Q5, Q7, Q8, Q9.
B = logistic coefficient; S.E. = standard error; Wald = Wald statistic; Sig. = significant level; df = degree of freedom; Exp(B) = exponentiated coefficient

Note:
Q4 = age
Q5(1) = male
Q5(2) = female
Q7 = income
Q8 = amounts
Q9 = visiting times

From this table, attributes, benefits, and country identity are significantly related loyalty. Where attributes discourages switching (negative relationship) benefits and country identity have the positive relationship with predicted probability of switching.

Using the stepwise procedure, removing non-significant factors (party, gender, health, amounts, images, visiting times, attitudes, age), the final logistic regression results are as follows:

Variables in the Equation

		B	S.E.	Wald	df	Sig.	Exp(B)	95.0% C.I.for EXP(B)	
								Lower	Upper
Step 1[a]	attribute	−.541	.182	8.843	1	.003	.582	.408	.832
	benefits	.421	.146	8.310	1	.004	1.524	1.144	2.030
	country identity	.387	.187	4.288	1	.038	1.472	1.021	2.123
	Constant	.503	.129	15.218	1	.000	1.653		

[a]Variable(s) entered on Step 1: attribute, benefits, country identity.

As benefits and country identity value increase, the predicted probability of switch will increase by 52% (for benefits) and 47% (for country identity) change in odds. On the other hand, increase of one part in attributes increases the odds of switching of 41.8%.

China sample BLR: Hosmer and Lemeshow tests

Variables in the Equation

		B	S.E.	Wald	df	Sig.	Exp(B)
Step 0	Constant	−.629	.165	14.432	1	.000	.533

Wald = 14.432, P value <0.001, brand loyalty/equity has significant logistic regression relationship with independent variables (see Appendix 18, Hosmer and Lemeshow tests).

Omnibus Tests of Model Coefficients

		Chi-square	df	Sig.
Step 1	Step	8.610	1	.003
	Block	8.610	1	.003
	Model	8.610	1	.003

Model Summary

Step	−2 Log likelihood	Cox and Snell	NagelkerkeR Square
1	199.431[a]	.052	.072

[a]Estimation terminated at iteration number 4 because parameter estimates changed by less than .001.

Hosmer and Lemeshow Test

Step	Chi-square	df	Sig.
1	1.460	2	.482

The chi-square for change in the –2LL value from the base model indicated the chi-square value was statistically significant at the 0.003 level. The Hosmer and Lemeshow measure of overall fit indicated there was no statically significant difference between the observed and predicted classifications (p = 0.48 > 0.05). Both tests provide the support for the acceptance of the seven dependent variables model and are correct for further analysis.

China sample BLR: classification tests table

Classification Table[a]

Observed			Predicted		
			choice		Percentage Correct
			first choice	second choice	
Step 1	choice	first choice	93	11	89.4
		second choice	41	13	24.1
	Overall Percentage				67.1

[a]The cut value is .500

Table of the case summary table for China sample

Case summary table

Choices			Classification %	25% higher
First choice (stay)	104	0.658228		
Second choice (switch)	54	0.341772		
Total	158		0.550072	0.68759

Unlike Australia sample, the hit ratio table for China sample indicates 89.4% correct classification for staying and 24.1% correct classification for switching with an overall predicted for the second preference brand, switch can be predicted 24.1% correctly, totally can be predicted for rate of 67.1%. It can be concluded that for Chinese sample stay with first preferred brand can be predicted accurately, but not switch off to their second preferred brand. The prediction percentage is 21% higher than the classification by chance 68.76%.

China sample BLR: variables in equation

Variables in the Equation

		B	S.E.	Wald	df	Sig.	Exp(B)	95.0% C.I. for EXP(B)	
								Lower	Upper
Step 1ᵃ	image	.055	.242	.052	1	.820	1.057	.657	1.699
	attitude	.090	.267	.1121	1	.738	1.094	.648	1.847
	attributes	−.235	.233	.016	1	.313	.791	.501	1.248
	quality	−.179	.269	.4422	1	.506	.836	.494	1.417
	health	−.369	.243	.297	1	.130	.692	.429	1.114
	benefits	−.044	.246	.0321	1	.858	.957	.591	1.549
	country identity	.285	.285	.002	1	.317	1.330	.761	2.323
	Q4	.112	.145	.598	1	.439	1.118	.842	1.485
	Q5	.252	.414	.369	1	.543	1.286	.571	2.897
	Q7	−.002	.001	10.682	1	.001	.998	.997	.999
	Q8	−.012	.050	.054	1	.816	.988	.897	1.090
	Q9	.105	.1682	.393	1	.531	1.111	.799	1.545
	Constant	−2.566	.974	.745	1	.388	.077		

ᵃVariable(s) entered on Step 1: image, attitude, attributes, quality, health, benefits, country identity, Q4, Q5, Q7, Q8, Q9.

B = logistic coefficient; S.E. = standard error; Wald = Wald statistic; Sig. = significant level; df = degree of freedom; Exp(B) = exponentiated coefficient

The parameters attributes table shows only one significant predictor: income. Attributes, health, benefits, income, amounts all have the negative relationship with switching choice and images attitudes, country identity, age, gender, visiting times have the positive relationship (although not significant).

Removing non-significant exploratory variables in a stepwise regression was obtain amounts, images, country identity, visiting times, benefits, attitudes, ages, health, gender, and, attributes.

Variables in the Equation

		B	S.E.	Wald	df	Sig.	Exp(B)	95.0% C.I. for EXP(B)	
								Lower	Upper
Step 1ᵃ	Q7	−.002	.001	7.894	1	.005	.998	.997	1.000
	Constant	.047	.281	.028	1	.867	1.048		

ᵃVariable(s) entered on Step 1: Q7.

After running stepwise logistic removing non-significant factors, the results show only income associated with their choice (brand loyalty); health reducing the probability to switch to the second preferred brand, also plays an important role in the beer users' choice but not significant factor (Sig = 0.087).

APPENDIX 10

ENGLISH QUESTIONNAIRE ADMINISTERED IN AUSTRALIA

A Survey on Beer in Australia

I'd like to ask your opinions about, and use of beer. This interview is being conducted as part of a research project for a PhD thesis. Your answers will remain confidential and anonymous. Your responses cannot be traced back to you.

If I offered you a midi size glass of beer now, please rate these three brands of beer in terms of your preference. Write down number 1 for your first preferred brand, and number 2 for your second preferred brand:

Tooheys new_____

Amber ale_____

Swan draught_____

Please indicate the extent to which you agree or disagree with the following statements by circling the answer that best describes your opinion.

Statements about my First preferred brand:

Imageries:

	Strongly disagree			Strongly agree	
1) I feel prestigious.	1	2	3	. 4	5
2) I feel cheerful.	1	2	3	4	5
3) I feel elegant.	1	2	3	4	5
4) I feel charming.	1	2	3	4	5
5) I feel trendy.	1	2	3	4	5

Attitudes:

	Strongly disagree				Strongly agree
6) I like this brand.	1	2	3	4	5
7) I like its taste.	1	2	3	4	5
8) I'm interested in this brand.	1	2	3	4	5
9) This brand attracts me.	1	2	3	4	5

Attributes:

	Strongly disagree				Strongly agree
10) It tastes good.	1	2	3	4	5
11) It has good quality.	1	2	3	4	5
12) It has foam and nice color.	1	2	3	4	5
13) It's refreshing.	1	2	3	4	5
14) It's suitable for celebration and party.	1	2	3	4	5
15) It's suitable for men.	1	2	3	4	5
16) It's Australian style beer.	1	2	3	4	5
17) It supports Australian economy.	1	2	3	4	5
18) It's very popular.	1	2	3	4	5
19) It's always available.	1	2	3	4	5
20) It's good value for money.	1	2	3	4	5
21) It's inexpensive comparing with competitors.	1	2	3	4	5
22) It increases Australian identity.	1	2	3	4	5
23) It has a creative advertising.	1	2	3	4	5
24) It can cool you down in hot weather.	1	2	3	4	5

Benefits:

	Strongly disagree				Strongly agree
25) It makes me happier.	1	2	3	4	5
26) It makes me feel cool.	1	2	3	4	5
27) It reduces my stress.	1	2	3	4	5
28) It makes me enjoyable and satisfactory.	1	2	3	4	5
29) It gives me energy and courage.	1	2	3	4	5
30) It improves my status.	1	2	3	4	5
31) It makes me sociable and let me make friends easier.	1	2	3	4	5

(Continued)

(Continued)

	Strongly disagree				Strongly agree
32) It's getting attention from others.	1	2	3	4	5
33) It can warmly welcome my guests.	1	2	3	4	5
34) It's good for health.	1	2	3	4	5
35) It's not getting me fat.	1	2	3	4	5
36) It's interesting and exciting.	1	2	3	4	5

Please indicate the extent to which you agree or disagree with the following statements by circling the answer that best describes your opinion.

Statements about my Second preferred brand:

Imageries:

	Strongly disagree				Strongly agree
1) I feel prestigious.	1	2	3	4	5
2) I feel cheerful.	1	2	3	4	5
3) I feel elegant.	1	2	3	4	5
4) I feel charming.	1	2	3	4	5
5) I feel trendy.	1	2	3	4	5

Attitudes:

	Strongly disagree				Strongly agree
6) I like this brand.	1	2	3	4	5
7) I like its taste.	1	2	3	4	5
8) I'm interested in this brand.	1	2	3	4	5
9) This brand attracts me.	1	2	3	4	5

Attributes:

	Strongly disagree				Strongly agree
10) It tastes good.	1	2	3	4	5
11) It has good quality.	1	2	3	4	5
12) It has foam and nice color.	1	2	3	4	5
13) It's refreshing.	1	2	3	4	5
14) It's suitable for celebration and party.	1	2	3	4	5
15) It's suitable for men.	1	2	3	4	5
16) It's Australian style beer.	1	2	3	4	5

	Strongly disagree				Strongly agree
17) It supports Australian economy.	1	2	3	4	5
18) It's very popular.	1	2	3	4	5
19) It's always available.	1	2	3	4	5
20) It's good value for money.	1	2	3	4	5
21) It's inexpensive comparing with competitors.	1	2	3	4	5
22) It increases Australian identity.	1	2	3	4	5
23) It has a creative advertising.	1	2	3	4	5
24) It can cool you down in hot weather.	1	2	3	4	5

Benefits:

	Strongly disagree				Strongly agree
25) It makes me happier.	1	2	3	4	5
26) It makes me feel cool.	1	2	3	4	5
27) It reduces my stress.	1	2	3	4	5
28) It makes me enjoyable and satisfactory.	1	2	3	4	5
29) It gives me energy and courage.	1	2	3	4	5
30) It improves my status.	1	2	3	4	5
31) It makes me sociable and let me make friends easier.	1	2	3	4	5
32) It's getting attention from others.	1	2	3	4	5
33) It can warmly welcome my guests.	1	2	3	4	5
34) It's good for health.	1	2	3	4	5
35) It's not getting me fat.	1	2	3	4	5
36) It's interesting and exciting.	1	2	3	4	5

Please answer the following questions to help us categorize the responses we get.

4. Your age:_____ (in years)
5. Your gender: Male ☐   Female ☐
6. Your country of permanent residency (e.g., where you live when not enrolled at uni)

_____

7. How much is your pocket money per month?

_____

8. About how many mid-sized (midi's) beers have you drunk during the last seven days? _____

9. About how many times did you visit this tavern in the last seven days? _____

10. To thank for your time, I would like to offer either of the following, based on the answer you gave earlier.

☐   You pay only 1 dollar for midis of your first preferred brand beer.

☐   You pay nothing for midis of your second preferred brand beer.

APPENDIX 11

MANDARIN QUESTIONNAIRE ADMINISTERED IN CHINA

啤酒品牌问卷调查

这是一份博士生的论文问卷调查，问题是关于您对啤酒品牌的观点，您的答案我们会保密。

请列出下列三个啤酒品牌的顺序，数字1表示你第一喜欢的品牌，2表示你第二喜欢的品牌。

燕京啤酒 ————————

青岛啤酒 ————————

雪花啤酒 ————————

请给出在多大程度上你同意或者不同意下列观点，用数字圈出你的意见。

当你喝你第一喜欢的品牌啤酒时（联想）：

	非常不同意				非常同意
1) 我感到尊贵有优越感	1	2	3	4	5
2) 我感到放松愉快	1	2	3	4	5
3) 我觉得很优雅	1	2	3	4	5
4) 我感到很有魅力	1	2	3	4	5
5) 我感到很现代时尚	1	2	3	4	5

你第一喜欢的品牌（态度）：

	非常不同意				非常同意
6) 我喜欢这个品牌	1	2	3	4	5
7) 我喜欢它的味道	1	2	3	4	5
8) 这个品牌我很有兴趣	1	2	3	4	5
9) 这个品牌吸引了我	1	2	3	4	5

当你喝你第一喜欢的品牌啤酒时，这个品牌的啤酒 (特点)：

	非常不同意				非常同意
10) 味道口感很好	1	2	3	4	5
11) 质量放心	1	2	3	4	5
12) 泡沫和颜色很好	1	2	3	4	5
13) 很新鲜	1	2	3	4	5
14) 很适合祝贺和聚会	1	2	3	4	5
15) 很适合男人口味的啤酒	1	2	3	4	5
16) 中国口味的啤酒	1	2	3	4	5
17) 支持中国的经济发展	1	2	3	4	5
18) 很大众化的啤酒	1	2	3	4	5
19) 它随时都能买到	1	2	3	4	5
20) 物有所值很实惠	1	2	3	4	5
21) 和竞争者相比很便宜	1	2	3	4	5
22) 提高中国在国际上的知名度	1	2	3	4	5
23) 它的广告很吸引人	1	2	3	4	5
24) 喝起来很凉爽	1	2	3	4	5

你第一喜欢的品牌 (益处)：

	非常不同意				非常同意
25) 使我高兴，放松，享受，满足	1	2	3	4	5
26) 让我感觉很酷	1	2	3	4	5
27) 减轻压力和忘掉烦恼（借酒消愁）	1	2	3	4	5
28) 夏天让我凉爽	1	2	3	4	5
29) 给我能量和力量（酒壮怂人胆）	1	2	3	4	5
30) 提高我的身份	1	2	3	4	5
31) 让我更容易交朋友（酒逢知己千杯少）	1	2	3	4	5
32) 在聚会上能引起人的注意（吸引眼球）	1	2	3	4	5
33) 更好招待客人（无酒不成席）	1	2	3	4	5
34) 对健康有好处	1	2	3	4	5
35) 它不会让我发胖	1	2	3	4	5
36) 很有趣且让人激动	1	2	3	4	5

请给出在多大程度上你同意或者不同意下列观点，用数字圈出你的意见。
当你喝你第二喜欢的品牌啤酒时 (联想):

	非常不同意				非常同意
1) 我感到尊贵有优越感	1	2	3	4	5
2) 我感到放松愉快	1	2	3	4	5
3) 我觉得很优雅	1	2	3	4	5
4) 我感到很有魅力	1	2	3	4	5
5) 我感到很现代时尚	1	2	3	4	5

你第二喜欢的品牌 (态度):

	非常不同意				非常同意
6) 我喜欢这个品牌	1	2	3	4	5
7) 我喜欢它的味道	1	2	3	4	5
8) 这个品牌我很有兴趣	1	2	3	4	5
9) 这个品牌吸引了我	1	2	3	4	5

当你喝你第二喜欢的品牌啤酒时, 这个品牌的啤酒 (特点):

	非常不同意				非常同意
10) 味道口感很好	1	2	3	4	5
11) 质量放心	1	2	3	4	5
12) 泡沫和颜色很好	1	2	3	4	5
13) 很新鲜	1	2	3	4	5
14) 很适合祝贺和聚会	1	2	3	4	5
15) 很适合男人口味的啤酒	1	2	3	4	5
16) 中国口味的啤酒	1	2	3	4	5
17) 支持中国的经济发展	1	2	3	4	5
18) 很大众化的啤酒	1	2	3	4	5
19) 它随时都能买到	1	2	3	4	5
20) 物有所值很实惠	1	2	3	4	5
21) 和竞争者相比很便宜	1	2	3	4	5
22) 提高中国在国际上的知名度	1	2	3	4	5
23) 它的广告很吸引人	1	2	3	4	5
24) 喝起来很凉爽	1	2	3	4	5

你第二喜欢的品牌 (益处):

	非常不同意				非常同意
25) 使我高兴，放松，享受，满足	1	2	3	4	5
26) 让我感觉很酷	1	2	3	4	5
27) 减轻压力和忘掉烦恼（借酒消愁）	1	2	3	4	5
28) 夏天让我凉爽	1	2	3	4	5
29) 给我能量和力量（酒壮怂人胆）	1	2	3	4	5
30) 提高我的身份	1	2	3	4	5
31) 让我更容易交朋友（酒逢知己千杯少）	1	2	3	4	5
32) 在聚会上能引起人的注意（吸引眼球）	1	2	3	4	5
33) 更好招待客人（无酒不成席）	1	2	3	4	5
34) 对健康有好处	1	2	3	4	5
35) 它不会让我发胖	1	2	3	4	5
36) 很有趣且让人激动	1	2	3	4	5

4. 请帮助回答下列问题:

1) 你的年龄 ———————— (岁数)

2) 你的性别： 男 ☐ 女 ☐

3) 你的可以自由支配的收入是:

(1) 100 元以内, (2) 101–500元, (3) 501–1000元, (4) 1000元以上

4) 过去一周内你喝了多少瓶啤酒?————-

5) 过去一周内你喝了几次啤酒?————

为了感谢你的时间,根据你的答案, 我想请你选择:

☐ 给你一瓶价值2元的啤酒,如果你坚持你的第一喜欢的啤酒品牌,请你自 付1元。

或者是:

☐ 如果你坚持你的第二喜欢, 给你一瓶免费啤酒。

INDEX